A PATH CALLED ALZHEIMER'S
... That We Walked Together

Christine Leys

FOREWORD BY DUANE KELDERMAN

WESTBOW
PRESS®
A DIVISION OF THOMAS NELSON
& ZONDERVAN

Copyright © 2022 Christine Leys.

All rights reserved. No part of this book may be used or reproduced by any means, graphic, electronic, or mechanical, including photocopying, recording, taping or by any information storage retrieval system without the written permission of the author except in the case of brief quotations embodied in critical articles and reviews.

This book is a work of non-fiction. Unless otherwise noted, the author and the publisher make no explicit guarantees as to the accuracy of the information contained in this book and in some cases, names of people and places have been altered to protect their privacy.

WestBow Press books may be ordered through booksellers or by contacting:

WestBow Press
A Division of Thomas Nelson & Zondervan
1663 Liberty Drive
Bloomington, IN 47403
www.westbowpress.com
844-714-3454

Because of the dynamic nature of the Internet, any web addresses or links contained in this book may have changed since publication and may no longer be valid. The views expressed in this work are solely those of the author and do not necessarily reflect the views of the publisher, and the publisher hereby disclaims any responsibility for them.

Any people depicted in stock imagery provided by Getty Images are models, and such images are being used for illustrative purposes only. Certain stock imagery © Getty Images.

Scripture quotations are from the ESV® Bible (The Holy Bible, English Standard Version®), copyright © 2001 by Crossway, a publishing ministry of Good News Publishers. Used by permission. All rights reserved.

Cover art: Christine VanDyk Art

ISBN: 978-1-6642-6345-1 (sc)
ISBN: 978-1-6642-6346-8 (hc)
ISBN: 978-1-6642-6344-4 (e)

Library of Congress Control Number: 2022906830

Print information available on the last page.

WestBow Press rev. date: 4/29/2022

"Lord, it's my deep desire always 'to teach others to observe all things that you have commanded,' and therefore, I ask you to empower me through your Holy Spirit to teach for lasting life-change. I invite you to work in any way necessary to develop an applier's heart in my life. Impart to me, therefore, your heart for the world."
Wayne Leys (February 4, 1993)

CONTENTS

Foreword ix
Prologue xiii
Preface xix

Part 1: The Long Slope

Chapter 1: The Gentle Decline 1
Chapter 2: Small Downward Steps 21
Chapter 3: Bigger Downward Steps 85

Part 2: The Steep Descent

Chapter 1: The Slide 107
Chapter 2: The Slide Continues 177
Chapter 3: The Landing: Memory Care, Fatal Illness 226

Afterword 245
Acknowledgements 251
Reading List 255

FOREWORD

I first met Wayne and Chris Leys in the summer of 1970 in Colorado Springs, CO where Wayne, age 26, was brand new in the ministry and Chris was great with her first-born child. I was on SWIM, Summer Workshop in Missions, a six-week summer missions experience for high school students in the Christian Reformed Church. Five other high school graduates from the Pella, Iowa area and I had the privilege of working in ministry alongside Wayne and Chris at the Cragmor CRC.

Wayne and Chris had a transformative impact on my life that summer. They embodied a joy in the Lord that was contagious. They were fun-loving. Christ became more real to me that summer than I had ever experienced Christ. The Holy Spirit was palpable in worship and in meetings we had with other high school students and college students. Discipleship and mission were not just concepts but lived reality for Wayne and Chris and so many people in that church. I left Colorado that summer for Calvin College where I enrolled as a pre-seminary student. I wanted the church to make a difference in the world, and I wanted to be used by God, like Wayne and Chris, to make a difference in people's lives.

Little did we know how intertwined our lives would remain forever. Within two years of my SWIM experience, I married Jeannette, Chris's first cousin! Over the years our paths crossed so many times. And, of course, with each year, we all changed and grew. We picked up some scars along the way. Through all the life experiences God had in store for us, my respect for Wayne only grew. Wayne's constant concern for the outsider, the other, his grasp of a kingdom of God that was large and glorious, his balance of concern for personal salvation and righteousness and justice, his deep trust in Scripture for knowing God, his practice of prayer that was life itself for Wayne, his good humor and radiant smile – all these things only blossomed more and more throughout Wayne's life and ministry and made Wayne a larger-than-life figure to me till the day he died.

Anyone who knows Wayne and Chris knows that they were a ministry team from start to finish. All of the things that make me so deeply love and respect Wayne apply equally to Chris, which brings me to this book. When Chris asked me to read the manuscript of this book and write a Foreword, I was honored. But I was not prepared. I'd like to prepare you for what you are about to experience as you read this book.

This book is hard to read. Many times, over the course of the three days I read it, I said to Jeannette, "This book is assaulting!" Let me explain. This entire book is woven together with entries from Chris' daily prayer journal. Little did Chris know that her prayer journal would provide this vivid record– day by day, sometimes minute by minute–of what Chris calls the path of descent that is Alzheimer's. This book gets you inside Wayne and Chris' home, totally inside, and inside Chris' soul, and gives you as close to a firsthand experience of Alzheimer's as I can imagine. And it's hard. Raw. Unvarnished. And it feels long because it is all so painful. At times I found myself protesting to God, Why does this have to go on and on? Exactly what Chris was feeling, but for a lot more than three days. Through the prayer journals, we walk at Chris' side through the travail. And with Chris, we often feel like it's all too much to take.

Before I talk you out of reading the book, let me explain that this book is also deep and beautiful. This book is a deep exploration of the vulnerability of love and the practice of faith.

Fifteen times in the book, Chris prays, "I bow down." Chris lives Coram Deo—before the face of God.

> Lord, I used to bounce back and go on. But I find I'm exhausted and just want to cry. So I come, Lord. For you are my Strength, my Fortress, my Rock, and I receive anew from you. No matter all these things or any other yet to come, I am your child, you are my Father, my Savior, my Helper. I look to you.

In many ways, this is a book of questions from a journey of questions. Every day Chris faced hard questions – for God, about what was happening inside of Wayne, what the future holds, what she should be doing today. So much of Chris' relationship with God during this journey was this safe and sacred space in which she could give voice to all of her questions, and then release them all to God as she went on with the next excruciating moment of her life.

> Lord, it's hard; and I know I can stay apart emotionally in order to avoid falling apart, but then that means I'm not sensitive to him, nor in touch with my own losses. So, Lord God, my Father, I come to you; I ask for help to 'deal' better, to be better support, and not a reactor only, to be better at assuring him. So please help me now to love better...

Often Chris writes things that are both raw and tender.

> I fell apart last night. It seems I spend all my time with him listening carefully, working to *hear* what he's actually wanting to say. . . . Wayne misinterpreted something I'd said and got ticked off and accusatory. I had to try to figure out what assumptions he made and why he was jumping to wrong conclusions. I was totally drained, however, and starting crying. I said, "I can't figure out anymore." Then he just held me.

Chris' deep desire is that readers of this book will understand more deeply what people with Alzheimer's and their families go through. The book certainly accomplishes that. But it accomplishes much more: it gives us a firsthand glimpse of a saint. Chris' selflessness, her submission to God's plan, her love for Wayne, her setting aside of her own preferences and desires to give Wayne what he needed – this is a book about a child of God living a life of deep faith and radical obedience. All of that, but no preaching, no moralizing. Just the rugged, raw, real life of one-foot-in-front-of-the-other faith and obedience.

I predict that before you finish this book two things will happen. They happened to me. First, if you are married, you will talk to your spouse about this book. No amount of talking prepares anyone for the journey of Alzheimer's, but it helps a little to just say, "No matter what I might do or say with Alzheimer's, you have to remember I love you and those behaviors will not be me." Second, I predict you will bow down. Bow down before the God of the universe whose ways are not our ways, and plans are not our plans. Chris' testimony shines a light upon one of the most amazing things about our faith, what one person has called "the gravity of joy:" that we can be overwhelmed with awe even in the middle of our suffering.

> . . . I bow in Awe – that you know me . . . that you help me . . . that you have abundance for me . . . O Lord God Above, I lift praise.

Duane Kelderman

PROLOGUE

12-28-20

"Dear Wayne,

My mind goes back to the first time we saw each other. It was at the home of the principal - what was his name?
    I'd gone to Sheboygan to visit my sister Jo and her husband George for a weekend before starting my junior year at Calvin College. That Sunday evening your church divided into small groups to help people prepare for the next Sunday's Communion participation. The school principal and his wife hosted the post-high young adults, and I was invited to join the group. So, I did. You, of course, came also. You were about to start your sophomore year at Calvin. All of the guests were asked to introduce themselves. When my turn came, I said I was Chris Greenfield.
    You leaned forward and exclaimed, "<u>You're</u> Chris Greenfield?" I just said yes, having no idea what you'd meant by that.
    We had a good time in Bible study and discussion and then disbursed. Since I had to wait to be picked up, I helped clean up. One of the girls said as we dried dishes, "I bet you start dating Wayne Leys this year." I didn't know what to say.
    A couple of weeks later we both found ourselves in the Cappella choir of Calvin College, and you asked me to accompany you to the choir's get-acquainted square dance. And that did it. Neither of us looked elsewhere after that.

Much later you told me you had driven around the block that night in Sheboygan, wondering about trying to give me a ride. And you confessed why you'd been so surprised at my being Chris Greenfield. A year earlier, as you prepared for your freshman year, your mom told you Miss Greenfield had a sister at Calvin whose name was Chris. At your first rehearsal for Radio Choir, you heard that name and turned to look; someone was standing, someone you assumed to be Chris Greenfield, and you decided to take a pass. No way, not that girl; not interested. Hence your shock at finding out the real Chris Greenfield looked totally different – in fact, totally good to you!

I love you, Chris"

Wayne and I were only apart two summers of the next three years of dating. The first he spent at his home in Sheboygan, WI and I spent at my home in Grand Rapids, MI. The second he spent in Minneapolis, MN working with Rev. D. Aardsma, leading a Summer Workshop in Missions team for Aardsma's church. By that time, it was hard to be apart. The third summer we were married, and he began studies at Calvin Theological Seminary, while I continued teaching at Cutlerville Christian Junior High School.

As he neared graduation, he met Rev. Cliff Bajema who had been sent to interview prospective candidates to succeed him in his pastorate in Colorado Springs. Cliff was given a list of possibilities by the Home Missions office; it did not include Wayne because someone there forgot that Wayne had asked to be considered by them. But a professor at the seminary "happened" to be talking to Cliff and told him he should consider Wayne Leys. We realized later the Lord had directed our steps, despite actions of people. We received and accepted a call to pastor Cragmor Christian Reformed Church in Colorado Springs, pending Synod's approval and the exam before Rocky Mountain Classis in the fall. We drove west with some fear and awe, he to pastor a church, and I to be pastor's wife, which to both of us meant partnering in ministry. He was 25 and I had just turned 26.

We, of course, had no idea what the Lord had in store for us. We just got next to people, thoroughly enjoying and appreciating them and their faith. It wasn't long before we were aware that the church people had a comfortability with the Lord that we hadn't seen before. Since I had no children and no job, I had no excuse for skipping the women's prayer group. But I'd never experienced anything like it, and I was quite intimidated. When they prayed, it sounded as though they were talking to someone they knew well. They seemed to think the Lord was very near, very real. It was conversation, person to person. I was "the pastor's wife," and felt obligated to join, but I also felt odd, as though what I said was empty. The same thing happened in the youth group. There would be a prayer time, and it was so comfortable for them, so easy to just talk to God. Again, I felt obligated to participate. I began to tell myself to see only the Lord as I "talked," to be aware of no one else. But as I did that, I'd cry, and that was uncomfortable. (I thought later that was just the self-protecting scales breaking down, falling out of the eyes.) Wayne had his own experiences of similar feelings.

In our second year there, the denomination was offering Renewal opportunities, making a visiting pastor available to each church. Wayne immediately signed us up, and Rev. Paul Veenstra came to us. When Wayne picked him up at the airport, Paul asked him what he wanted to see happen in his church these three evenings (and two daytimes). Wayne laid it all out, and then Paul said, "That's very good, and it's obvious we need to start with you." He was right, and the Lord used him so greatly in both our lives that we consider those days the foundation of our faith life. I don't mean to diminish the effects of our early lives in Christian families, in the church and in Christian schools; those were also foundational. But moving from knowledge about God to relationship with him began in those three days in Colorado Springs. We were never the same; we both came to assurance of our salvation. We blamed no one for us not having it before that; we just didn't receive it. We now knew the one who knew us, personally.

After five formative years in Colorado Springs, we sensed the Lord calling us to Elmhurst Christian Reformed Church (ECRC) in Elmhurst, IL. It was very hard to leave Cragmor, but in the fall of 1974 we arrived in Illinois. ECRC had been without a pastor for two years, so they were ready to accept this young maverick, though they'd heard strange stories about his ministry. Here too the Lord met us, taking us and many others deeper in knowledge of him and in opening the church up to minister to its people and its community in new and powerful ways.

It seemed to be humming along really well, when the Lord broke through and showed Wayne first, then me, that he wanted yet another path for us. It was a path some would have called "downward mobility." He asked us to leave a sizable, well-functioning church and go to an eight family Home Missions plant in the Atlanta area, New Hope Church of Dunwoody. We knew we were to do it, even though we felt yanked out of Elmhurst. So, in the spring of 1983 we headed south and began searching how to live and minister in Dunwoody, GA. We soon discovered that the move was also a family move. In Illinois, we had both allowed our schedules to become more and more full, and now, with this move, we had time, a lot of it, and it was good. (Our kids, Jeff, Sarah and Maria, were 12, 9 and 5 when we got there.) The church became family as well. Since most who came were away from physical families, they looked to the church fellowship to be family. So, we grew together, and together we grew in worship and the word.

In the summer of 1989, we believed the Lord was sending us back to Colorado, to Denver this time, to Ridgeview Hills Christian Reformed Church. There we started by getting next to people, bringing them the word, emphasizing worship, welcoming and coming alongside the ones the Lord started to bring to us. After six years we were moved by the Lord to go to Lockport, Il., to Community Life Church. There again we were a family, one that also welcomed and ministered to broken people, that expected the power of the Spirit of God to help. During those years Wayne started leading Bible studies in the Will County Adult Detention Facility. That led to him becoming chaplain of the facility, along with pastoring, and later to be Executive Director of the Center for Correctional Concerns (CCC), the agency inside the jail that served the population with chaplaincy, GED, drug counseling, social work, library, among other things. After retiring from the church in 2010, he did that full time, and I joined him as well.

We thought we would start cutting back, reducing hours and letting others take the lead at some time. But in 2013 the Lord made it very clear that we were to stop jail ministry altogether, which we then did in July of that year. How good of him to lead so graciously; he was sparing us the experience of Alzheimer's Disease (AD) becoming obvious to others in the jail and court systems, but we weren't conscious of that at the time. I just knew the last year there had been hard for Wayne, and he was depending more and more on me.

I wrote the letter that began this prologue after he'd entered Memory Care. The idea came to me to recapture our pre-Alzheimer's life together by writing a series of letters, which I then wanted to read to him as I visited. I only got two such letters written, for COVID entered the facility and I wasn't able to see him inside. Later, when he was in Hospice care, I could be with him and I spent time then remembering for him who we had been together.

PREFACE
Introducing the Path

The following narrative was compiled from my writings in the years 2012-2021, with a few remembrances from earlier years. At my daughter's suggestion in 2012, I started making notes of the changes I saw in Wayne, thinking I'd then be better ready to describe them to a doctor, if the need ever arose. I also have inserted here my thoughts, questions, feelings and fears about those changes that I'd taken to the Lord in my prayer journal during those years. These are excerpts only, not the entire journal entries.

Prayer journaling was a practice of mine and Wayne's long before the challenge of AD came into our life together. It was something that developed naturally for me. At first, I decided to make myself write something about the daily scripture reading (we followed a schedule of reading through the Bible annually), for otherwise it could seem so familiar that I'd just read it and leave it. As that habit of writing a response developed, I found I was starting to address some of those thoughts to the Lord, discovering that writing was a comfortable vehicle for "talking with him."

I discovered it a good way to "cry out to the LORD...and pour out my complaint before him..." (Psalm 142:1-2); it was a way for me to "cast...anxieties on him..." (I Peter 5:7). This practice helped me to get at feelings and inner thoughts, to come to some understanding, to give them over to him for that day, to receive assurance and enabling to go into the day in trust that he would supply. I could be very honest, raw, weak (for no one else ever saw what I wrote), knowing I was heard and received and helped. Madeleine L'Engle, writing the Foreword to <u>A Grief Observed </u>by C. S. Lewis, says about journaling, "It is all right to wallow in one's journal; it is a way of getting rid of self-pity, and self-indulgence and self-centeredness. What we work out in our journals we don't take out on family and friends." (p. xiv) Some people, I think, saw me as a strong person; prayer journaling explains that. It was not my strength; it came from the Lord as I unveiled myself to him. This will be apparent in the following pages.

The practice was so entrenched in Wayne that he daily sat at his desk, Bible open, writing in his journal until he left for Memory Care. In fact, we sent a small desk, his chair, his Bible and journal with him there. The caregivers knew of its import to him and encouraged him to do it. But that move affected him deeply and he was no longer able to do it.

As we grew in the ability to connect with the Lord through the journaling, we both grew in the expectation of hearing back from him. This could come from a strong inner sense, an actual "word" from him that gave encouragement and building up (this type of thing came mostly to Wayne), or dreams (which often came to me). We learned to pay attention to what we were sensing and to dreams that we could easily remember. You will read of all of these in the following account.

You will also read of "Wayne's devotional." Many years ago, he began emailing his thoughts on a given Bible passage to our son, Jeff. Jeff would often send back what he was thinking of that same passage. In this way they would go through a book of the Bible for a month, then repeat it each month in that calendar year. After a while, Wayne decided to forward it to others as well, and that list grew. This practice was also very entrenched in Wayne and he continued trying to write something till just a few months before memory care. In the last years he knew he needed help with it and gave it to me each day to edit, at first, then to rewrite, trying to capture and convey his insight.

There is evidence in these pages of the fact that I did not understand everything happening in the moment, though I sometimes did after the fact. But some things I didn't understand until I was no longer in the midst of caretaking. Some insight is still coming to me.

I offer this account first with the hope that the reader will see the indignity pictured here as being from the disease and not the person; secondly, with the understanding that the aloneness described in it is inherent to an AD journey; and thirdly, with the hope that some in the Lord's church may come to know this journey better and determine to come alongside others walking this path called Alzheimer's.

PART I
The Long Slope

CHAPTER ONE

The Gentle Decline

(PRE-DIAGNOSIS)

It seemed my once confident, fearless husband wasn't himself. As we finished the last church year of full-time pastoring (2009-2010), he didn't seem to be in the moment many times; he missed things, his driving was erratic, and he got angry at me if I said anything about it, making me the problem. I noticed he was using a lot of pronouns when he preached and when he conversed with others, giving no reference to an antecedent, often just stringing a lot of phrases together. Both were confusing to the listener, and his point was hard to follow.

I found myself often restating what he'd just said to someone, sensing that the listener hadn't followed his thought. At the time I wondered if keeping up with the church besides being full-time executive director of the Center for Correctional Concerns (CCC) at the jail was causing so much stress that he couldn't always function well. But it continued after retiring from the church and going full time to the jail.

May 2011 I found myself reaching to the Lord, "Lord God on High...I admit I'm tired of this *work*, this life we're in, so tired.... because of living with an absent-minded husband...it's worse than when we pastored full time!"

A couple of years later we accepted the fact that the responsibilities indeed were too much, but we still didn't realize AD was the cause of this change.

2012

I started writing down small changes that were showing up, things that were new to our life together:

Wayne referred to our neighbor Millie as Edie. (We'd been there many years, and he knew her well.) He stopped helping me make dinner (we were both working full time), reverting to a past assumption, a default position: one's wife provides the dinner. He couldn't remember what all should go on the table when setting it for dinner. He instructed me in obvious things, as if I was six years old. When driving, he was uncertain of the way and would ask, "Should I turn here?" though the route was familiar. He didn't actually listen when I talked, also a new thing, and could act as though he already knew what I was going to say. Perhaps he doesn't have strength to listen to me after listening to so many at the jail?

These years we seemed to be getting separated from each other, as the load of the jail ministry pressed heavily on him. This too was new for us and scary.

In September he shared during our Door County vacation more deeply than he'd done in a long time. He expressed sorrow at having no reason to stop in Sheboygan, for there was no parent, no sibling there. He said he was afraid to have contact with people from the churches we'd served because they might be expecting something from him, some help, some encouragement from scripture that he'd always been able to give but that he now thought he couldn't give. He was too tired and had no strength for that.

That confession, with its accompanying fear, was an early precursor of things to come. But we didn't recognize it then, and

I was hopeful this ability to connect together would continue as we returned to our home and to our work at the jail. However, such was not the case. When we got back to Lockport, he returned to being a pressured, pressuring person, challenging me, complaining, and grumbling. Sometimes he was mean and unable to stop worrying or to listen to my attempts to communicate anything. It seemed he was just too tired. This was not the Wayne he'd been.

2013

In the first several months of 2013, I had dreams that seemed to be revelations from the Lord; each pictured the possibility of pastoring a large church, and each had Wayne and me getting separated.

> **January 30**
> Lord, thank you for the dreams you give that lead us. Last night I dreamed we'd moved to pastor a large church, and I was getting ready for the first service in one dream and getting ready to put our things into the parsonage in the other. Are you revealing that you have something large ahead for us, something for which we're getting ready now? Please keep us, me, in your hands, on your path, in this readying stage, I pray.

I sensed it was not actually about pastoring a church, but about the Lord giving us an unknown, yet large assignment of some kind. This thought of getting ready, and the reality of being readied by the Lord came again a year later and then many times thereafter. Looking back from the end of the path, I marvel at his preparation of us, of me, for us, for me along the way. I came to know his "very present help in [the AD] trouble." (Psalm 46:1)

Wayne also experienced dreams in these and subsequent

years. His were about ferocious animals attacking us. He would actually strike out at the animal, wanting to keep it from hurting me or sometimes himself.

> **June 3**
> Lord, what is the danger being revealed? Is the destroyer out to stop him? Is it symbolic of the attempt to wreck your church? Or is it about more coming, with this being warning? If so, there were three warnings, in three dreams, last night. I plead for you to protect him, us, me, the church, our kids and their families; and ask you to identify danger and destruction ahead.

The year 2013 also brought more times of Wayne struggling to grasp what I was trying to explain. Since neither of us understood why this was happening, we didn't do very well. It was very frustrating for me, and at times I got angry. He would accuse and say I was the problem.

Fear came between us in these days, something Wayne had never displayed and very seldom felt. But now he was afraid "someone had come into the house and taken his billfold," and things like that. The Lord led us to sell our house and move to Michigan, and this caused great fear and anxiety: we'll lose our money, "they" will deceive us, we can't trust them, and so forth. This was all very new for him and hard for both of us to deal with. He agreed that the Lord was leading us to move, but he turned the responsibility and workings of it over to me. He just couldn't take hold of anything. That too was new. So, I took it, hoping it was temporary and would all settle down once the move had occurred.

2014

But it didn't. By the next spring there were even more changes to note in him, in his actions and thoughts.

March 28
Lord, I bring you my fear regarding Wayne's confusion and inattentiveness to his surroundings (leading to knocking things over, and so forth). There's confusion regarding the adding and subtracting in the check book, and he doesn't understand explanations. O Lord, what does this mean? Is it the beginning of Alzheimer's? Do I keep trying to correct new, bad, harmful habits, or just accept the actions and clean them up? Do I fight for clearer thinking, or let it go? Please help me, I pray.

April 5
Sovereign Lord, I bring also my hurt at his refusal to listen to what I'm saying, believing apparently that he knows what it is. Then he lectures on and on, on a topic different than what my question had been. This happens repeatedly. I find I end up feeling hurt because he's been dismissive of the real me, and it seems I feel very alone in those moments. Then I feel a strong desire to get away from him, thus to stop him misusing me. Lord, I don't know...I need your help to relate, to communicate, and especially to love him when I'd rather protect myself from being hurt again.

Again, the Lord met me in a dream and got me ready to keep worship through song a possibility in our home. I dreamed I was getting songs ready for a worship team. Jeff said he was going to give me sheets of songs and talked of what he'd do with them. Then he said, "I have to prepare you to die." I didn't think the dream meant that my physical death was imminent but that staying active with worship music would prepare me for heaven.

Lord, is that your message through this? Somehow, I sense I am to prepare my worship music – I will put it all in binders, Thank you!

Wayne's driving again worried me, and I noticed he was also becoming more confused about recording financial transactions, which we did in a ledger that he'd set up. This was hard to see.

> **April 22**
> O Lord, I bring my great concern regarding his driving; please surround and protect us on the road. Give him awareness and me patience. Please keep and protect, carry and cover, I pray.

One day an online article we received said for people to "get ready to embrace many changes." It struck a chord in me – "Lord, I ask you to show me what is needed to get ready."

May 4 My devotional reading that day was from Mark 10:51, where Jesus asked, "What do you want me to do for you?" I sensed the question being asked of me and answered:

> Help me *see* the path you've assigned for this season, with the primary need being to love and respect my husband though he seems to be changing. It just dawned on me that respecting him could do more for him than scolding or instructing him to stay aware and attentive. Thank you! I will need your help, your strength; fill me, I pray. I "haven't walked this road before." (Joshua 3:4)

I tried to sleep in the living room since his restlessness was keeping me awake. About two am, he called out, "Chris!" I went back to bed, he lay his head against my shoulder, kept his hand on my arm, and went back to sleep.

> Am I his crutch for life needs? In the morning he has no memory of it. What is it all about? Please continue supplying for me what I need so I can be his helper now. Is there fear in his spirit that I might not be there? Lord, provide our supply, I pray, especially for today.

Wayne asked me why we're leading worship at a local church. "What are you wanting to come from it?" I said, "I'm just trying to obey what's been given me."

> Lord, I bring his *why* questions... He keeps raising: Why are we doing this? What is the purpose, the result, you're looking for? He seems led by fear and everything he encounters evokes fear. So, he fusses, worries, questions repeatedly, and depends on me. Is it because deterioration mentally has actually robbed him? Or because a stronghold of fear hasn't been broken?

July 27 I dreamed that Wayne had a woman assistant and wondered what that would be about. Much later he would think of me as his helper and caregiver, not as his wife. Was this dream foretelling the AD experience of thinking I was helper, assistant?

August 6
Gracious Father...I bring to you the thoughts about disability, wheelchair living – there too I've said "Not I," haven't I? But only you know what's ahead for us – a deteriorating disease or disability from an accident – if you have such for me or Wayne, I know you will still carry me, still help, still be *for*... "So, teach us to number our days...that we may get a heart of wisdom." (Psalm 90:12) "Look carefully then how you walk, not as unwise but as wise, making the best use of the time, because the days are evil." (Ephesians. 5:15-16) Thank you for the "Get ready (be ready)" message and for leading me in it – ready to host guests and family, ready to help with worship, ready to help kids, ready to bless our family and teach the next generation to know you...

September 16
Lord God, it's hard to experience his pressing, his anxiety, and such things. Even a power failure, with loss of internet service, causes fear. So, I come and seek renewing from you...

I started thinking the "Get ready" message was also for preparing for the future – lawyer's work on our will, funeral and burial plans, and other information the kids would need. And I asked the Lord to "make this way also."

Wayne is often confused. Today he thought things still operate the old way; for example, our 815-area code is long distance for people who call us. He responds to something I say (apple) with something totally different (orange), with there being no possibility for me to get him to the "apple" understanding. I find I get really frustrated, and he can get angry. Yesterday, he couldn't find his car keys, so he used his cell phone to call the home phone, convinced that would show him where the keys were.

And then there's word substitution, using something from the past, such as "I'm going for a *quart* of milk." One day he called the turning lane "the middle aisle." When we were watching a playoff baseball game he wondered if a major league team still calls up minor league players at this time of year. But instead of saying "major" and "minor" he said New Testament and Old Testament.

December 2 Wayne is still having dreams of being attacked, where he ends up hitting me or shoving me strongly, apparently thinking he's hitting an attacking animal.

> Lord, is it a warning? Or is he still remembering the attacks against us from years ago? Still thinking he needs to protect his own, including me, by defeating the intrusion?

2015

Wayne had a dream of singing in the jail, and he actually sang out loud. But it was in a feeble, crackly voice, not his regular singing voice.

Lord, does that mean he'll be ministering in such ways even when he is very old, when his voice will be feeble and crackly? O Lord, thank you for whatever it is you're doing, whatever doors you're opening. Use him yet in broken lives and in your church that's lost its way.

This is, in fact, exactly what happened. When he was in the hospital at the end, so unsure and afraid about what was being done to him, his coping mechanism was singing and praying. He would close his eyes and just talk (out loud) to the Lord, moving into spontaneous song while raising his arms. And yes, the voice was weak, sometimes crackly, but many working on that hospital floor, and in memory care, heard his dependence on and love for the Lord.

January 23
I bring the "what-ifs" to you – nursing care, payment for it, Medicaid, and so forth. You know it already and already have a plan. Thank you. Please lead us to be responsible, and prepare the place where we'll live in dependence, if that is in your plan, even as you prepare a place for us in the Father's house.

My concern about Wayne's driving continued throughout this year – though acknowledging the existence of blind spots, he drove as though there were none. He didn't make use of the left turn lane, saying he didn't see it. He also missed a lane ending and a stop sign and then said that I made him tense. One day he said he'd figured out why he had trouble on the car brake: the pedals were positioned differently than they used to be.

As AD progressed, he gave various explanations for riding next to the left lane line or on it – he couldn't tell how close he was to the right side of the road and was afraid of going into a ditch, or he blamed me, "I thought *you* wanted me to do that."

When we bought a new car, I saw anxiety rise up. Can we trust them? Will they take advantage of us? Shouldn't we give them the garage door opener that goes with the car we're trading in?

He began having confusion about typing his email devotional, which he sent daily to Jeff. He'd ask, "What do I use if I write something to Jeff? Where do I type it?" forgetting he always used the iPad. He started struggling with the name in the address line, with the date versus the chapter number, and the chart I'd made confused him. He wrote once about the "assistant priest." When I asked him about it, he laughed heartily. Laughing at his own mistakes used to be easy for him; now it was becoming harder, so this was good to experience.

April 7
Lord, what do I do about these lapses that I observe? Please be merciful to us, to him; keep him, I pray, and please help me.

I started seeing a reluctance to attend grandkids' programs. It first came as we were headed to the high school performance of "The Creation," and continued with other events. He admitted years later that he was afraid some unknown, uncontrollable change would happen to/in him while in public settings, and that could be hard to experience.

April 20
(I Corinthians 13:5) "...love is not irritable or resentful..." (7) it "bears all things...endures all things..." O Lord, please be love within me for this season of helping, as he's more and more dependent on me, needing things repeated more and more. I "haven't walked this way before." (Joshua 3:4) Please fill me today for the tasks: patience and love to show, wisdom to know what choices, decisions to make.

April 21
Your good still pours out to us and we have been able to do some updating – please lead regarding more – and

the readying for life ending issues (will, burial plots, funeral payment too?). Please continue to lead in this regard. Thank you for helping me yesterday, for love renewed. How good and faithful you are. Please continue to provide your way for us.

May 5
(II Corinthians 4:16) Our "outer nature," earthly life, is "wasting away." But our "inner nature" is also "being renewed day by day." Thank you for life within, your life that will not ever end. Please lead us on its path today and in these days of senior years! And Lord, is the "outer nature" heading into Alzheimer's for him, and caregiving for me? Or is what I'm seeing in him just "normal," his normal – needing to have things repeated, needing reassurances...He always had doubts about going somewhere new, but then he wasn't afraid of making a wrong turn and figuring out how to fix it as he is now. There was always a fear of mathematical mistakes in our finances – has that merely increased to cause fear of putting the figure in the wrong place, with *fear* actually causing mistakes? Therefore, a blossoming, so to speak, of what was always there? Still, I pray for help from you in walking with him, in handling it rightly...

June 25
Lord, I bring my mixed feelings this morning: I am grateful to you for giving us all a good time last night at church (as we led a Bible study there), along with the realization that Wayne's confusing thoughts and expressions are seen more. Also, he didn't bring a word from you at the finish, as I'd looked for. So, it feels that I should come with more from you, beyond information. And it feels this morning as though I've been yanked out of a bubble where I'd been living as though this (AD development) isn't happening, thinking, "Why should I actually plan on it happening?" So, I come...please help me know, and know how to proceed. Please protect the good work you have in him, in me...

Wayne demonstrates confusion in more areas and repeatedly suggests taking the new computer back because we don't fully understand Word. He thinks that's the way to deal with it. He also said he wishes we had a copier, so we could just put a piece of paper in and get a copy. We do!

July 1
(2 am) Please help me; it feels as though I must carry it all. He struggles to get one of the songs (for our worship leading), saying the songs "should be simple; there's many songs much simpler than this." I sense accusation of me, because he can't get things. O Lord, please give him your ability to help those who come (to worship), and please give me awareness and ability to know the way...

Not only was Wayne reluctant to go to events, he also displayed a reluctance to taking leadership in the Bible study. This was new. We had agreed to lead a seven-week study on Philippians in our church, and I felt him dragging his feet and not taking hold. Today he said he didn't know what to prepare: "Tell me which verses you'll handle and what you want me to handle." This was so different for him, and it "threw" me a bit.

July 13
Lord God Above, I pray that you ...help me to get prepared for Wednesday night's study. Is it in your plan that I carry it, not he? I looked each time for him to bring a sense of your anointing, only to see him seem to back off and look to me. So, Lord God, please help me to know – shall I take it? Shall I look for you in his expression? Is he being changed, or is it lack of use, that is, lack of leading, as he suggests? Help, I pray...

And then there is reluctance to leaving home. We were planning to go to Rockford, Illinois, to our daughter's family, and he kept saying it was a long drive and asking why we couldn't come home Saturday? Why not Sunday? He checked his cash amount, worried about it; I said we could use credit card if needed. Later, he came saying, "I can use my credit card if we need to."

Fear about money can overcome him. Today he got really worried because our investments lost money this quarter. "Our rating has been lowered and we're where we are because of our rating!" He thought our credit rating would drop because of the stock market loss.

July 14
I realized yesterday I've come to know some loneliness, as I have no one to talk with about the situation here. Our kids are totally involved in their worlds, and there's no one available. But you know, you see, you have your plan. So, I plead anew for help on this path; especially prepare me for the Bible study...

July 16
Lord, I come...You know I've been avoiding you... Was I all right last night? Coming home I just wanted to crawl in a corner and block everything out. I think my greatest concern is not necessarily the slow driving speeds but the inattention they reveal. I was so upset by it, saying things I've only thought before – "This will never happen again, for I'll drive!" He said, "NO!" "I'll talk to a doctor!" He said, "NO!" And in that frame of mind, we led worship and a Bible study. Because you were merciful to me, to us both, it seemed to go all right. But it also seemed that I'd put my *self* out there, a great risk, and I wanted to cover myself fully. I wanted reassurance; I know. But I cannot get that from him anymore.... Please, Lord, help me today on this path, as I accept... and I want to be *with* him... Help us go forward as *us*, overcoming this separateness that has crept in. Again, I ask: Should I bring it up?

Again, Wayne struggled entering checks into the ledger, actually walking away at one point. He returned and got at it again, knowing however he was making mistakes. When he walked away, he said, "I don't get it; I don't understand." That struggle continued, but each month he'd work at it, though continually coming to me with questions about it.

July 17
There's still the elephant in the room, and there's distance between us regarding Wednesday night's driving experience. So, Lord, please help me, for it seems we should acknowledge the elephant.

Sarah urged me to have a conversation with him about the things I was seeing. I told her that each time I tried to say something, he would get disturbed, even angry. But she said we needed to have things considered – maybe there was a physical explanation for these things. So, I braved it and asked him to talk with me about changes that were apparent to me. This time he was actually relieved to get it out together. I had feared his response, and he admitted he had feared making it more real – maybe it wouldn't be true if we didn't acknowledge it? We both felt great relief in doing this and knew we had finally reconnected after so long a time of being in our own worlds about this. Still, he asked that we keep it to ourselves for a while, not even talking to the kids about it.

July 22
I praise you, Lord God Almighty; there is none like you. You have heard our hearts' cries and restored us to each other, giving us hope for the time we have here yet. I ask anew that you direct our steps on this path, and bless them. Protect us, I pray, as we drive again today, and as we open up your Word with this group. Set him free to hear your voice with his "Thus saith the Lord" gift again, I pray.

August 9
Lord, I bring to you last night's discussion regarding his mental changes, and I plead for your protection as he

insists there's no change in his driving (it's my fault, he says; when I'm not in the car he's less tense and makes less mistakes!). He also says he lives knowing there's "accusation and a critical spirit" within me. He says that gives him the right to dismiss everything. Again – it's all on me. He's angry about wives who limit their husbands' driving, and is on the lookout to make sure I don't do that to him. So, Lord, please help today; help me to be honoring, and protect us, I plead.

Another new experience these days is his hearing voices during the night. It makes him get up and check around the house.

Lord, thank you for your protection through the night – what is happening when he gets up saying he's "heard voices?" Are you beckoning him? inviting him to receive something from you? or letting him know you and your hosts are near, for us? Please reveal what you want us to know.

August 13
Anniversary Forty-nine! Please lead us in this new year of being together, especially as we explore changes in mental capacity. Please protect each of us in all that and the *us* of us; keep us with each other, I plead.

August 22
O Lord, please open my eyes, enable me to see you, to receive what you have for me, us… and I plead for your help…in what my steps are to be in this chapter of deterioration. Most of all, teach me how to love in the midst of things that cannot be corrected. How ironic – I am so good at that (giving correction), and he hasn't let me do it for him for fifty-two years! Teach me, I pray; I give myself to you for your use here.

August 23
Lord, it seems my present assignment is more and more moving to the "good work" of taking care of everything

here, including him. How do I do this? Especially as he denies and demands I keep silent and insists our kids should stay out of it. And he doesn't want medication. Lord, I feel very alone, since I can't have the kids' help. Help me know what steps...what words...what things to avoid...

August 30
Lord, the kids have been busy, and I miss talking with them. Perhaps that's why it's harder to hang on to grace; I'm needing them for it (and it seems Wayne can't give me the assurances I used to get from him). Probably it was time to stand alone before you, stripped of all others. I hadn't even known I was looking to you *plus* others. Thank you for your sympathy with my weakness (Hebrews 4:15).

Questions, my day is spent answering questions. And sometimes there's pushback. He got mad at me again yesterday for pressing him to clarify what he was saying. "You know what I'm saying..." But I didn't. Maybe he didn't either?

October 2
Lord, please lead us in this chapter, as he struggles with the things he does (not remembering how to do them), and I more and more carry things. As he said this morning, "It'd be nice if the kids would just check in, see if we're okay, let us know they are okay."

October 4
O Lord, thank you for our life together. Please help me make the most of it while I still have him in awareness. And help me love and honor and respect him and not just give deference... Help me learn to love, and to find ways to show love...

October 5
Father, thank you for our talk this morning. Please help us on this path – toward Alzheimer's? Still, thank you.

I'd felt so alone, with Wayne denying, accusing me of it being just "my problem," with the kids and others being so busy.... Thank you, Merciful Lord, for receiving me and these things, for helping Wayne and me to talk, for seeing me here, in this. I look anew to you.

I realize he's unsure of himself often, and leans on me so much more. He gets confused regarding the numbers on the TV screen during a baseball game – the score, balls and strikes, the inning, and so forth; he isn't sure much of the time. He went to get a sports pass to attend athletic events for our grandkids and realized, after coming home, that in confusion he'd listed his birthday as 12-44 (it's January 12, 1944). He went back to correct it. He struggles to express his thought; he can't think of the word, so he either uses a wrong one or a bunch of pronouns.

October 17
Thank you for yesterday's conversation regarding brain health, initiated by him! Help me know what we should be doing to prepare for the future. Please lead, and provide the way.

October 18
Fear came to visit last evening as I lay down to sleep. Fear now about what the future holds for us, for me, if indeed we are brought into an Alzheimer's chapter. I suddenly felt the weight of having to make all the decisions by myself. I've been so blessed in being able to lean on him, to face things with him, to be supported when low or uncertain. And I felt again the aloneness of it all, as our kids remain heavily involved in their worlds.

Alone also because I have no one to talk to. I can't process out loud or think through something with someone or just be heard. There's no earthly support right now, which I've always had from him. This is so new for me. Yes, I "haven't walked this way before."

And now he is asking that I write down all the steps for things I do, for example, paying bills, so that if "something happens to" me, he'll know what to do. That seemed to add to my sense of fear last night. Now I have to have even more made ready? O Lord, help…lead me in these things, sort it out for me, I pray. (I need to finish estate-planning folders for our kids…continue sorting through file boxes in storage…)

Amazingly, on the way to church after I wrote the above, he asked me if I was okay. So, I told him those fears. He graciously said we should see the doctor, so that neither of us is alone anymore.

October 20
Lord God, thank you so for meeting me these last couple days since the weightiness of the coming years hit me, causing fear. You spoke to that in the worship service Sunday and then yesterday sent C____ (via the phone), showing me that she knew! Therefore, she reached out to me. I marvel yet – how good you are, how very good. You also led me to mention it to Wayne, which led to honest talking between us, which led to setting up an appointment with the doctor. O Lord, thank you. Please prepare us for that and prepare the doctor with wisdom.

October 22 We saw the doctor today, and he was blunt, "It's Alzheimer's and it's not going to get better." He explained life would be like a stairway going down; sometimes the AD would plateau or stay on a landing, other times it would progress down the steps one at a time. He told us some medications can help plateau the disease for a time, but one can never know how long that would last, or if it would even do that.

(10:30 pm) Thank you so for the discussion with the doctor, for a pathway now for help, and for his agreement that things "are not normal, though minimal yet." He's ruling out medical causes now. It feels good to have someone else aware, someone who can advise and help.

October 26
Lord, we look ahead and wonder about how this disease will go, for both of us – will it be a long, slow deterioration, a long goodbye? We are both thinking he should take medication to have more "quality of life" for a prolonged time – is that right? Or should we let it develop normally, and perhaps bring heaven to him sooner? Please lead us, equip us for this assignment, I pray.

October 27
Lord God above, please help him going through this MRI, a completely new experience for him. And then the report – will that bring a recommendation of meds... and should we seek our kids' thoughts on the matter? If it is indeed Alzheimer's, should we let the deterioration occur or hold it off for a time? Please be gracious to us, lead us, and help.

(11:45) Thank you for helping him, for times of talking things out. I bring other questions affecting me – if it gets to a point of him needing a facility, will we have money? And will I have physical functioning to care for him? What does the future look like? I don't know, but I know who holds the future, and I will trust you. You led us to work together for one salary all those years, and we believed that you assured us you'd provide in these years we're now in. So, I call for that now and thank you, Lord God.

The test results confirmed the doctor's diagnosis of Alzheimer's Disease. His brain was not being affected by any physical cause.

TAKING A BREAK
(1)

One thing I referred to repeatedly may require some explanation. I mention that Wayne entered paychecks into our ledger. Some may wonder about him doing that. When we were first married, I handled such things. But then he decided one day, seemingly out of the blue, that he should do it; it was his responsibility. Naturally, I balked. I wasn't making mistakes (my math is actually better than his). I'm perfectly capable, but he insisted it was his to do. It felt like a slap to me. Nevertheless, he took it over. And I discovered I didn't have to have that in order to be considered of value.

He discovered that his math needed to be checked and that he didn't like reconciling bank statements (ah, a place yet for me!). He also regularly informed me of our complete financial picture. He continued handling it until we switched to online bill pay in 2012. He couldn't figure out how to do that but he knew it was a good step to take. He agreed to have me do it, but didn't like being removed. He remained involved by entering the pay checks into the categories of the ledger, trying desperately to preserve who he'd been in our financial world. That is why I encouraged him to keep doing it, even though I needed to give him more and more help along the way.

CHAPTER TWO
Small Downward Steps

(POST-DIAGNOSIS)

2015

November 3
Heavenly Father, you are my provider and always have been. I bring to you the thoughts and fears of the night – if he must go into nursing home care, they'll take his Social Security and pension, leaving me ____ to live on each month – is that possible? No! If I take ____ from savings each month, I could perhaps do it – will they commandeer that also? Okay… Now I feel better. If they don't take that I'll be okay for a time. I lift this to you with thanks for the savings and with trust renewed that you will provide for me. We believed all those years, when not taking pay for me and helping others, that you would make our way when we needed it. So, I give you this fear. I trust that "the thing that I fear" does not come upon me, that "what I dread" does not befall me, that I will be "at ease…quiet…at rest…" (Job 3:25-26), helped in trouble.

November 4
Thank you for helping us through more feelings and thoughts regarding this new assignment, Alzheimer's

Disease. O Lord, please help each day and prepare our kids...

November 5
(John 9:1–12) O Lord, how good to revisit this passage now. It seemed to be for me for so many years, for I too was born with an abnormality, not because I sinned, or my parents did, but because you wanted to display your works in me! (3) And you have! And still do, and I praise and thank you for your strength – carrying, filling, equipping me. Now I ask you to display your work in Wayne, to show that you are greater than this genetically-induced memory losing. Please bless our conversations with our kids about it and lead regarding praying together for healing work on Thanksgiving Day.

Now that we knew the diagnosis, we set about sharing this news, starting with our kids. We talked with Sarah and John, Maria and Ben by phone, as none of them lives nearby. They were most supportive and loving, as were Jeff and Shelly who came over, Shelly carrying the book *Stop Alzheimer's Now* by Bruce Fife. That was a visible reminder that they all knew it, which had been expressed some to me, but now Wayne also knew they knew. He felt their love and was encouraged as they prayed for us. We called our siblings and told them (none of them lives here either), then told friends as we saw them. Wayne did not want to hide it; he knew there was no need to feel shame in this, so he was quite open with friends and family. Beyond that, in general with people, we didn't hide it, but we didn't broadcast it either. Maria and Ben were our pastors and they took care of informing elders and those who needed to know.

November 11
(John 10:1–10) "The thief comes only to steal, kill and destroy. I come that they may have life and have it abundantly." You are abundant life. Though the thief

has come to steal mental capacity, your abundant life remains. It cannot be stolen, or put to death, or destroyed. I praise you anew, Heavenly Father. My life, Wayne's life is in your flow of *life*. We remain in "the abundant."

November 14
(John 11:1–6) Lord, it seems you've done something similar for Wayne (similar to your waiting, though you knew Lazarus was sick, before doing something.) A deterioration had set in, and Wayne seemed entrenched in it for many months. But since we "faced the giant," named it, yielded it to you, spoke of it to family and accepted meds, it seems to have lost power over us. I praise you; it is "not…to death," (4) at least not until you say so. Thank you, God who is greater, who is *life*. I pray you keep us alert to the moment, to *life* in each day, to draw from it. Thank you.

Wayne wants to learn to access the bank account online, but needs me standing there, pointing out each step. Still, he thinks he's learning. (Being teachable was very important to him all his life, for himself, for others.) I get frustrated informing him of things, for he listens only until he figures he knows where it's going, then just lets me keep talking. So without hearing me he later says, "You said such and such…" when I hadn't at all. Or he interrupts, thinking my talking was heading to "A," and starts giving his view of "A," when actually I'd been heading to "B," something totally different. In the past he admitted this was a lazy habit. Now he is actually unable to follow something all the way.

Our family gathered here for Thanksgiving Day dinner. I'd sensed we should pray as a family for healing for Wayne, which we did. It was a good time.

December 30 Wayne dreamed again that he was being attacked, ferociously. And as he's done so many times in the last years, he swung his arms and kicked his legs at the "attackers," hitting me in the process. I had no warning this time, as there was no physical agitation from him, so I couldn't try to awaken him before the blows struck me. I cried out, and he finally stopped. In the morning, he had no recollection of hitting, nor of swinging his arms. This was new.

> Heavenly Father, please protect us and bring understanding. It's been clear with these repeated episodes, that he discerns evil, danger, and is willing to go after it in order to protect others. But why does he make me his assailant? Does your enemy, and ours, get into what you are doing, and twist things? Or does Wayne wonder whether I'm on his side? O Lord, help me demonstrate it so that he *knows* deep down, even though it's now more difficult because of AD...

2016

Today I commented on him spilling water on my Bible and he used a vulgar word to describe me. I said, "If you'd think about what you're doing, I wouldn't have to be that; but that's a foreign concept." This was a totally new experience for us; neither of us ever used that word. Clearly, our new assignment was affecting us.

Two years ago, he got things ready for filing taxes, and I checked it. He went to the appointment with our accountant in Chicago by himself. Last year, I did most of the readying and went to Chicago with him. This year, it's totally my project (and I mailed it to Chicago).

> **January 18**
> Loving Lord, there is none like you in giving love. No human has the capability of initiating selfless love, of giving purely, unless filled by your character. I marvel anew, realizing anew how hard it is for me to receive love, how I can even fear initiating and giving it because

what if it's not received? O Lord, what factors produced such carefulness, such protection of self? I'm haunted by the question, "Did you learn to love?" Maybe there's a bit learned, but may I have more time to overcome carefulness? Thank you for amazing love...

January 22
O Lord, I marvel at your grace poured out anew on me, on us. You worked through the surgeon to indicate there is no cause for concern (regarding a pancreatic cyst I've had for years)! No apparent cancer! How good you have again been to us. Thank you for continued health to stay with Wayne and with the things you've put before me. You pour out good.

I've noticed occasionally Wayne forgets to flush after urinating. This is new. He's definitely less sure of himself; he holds back and looks to me. He now asks if the iPad is usable when he could check himself if there's battery power. He admitted his frequent questioning could be from fear of getting something wrong. He's reading the novel *Shaper* (John Timmerman), but he says it's hard to follow.

February 8
Lord, seeing our neighbor taken by ambulance and her husband following in the car (after having just talked with him this morning) shook me a bit, I admit. I shook for them and the difficulties obviously there, and their question regarding paying for care..., and for us, wondering what's ahead, and how can we pay for anything. I admit I always assumed we'd have my parents' experience with no need at all for nursing home care. But is Wayne on his dad's path? What is going to happen? And will there be money? Have we been poor stewards? And were we wrong to interpret scripture so that we'd give to someone in need if we had it, rather than save it all for ourselves for a future, possible need? I look to you and ask again for your guidance in these areas, this life chapter. Please

protect, provide for us, and equip me for this day, this week, this season, this year...

Wayne is doing the brain exercises we've read about but can't always figure out what's being asked of him. His logic is even worse than it used to be! He got a chest cough on Monday, and I awakened with it this morning. He blamed it on including a coffee stop with his sister Ruth and her husband Pete in our trip to Rockford. Yesterday he'd stated strongly he doesn't like seeing people on the way there; he just wants to go straight there and back. His strong likes and dislikes continue, but now he also depends on me to make decisions. Then he balks and complains. He's probably not liking having to depend on my decision-making, hence the crabbing about it.

He now complains about being away from home. Last week, though the decision to stay with Ben and Maria in Paw Paw for a chili cook-off was his completely, he tried repeatedly to change it, even as we drove to Maria's after church. He's now objecting to staying there this week for a high school concert after a meeting for Bible study leaders.

The first year after we moved here he felt guilty about not having people over more often, saying "we should be" inviting others over. Now he balks about doing it at all.

The writing of his devotional this morning made no sense. There were several lines of typed words with no punctuation; it was a mess. I asked him to redo it, but then I still made major changes. Yet, in some ways it seemed he was doing better. I was sick this weekend, and he went willingly and alone to Jeff's for a birthday party on Saturday and to Paw Paw for Marissa's musical on Sunday. There was no trouble! Yes, he's very familiar with going to those places.

I notice an inability to stay with a full news report; often he starts talking in the middle of it about something else. Besides not flushing after using the bathroom, he's now also forgetting to turn off the light after he's been in the garage.

He took Topher to the airport this morning, and did well. But he had fussed about it and wanted to see the map over and over and over again. This is so different for him, who'd always said, "I know the general area; it can't be hard to find."

April 6
(Joshua 14:6ff) Lord, years ago (already in Colorado Springs) Wayne declared he wanted to be Caleb at eighty to eighty-five, still "taking the hill." I believe that was of you, and I pray you give him physical and mental strength (v. 11) for many years yet. Thank you for our life now; these are such good days.

His reading out loud has become halting; he says his eyes jump lines. Perhaps. I also know he jumps sections and puts into the jumped-over section what he assumes it had said.

Saturday, we had guests here and the subject of Wisconsin Dells came up. I said I'd never seen it. He was surprised. "No? Didn't your family stop there on the way to Iowa?" He'd forgotten what I know he knew.

Wayne had a nighttime vision in which the Lord showed him the place in his past where he experienced great accusation; more was being hurled at him now. He spoke – out loud – words that the Lord had given him. He sighed deeply when the vision was finished. He realized in the morning that the Lord has countered, silenced, finished the massive accusation that had lived on in him from the past. He said the Lord seemed to say, "Your 'mission,' what you stood for and pursued – helping and encouraging the wounded to find The Rock – was right! You did not cause the struggles you endured. And now, no turning back from that mission!"

April 6
Wow, Lord! How awesome, how good, how gracious and merciful you are. Healing has come to his soul. All these years of dreams in which wild animals were

attacking, causing him to swing or kick at them (usually hitting me) – was that all about this accusation? You've shown him it's gone. On Thanksgiving Day our family prayed for healing for him – you have powerfully given it. Thank you so… what a good and faithful God you are.

Wednesday evening, we had an honest, transparent conversation. He talked about preaching, saying he wondered if he could still do it, without notes, as he always had. He got the thought while jogging that he should write some sermons, preach them while alone in the house to see how it would go, to see if they're "coherent." He talked about driving, saying he knows he's always done it automatically and that he now needs to give full attention (and not look around as he'd always liked to do). He has wondered about his foot not transferring from the gas pedal to the brake smoothly and in time. He thinks his shoe's sole slows him down – it "gets stuck." He also admitted he was never, nor ever considered by others, a good driver. (He didn't ever write those sermons; apparently, he forgot about it.)

It's been a long time since he's asked to go online to our bank account. At one time he wanted the steps written down for him, I did that and put it on the desk. But each time he wanted to do it, he'd call me to be there. I realize now he was unable to follow the steps. It's been months since he wanted to try.

He told me again that he drives on the left lane line because country roads in Wisconsin (back when he started driving) had curbs, causing the shoulder to be higher than the road. It was scary for him, and now he remembers that fear.

April 17
Lord…I didn't sleep for a portion of last night. I suspect that the book (of a personal experience with dementia) has stirred discomfort deep within, too deep to know the specifics of it. I confess I thought it easy for them to have cancer take his life just a couple of years after

the AD diagnosis. Thus, they didn't experience or deal with greater mental limitations, or with the question of when to stop driving. It seemed great mercy on your part to end it early. But such is not my call to make, or to demand, or to covet. So, it left me with unvoiced questions (that I recognize now) – what then for us? If no physical illness cuts off AD, how prolonged will our parting be, and how devastating? Or will your mercy continue the measure of healing you've done already and keep him "functioning highly," as the doctor put it? I admit you're helping us so much that I can forget the diagnosis; or is it trusting you've worked healing? I go on normally and then respond wrongly when I've forgotten he can't grasp what I'm trying to explain about something. I am so grateful for your help, your provisions (regarding meds, diet, and so forth), your leading in conversations. I plead for you to keep me alert so I catch what you want me to see and receive from you the way to respond. Please pour out your Spirit, on me, in me, with grace, mercy, blessing flowing then from me.

April 18
Thank you for meeting me yesterday with renewed peace. This leg of the journey is known to you and you will lead, supply, carry us. You have always done so.

Wayne enjoyed a trip to North Carolina to see his brother Ken and his wife Carole with Pete and Ruth, though it was hard on him to be driven around, to accept not driving himself or have his own car. Now he's very glad to be home. We're planning to go to Rockford and he wants to cut it short. He was *down* this morning. He'd scraped open his leg on Saturday and it's still draining. That, along with yesterday's discussions about trips and the financial accounting struggle, piled together and he said, "Sometimes I just want to be done with it!" apparently meaning AD.

May 7
Thank you for your amazing care of us, for leading me to the article on Facebook (from the New York Times) which showed me Wayne isn't yet that far into the Alzheimer's journey. Thank you for the measure of healing you've given, for the level of functioning he has because you provide. How good you are to us. I ask for good functioning for the Calvin reunion, the Chicago Cubs game and outing for our anniversary. Thank you, Father. (We were planning to take our whole family to a Cubs game for our fiftieth anniversary.)

Maria was riding with us on a country road when Wayne continued full speed though there was a car stopped up ahead. She cried out, "Brake!" He then did, explaining he *was* braking and had started it "way back there." But he hadn't. I was very thankful one of our kids had now experienced his lapses in driving.

I'm also noticing his uncertainties regarding outfit choices – what goes with what – and he is asking me! This is totally new; he was the fashion expert, not I!

May 13
Loving LORD God, giving self for another, desiring the highest good for the other isn't based on merit, worth, or the response of the one being loved. Lord, I know I fall so far short. "Have you learned to love?" still comes to me. I suspect you are the one asking and giving me opportunity to learn. I get so focused on my duty list and so automatically operate out of self-protection. Thank you for more time (!), for this day to practice; please remind me and release me. I read recently one loves because he's been loved. I know I've learned some because he has loved me. Thank you so for that and particularly for your great love, "while we were yet sinners" (Romans 5:8). There was and is no deserving, no meriting. Flow to me, through me today, I pray.

Wayne really struggles with new things. Trying to learn the Meistersingers music for the fifty-year Calvin reunion has been really hard. He doesn't remember which line to follow and always defaults to tenor (he's supposed to be singing baritone). The difficulty entering checks into the ledger continues, as he added several times when he should have subtracted or vice versa. Word substitution continues as well. As he left to get blood work done, he said, "I'm taking a billfold just in case." A billfold? "Yes." My billfold? "Well, it's yours, and it's mine too." Then he took the checkbook out his shirt pocket. But a new thing I've noticed is that he forgets to unlock the car (as we return to it) and tries to open the door; then he remembers he has to use the keys. Forgetting and sequencing difficulty – both are AD-influenced.

Another new thing popped up – he wondered, as he was leaving to meet his friend George for coffee, if he knew how to find Panera Bread. After that I asked George to pick him up, or have coffee with him here.

June 13
O Lord, I just heard regarding the mammogram – I must go back! Lord, I look to you… On the one hand I like the idea of a door opening to enter heaven; on the other hand, I'd like to care for Wayne and not see him experience something stressful, something causing anxiety (such as not having me around). So, I ask you to lead, to carry us through this, to protect, to allow only what is according to "your good purpose." (He mercifully gave me a clear report.)

June 14
(II Kings 2:9) Elisha asked for a "double portion…" Lord, I was given the word years ago that you had given me a double portion. Again, thank you, my Lord, my God. I marvel anew. I have wondered if it refers to my two daughters who both serve you by helping people who need it. I wonder now also if it's about extra

health protection, with strength to yet be of help to people physically (with hospitality) and spiritually (with encouragement of lives and faith walk). At any rate, thank you for your good hand on me.

June 20
Lord, I ask for wisdom regarding spending. I saw again someone denying self dramatically in order to squirrel it away – why? For nursing home expense? Or so that their kids can have all that money? So, I wonder, and I am thankful you taught me (through Wayne) to have open hands to receive and give, and to avoid living in fear, or being led by it. Still, I need to be responsible, and I need to "plan for the future" also. Please lead me, I pray. I remember being led (I believe) to know you as our inheritance, as with the Levites (Numbers 18:20–24), and I continue to look to you for provision and help. Thank you for amazing care and provision already, the abundance of this home, the ability to get to our kids. Thank you.

In our empty nest years, Wayne helped a lot with dinner and dishes, but now he doesn't think of it and just accepts my doing it all. It seems that too is a "forgetting?" Or maybe he's too tired? He told me his frustration in writing the devotional is that he gets a thought in scripture, starts to write it, then before finishing it he looks back and gets another thought, which he then starts writing. The end result is two thoughts mixed together in one sentence.

July 17
Lord God Above… it was really good to be with couples here this week, to be able to do the work for it. I thought I'd spaced it out well enough to avoid getting overtired, but is there more going on now? It seemed I not only did all the planning, preparing, cleaning, and so forth, but then also carried the conversations – is that possible? I carried much more than I used to, I know, and I'm more tired.

July 22
(Luke 12:19) "...ample goods laid up for many years; relax, eat, drink, and be merry." Now in these latter years, as we see what our contemporaries are doing and hear the next generation being told to store up for retirement ease, we reflect that our understanding was instead "Share what's been given to you, don't hang onto it all for yourself." Were we right? If you took Wayne, I'd have to supplement monthly income with savings – but that's what it's for! Not for hoarding, nor hanging onto in fear. Still, what's being responsible? Please lead me, as most seems to be on me. Thank you for all you've given, all you've provided.

July 26 Wayne dreamed of an attacker coming at him again.

Lord, please reveal what this is about. It seems it isn't about protecting me as it used to be. Is he, as your watchman, being given warning? (See Ezekiel 3:17) Are you showing him something that's a message for now?

August 13
Lord, thank you for insight you've now given. After all these years I understand better what "take up your cross daily" means. It is about paying the consequences of someone else's actions. Rather than harp on Wayne about his inefficient or sloppy ways (because I'll always have to do the cleaning up), instead forgive and clean it up! Don't hold it against him or try to correct his approach. It took so long for me to see that – over forty years since you first impressed me with Luke 9:23. How patient and faithful you've been to me. Please grow me in this, and may "the latter years," this time of living this way with him, be "greater than the former," though shorter.

I've been quite sick. I stayed in bed all day sleeping, emerging finally in the evening. Wayne was anxious and a bit "lost:" he went to the store for chicken soup for me but got the wrong kind; he couldn't fix food for himself; he was too anxious to eat and lost two pounds. We cancelled going to Rockford because he didn't like the thought of not being in full health away from home. Still, the Lord met him as he read, and he felt understanding in his spirit, he said. That was so good.

September 8
O Lord, my Lord, how good to be up again, even if briefly. That was an incredible day of flu misery. Thank you so for hearing my cries, for giving sleep and restoration during the night, for carrying Wayne through the day (and mercifully keeping it to one day), for showing me anew that things have changed and he really struggles when I am sick. So, I ask again that you give me enough health to be here for him, to help with what he needs. Thank you for being our shepherd; you know our needs, and you hear our cries. I look to you...

September 9
Lord, my Lord, thank you for lifting me up again. But Lord, what of the night? I got very little sleep, and when Wayne woke me saying I'd called him, I got mad, rather than stopping myself and asking you if you were calling him. Were you? and the knocking at the door that he "heard" the previous night – is it you, for him? Regarding something specific? An assignment? A word?

Wayne's reading for dinner table devotions was again halting and with more word substitution, saying "pressure" for "presence," for example, or saying what he thought was coming ("what our imaginations can imagine" rather than "comprehend"). Later he said we should make a list in order to report such changes to the doctor. He also confused stories from the past with something that's happened more recently.

New things confuse him. For example, switching our Verizon plan to Jeff and Shelly's account made him think our email services had changed, and he was sure "that girl" didn't include his phone. When I got the kids' texts and he didn't, he again accused "that girl" of messing things up. He was thinking of texts as if they were emails which should automatically appear on both phones. "Where's the phone that was in the kitchen?" I explained what we did with the home phone (we'd switched to using mobile phones only). "So, I can't ever answer a phone when you're gone? I won't have a phone to answer? It all goes to you?" I told him people would call him on his phone. One day he looked at his phone and said, "This is a mistake; I shouldn't have this." It seemed he meant he didn't know how to use it; the switching had really thrown him off. Actually, he'd prefer it if nothing changed and everything stayed familiar.

And now there's more confusion when watching sports: the scoring of tennis is too hard to understand, as is the FedEx Cup tournament set up.

> **October 5**
> I plead for your help here – why is he losing weight? – and for help in responding rather than reacting. He's been pretty placid, and now all of a sudden, he's taking charge ("I *need* bacon and eggs..."). He's also complaining that our meals aren't varied enough, and that there aren't enough good-tasting beef meals. Has there been a switch to less self-control, to more "I want" reactiveness? Lord God who sees, please lead me today...

Driving home from Holland Christian's Powder Puff football game, Wayne got confused when the road curved to the right; he didn't know what to do. A left turn there would take us into Kollen Park. He headed right between the two. I yelled, "This way" pointing right. But he didn't look at my pointing, just said, "This way?" and turned left into the park, driving fast. Fear of him, in confusion, driving straight through the parking lot into Lake Macatawa flashed through my mind.

Last night, he fell, forward, out of bed. I heard it, and yelled, "Wayne!" at least three times before he answered. Finally, he said, "I'm all right. I was dreaming." He checked his head, for he'd hit it - on the chest of drawers? Then he said, "I'm always on this edge." I realized he was blaming me, for I'd asked him to roll over due to his snoring. But I didn't say move to the edge.

He was also upset again about our changing to mobile phone use only. My phone gets notices from ESPN, so he hears the notification. His phone doesn't get them so he's upset that all communications now come to me. He gets nothing. He's sure he's missing out. So, I put ESPN on his phone, and we named favorite teams. When notifications came, he was confused, again thinking they were emails. Over and over, I explained and demonstrated, but he couldn't grasp it; I got down about it. Spam doesn't catch everything on his phone, so he believes "someone else has been on the computer." He wanted to enter items in his phone's calendar, but couldn't remember the process, even though doing it repeatedly. I had to give each step, every time.

He quit watching the Cubs game (on TV) and went to bed, mad at them and at me for "being faithful" to them. In the morning, he explained that he was feeling the heaviness of not being what he used to be, of getting to feel almost physically sick if he stays up and gets tired, of aching all over on awakening so that he doesn't want to get up (which goes away when he starts walking). He read later "Four Signs of Dementia" and realized he has all four, including not doing new things. So, he determined to be more proactive, to reach out to people via email, thus not giving in to listlessness (and "I'd rather just sleep").

One day he was confused in handing me his devotional; he thought he'd mixed up the scripture phrases with his thoughts, but he hadn't; it was fine. Still, in talking about it he said, "It felt strange…" Then another day, when starting it, he said, "Usually the first thing is 'Good morning, Jeff' but today that isn't bringing up his [email] address." This is the second time he's typed the greeting into the address line. At lunch with friends, he couldn't formulate a response to what they'd shared and just repeated what they'd said or spoke with enough pronouns to keep it vague. He'd been asked for his theological opinion, but he couldn't give it.

He admitted he's more and more desirous of staying home, that he's fearful of driving home today from Maria's in the rain and the dark. I'm not a fan of that either, but I believe we shouldn't say No.

I mourned a bit last evening at Isabel's band concert. A woman in front of us was trying to get a picture of a grandchild but didn't have the right angle, so her husband got it on his phone. It struck me that I don't have a husband who knows how to do things anymore. So, I *felt* loss in that moment.

December 21
Lord, help me linger enough these days to *see* you in the midst of this assignment. I confess I've been so distracted by needed tasks the last days that I couldn't see. Thank you for mercy, for your supply to me of ideas and help to get so much done (including walking Wayne through the steps of making Chex mix, something he used to do by himself. You gave me understanding and prevented any fighting to arise in me). Lord, I bow in praise and great gratitude. Because you came, I can have strength beyond what's human; we are able to have our family together.

Twice yesterday he focused on an object and missed what was right in front of him: he reached for a screw driver and didn't see the container of nails in front of it, so it spilled; he reached for the glasses cupboard but didn't see the open dishwasher door, so he banged his leg into it. One thing at a time, just one thing. I need to understand that as well and that it's so hard for him to understand explanations. He also struggled to grasp the schedule I made for him, at his request, for his 2017 devotional writing.

2017

January 1
(Genesis 2:20) "...a helper fit for him..." Lord, you know I've bucked that concept all my life, especially when Mom Leys' last words to me were, "Be a good helper to him." But now I ask you to make me that, to increase my awareness of what that would call for, and to enable me by your Spirit to grow in it. Help me, Holy Spirit (Helper), to be helper, I pray. Were *you* saying it through her with these very days of Alzheimer's needs in mind? I pray for you to keep me in health to do this...

January 2
I bring to you yesterday's failure to receive the help I'd asked for as I tried to correct him about the garage lights. Thank you for having me back off, realizing the situation...

He's been putting things like his glasses and used tissues next to the sink I use. So, this morning he grabbed my contact case and put one of my contacts in his eye. Because he couldn't see with that lens, he thought it had either dropped or moved off the pupil. It took a while to straighten that out. Another new thing has surfaced: he often leaves the door open to the garage when going out there, letting heat escape. Prior to AD, he'd never have done that, because it costs money. He also leaves lights on.

We were able to talk together over his birthday dinner about us both sensing more deterioration. There are more times when he doesn't understand something, more things confuse him. He puts dishes away in strange ways now and then! It was so good to be honest and open with each other, to connect, rather than just *deal* with AD's life.

Early one morning, in the dark, he fell down the basement steps. He'd come from the kitchen, heading he thought to the bathroom, but turned too soon. I heard the loud noise and went running, calling for him. Amazingly, he was standing at the bottom of the steps, completely unhurt, not even scratched by the broken glass from fallen pictures. Shelly then found motion detection night lights for us.

January 14
Lord, I plead anew for your help in this AD journey. Thank you so for protecting him from broken bones in his fall down the stairs, for alerting me to the fact that it's time for me to be more aware, to take precautions, to take hold more. Please, Lord, help me see what... and think of things...

January 16
Lord, thank you for helping me through that experience (having a CT scan). There were several failed attempts at finding my veins and I feel so drained. But maybe it's from the pile-up of things: his losing a contact, his falling down the stairs, his losing the loner contact, his driving poorly, this CT stuff. I used to bounce back and go on. But I find I'm exhausted and just want to cry. So, I come, Lord, for you are my strength, my fortress, my rock, and I receive anew from you. No matter all these things or any other yet to come, I am your child, you are my Father, Savior, Helper. I look to you.

(Matthew 6:34b) "...sufficient for the day is its own trouble." Yes! Especially when several days pile it on! But you, my heavenly Father, know what I need. (32) I am comforted, I am kept, I am watched over. I turn anew to seek you first, and receive your help for this day.

For several days now, Wayne has come to me to check which Bible chapter he should be writing on. He also said that his mind thinks of the song "Awesome God," but he can't come up with the words. It so discouraged him.

January 22
Lord, I lift up my husband, as he retreats in some ways to being a child. Remind me, I plead, to respect him, to be merciful rather than corrective. Forgive me for failing, as correcting and instructing are natural inclinations. So please show me the way today...

February 4
Lord, thank you for _____, for her strong walk of faith, for blessing her now with *finished rest*.... It reminds me about our coming closer to The End – Lord, should I get more ready? Always be ready – yes! But having put more in order...? – I'll go through my prayer journals; thank you.

Wayne was confused as our son-in-law Ben preached. Ben would refer to something in the passage, and then Wayne would ask me, "Where is that?" That happened several times. He skipped a day with his devotional (we were in Paw Paw), so he was confused when he returned to his schedule: "Why isn't II Kings 24 on Feb. 24?" He's also trying to keep names of towns in his memory: he came up with Allegan and Allendale, but couldn't name Hamilton.

February 11
(Matthew 14:28–31) Peter joins you in your exploits (beyond-human accomplishments) by walking on water, until he remembers he's human, limited, battered by earth's elements, and fear hits causing sinking. But you called it "little faith...doubt." I wonder how often this happened in my life and I was not even aware? I just gave in to the fear and retreated. Lord, are there still "exploits" for me, for us? Perhaps it's wherever I move instead of letting fear stop me. Lord, as I take over more and more here, please equip me more deeply to lead while still seeing Wayne as my husband and not as

my child. Leading full time is new for me, Lord; please strengthen me in spirit...

February 18
(Matthew 18:6, 10, 14) "Little ones" are dear to you, and we've appreciated, even enjoyed that concept through our years of ministry. Thank you for that perspective. Please continue to open our eyes to such, to those you want us to care for. And Lord, as I observe my husband reverting to some childish characteristics (looking to me to take care of something he would have done himself pre-Alzheimer's), I wonder if he's at times a "little one" for me to "not despise"(10) but to help in a life-promoting way. (14) Thank you for your presence with us in this, a way we have not walked before. Please fill me to respond to the "child" with loving help and at the same time to honor the man he is.

He gave me his devotional saying, "There's something wrong with it; I tried to fix it but couldn't." Then again, its schedule confused him, so I'll have to type it differently for the next two months.
Conversations can get wearying, as he assumes I'm saying something different than I am. Frustration comes to me as I "explain," and then I want to have it over and go do something by myself.
He keeps leaving lights on!

February 28
Lord, thank you for...our time together here, though it seems harder to know what he's saying sometimes. Is that possible? These have been long months, with long days of being just the two of us. Help me know how often to schedule guests now...

Wayne was very worried the dentist would try to take advantage of him and make him go through expensive treatments just to get money from us. He's afraid we won't have money for medical needs. He'd always been inclined to distrust when dentists, doctors, auto mechanics and such would tell him of necessary work or repair, for he didn't know their subjects. But now AD was taking it to a new level, developing into paranoia that increases as time goes on.

A driving incident showed me he could no longer multi-task. He was driving as we went through Allegan. Up ahead two cars were stopped at a crosswalk, with a crossing guard standing in the street. He kept going at the same speed. Finally, I cried, "Stop!" He of course said, "Did you really think I didn't see that?" but then added, "I was seeing it, thinking, 'I wonder what's going on up there.'" So, it seems he sees, tries to process what the situation is about, but isn't able to remember that he must also slow down and begin to stop; he can't do "all of the above" anymore. Then a few days later something similar happened. He was going full speed, though there were stopped cars ahead. I finally put up my hands, crying, "Stop!" Afterward, he said, "Do you think I didn't see that? I was thinking he'll turn and I can keep going." He was "figuring out" the situation, but his brain did not say slow down, stop accelerating, you're getting too close.

March 12 I had a dream of us being in Colorado, in line for tickets to some event. I realized Wayne wasn't joining me in line, so I looked for him. I could not find him anywhere and found myself saying to the woman selling tickets, "I can't find my husband... He has early Alzheimer's."

> O Lord, what is it? Am I deep down saying I can't find my husband anymore? That he's being changed by Alzheimer's and isn't who he was?

> **March 23**
> Lord, I bring to you a comment I heard. Someone said he doesn't visit a certain person anymore because that person has dementia and no longer knows him. He

also said one might as well not visit because you can't have a conversation anymore. Lord, it's so wrong! And self-protecting. There's no thought here of bringing blessing to the person with dementia and certainly none of ministering to his spirit or to the caregiving spouse. But I realize I've done this too in the past, stayed away because of wondering how to converse. Lord, thank you for the friends who don't (won't) do that. Will anyone else stay with us, not abandon us?

Wayne really stumbled while reading the Psalm tonight, often saying what he assumed it would say. Then when he realized it didn't, he'd get confused about which line he was in, jumping to a previous one. Several times now he has haltingly made it through a sentence but said, "I don't know what that's saying." After supper he went in the office and read out loud. He asked me to read *My Utmost for His Highest* (Oswald Chambers) with him to practice reading. He was so stressed he couldn't find March 31, and didn't know whether to go forward or backward from March 21. The attempt at reading then didn't go well either.

March 31
Lord, what does it mean? If he can't read, what will he do? all day long? There's no one to take him for coffee, no one to respond to us…

He believes it's back! Even during the night, he must have tried to read, coming back to bed saying, "My reading is back!" and then doing the same after making coffee this morning.

April 12 I had a dream: A radio was on, and I heard a woman's voice say she was going to quote something "from Christine Leys, a new author, from her book…" I marveled, "Lord! Should I be formulating something?"

April 23
(Mark 8:34) "If anyone would come after me, let him deny himself and take up his cross and follow me." Lord,

I've tried to keep this verse in front of me since early Coffee Break days at Elmhurst Church. Yet, it seems *self* is just as big as ever. Reading old journals, I see it looms large, but perhaps that was the method you gave me of unloading it, "denying" it, for a time. Thank you for your "good hand" on me all these years, for meeting me, and lifting me above...

What book of the Bible Wayne is in or which chapter to use for his devotional writing continues to confuse him. I keep trying to simplify the schedule I've made for him, realizing also that my directions need to be given just one fact at a time. He's also wondering about preaching?? He's thinking the Lord is telling him to do it.

May 4
Lord, I remember some of a dream: I had a baby with me and was studying to lead a Bible study. I felt pressed and not ready, for I was caring for this baby, whom I loved. I thought it strange he was eating only what I spoon-fed him, and was not drinking milk. I thought, on waking up, "Is this what I'm feeling it's like to care now for Wayne?" I ask you to help me, Lord, to give me patience and strength, but also caring, understanding, respect. My parents were also in the dream. I wished they could take the baby while I led the Bible study, but I knew they couldn't. The baby had to stay with me.

May 6
Self-Sufficient Lord God, all capability is within yourself. You have no need for outside assistance; only you can be totally independent. Lord, is it ironic that one who lived his life so independently now is becoming so dependent? Yet, some independence is right as we reflect you.

We were anticipating a trip to Wisconsin in another week or so, and one through Grand Rapids for me the next day. I knew I'd have to drive a lot on the Wisconsin trip, something I was not used to doing because Wayne had always preferred doing it. Now, however, I knew it was needed. During the night I sensed I was being addressed: "You can drive Grand Rapids, and you can drive Milwaukee." I immediately said, "Thank you, Lord!" and went back to sleep. From that time on I had no fear driving highways.

May 27
O Lord, please continue with us (I know you will!) in this assignment of living and loving with Alzheimer's. Wayne was mad this morning, thinking I was talking about him behind his back with someone via text. I guess that'd be frightening in a way. Please help me assure him today and let go my pique at being distrusted and resented wrongly. Help us navigate this road in an honoring way, of you, of him.

I added coconut oil gels to our daily supplement intake, and it has confused him. He asks about it each morning. He took an office screen out yesterday and then couldn't get it back in. He needed to review next week's trip schedule and balked at the decision to stay three nights with his brother Rog and his wife Julie. He went over and over and over all of it.

June 1
(Luke 1:13) "Do not be afraid..." the angel said to Zechariah. Lord, I recognize some fear this morning. Hearing our neighbor's daughter describe her father's condition – he had dementia – of having to be fed, and so forth, brings our future front and center again. It's easy to forget it, to live in and enjoy what we yet have. But will our journey look like his? Only you know, for you know all and have planned it, and hold it also in your hand. I "can face tomorrow because you live." Please alert me when I need to let go of an expectation of him being able to do something.

Wayne did well on a trip to Door County. He shared his life and thoughts regarding it with Rog on a long walk. He believes he can still drive; I agree but would like to talk with him about him needing and accepting help.

Today, he spoke of "feeling good today," as opposed to that other day when he said, as he was looking out the window, "It all looks heavy." At the time I thought he was referring to the air being heavy from humidity. But today he explained he was talking about himself, saying he'd felt heavy, sensing the load that's on him as described by the book on dementia he's reading. It was also a day in which we saw no one, and because it was very hot, we had to stay inside.

He told the eye doctor he's wondering about ending preaching (as though he's still doing it), also saying he still leads groups. Later, when with retired pastors, he responded to the question "Are you preaching?" by saying he's participating with Ben, helping out there. He meant to be vague, but the questioner took it to mean that he was in fact preaching.

June 23
My Father, I pray for your hand to be on me...for you to give me patience and strength to continue serving him. Lord, it was hard to see him with other pastors, not able to admit he's not preaching. What an assignment you've given him, us. But we are yours, and you are here...

When Wayne got up this morning, he believed he saw ants, saying, "It's all ants here!" I looked and saw nothing. But he got the spray and covered the area next to the bed. Hallucination? Or a normal result of worrying about ants in the house (which we've been fighting in the kitchen)?

June 24
(Philippians 4:13) Lord, sometimes I wonder if we're getting closer to my having to decide to do something, even though he's firmly opposed to it? (That's totally

new.) I look anew to you, remembering "I can do all things through Christ who strengthens me."

He was checked again by the eye doctor regarding the reading problem of jumping lines. His eyes are going outward (which the doctor says could be related to Alzheimer's), and when he reads, the eyes strain to come together. We ordered new glasses with prisms in the glass.

June 26

Father, I bring my anxious thoughts. In driving today, Wayne made some bad decisions. I know his mind was focused on learning this route, but what will happen when he takes it by himself tomorrow? Will he pay more attention to conditions then? Will I know when he shouldn't do it anymore? Should I describe things to the doctor? Is he just not capable of total focus or having multiple things in view, as is necessary when driving? Please protect us, and others on the road also. And lead us, me especially, in taking responsibility more and more.

At yesterday's semi-annual doctor check Wayne mentioned he's having more trouble understanding things. We spoke of his trouble focusing on one thing, using driving incidents as examples of not multitasking. (He was mad at me most of the morning for also mentioning his falls, especially the one while playing basketball with Asher.) The doctor offered more medication, and Wayne agreed to take it. So, Namenda was added to his daily intake. Today he's depressed about it and wants to quit taking anything.

July 1

Lord, things suddenly seem harder here as he seems down, angry, and isn't feeling well physically. Thank you for your presence with us as we walk out life as old people: adding dementia meds, scheduling my cataract surgeries and all appointments, checking his eyesight also... I pray you help us at each step and protect eyesight for both.

July 2
Father, thank you for time here in Paw Paw, but Lord, there's again complaint about staying another night, a reference to feeling "drugged," He's not feeling well and prefers to be home. Please help me know if I should not have us go anywhere anymore. So, it escalates...and I pray for help.

I've been reading *My Journey into Alzheimer's Disease* (Robert Davis). He talks about making sure the Person With Dementia (PWD) is fully listening when talking to him, for he won't be able to fill in what he misses. I experienced this greatly 2013-2015, before we addressed the disease's presence. I was helped by his pointing out that depression and irritability can be a normal part of AD. Wayne displayed this also, but those moods improved after we "named the elephant." Davis is also saying that the middle stage causes increasing difficulty in coming up with the right word for something. I think this is happening. Wayne is also saying that as he talks with people at our church and they ask him questions, he wished they'd ask someone else.

His attitude is so much more positive now. A couple of weeks ago I said to him, "Walk with purpose!" He'd been going slower and slower in the house and on our walks, and I challenged it. It seems to have helped him beyond walking, as though he lives ("walks") each day believing God has purpose yet for him in that day. So, he chooses to be ready and act on what's put before him. That change helped me go through cataract surgeries and take care of the boys in Paw Paw. It's been really good.

August 22
O Lord, my Father, I come, for you are The One who has help...Lord, I miss R___; I remember all he's done for us over many years. He was one who exhibited "I've got this," as did Wayne (but who is now not able to be decisive and is no longer an "I've got this" person). But you are. It has always come down to that, but it seems so apparent now. Hearing my brother describe his growing weakness added to this sense of having no one around who's "got this." I know Jeff could, but his family needs it all, as does Sarah's, and Maria's too. I don't think these thoughts are coming out of fear for self, but out of acknowledgement of R___'s contributions to us, and of the growing realities of life at this stage. I turn therefore to you, thankful for the words this morning: "The Lord is my strength and my shield." My heart has trusted, will trust; I am helped.

September 7
Father, how good to enjoy each other yesterday and to receive all the birthday greetings. Thank you! and for seventy-four years! and for amazing health, strength, and ability to walk! Thank you for Wayne's health and strength as well, and for the ways you're keeping him from slipping further away. Truly you are merciful, gracious, good.

Things continue to be quite good, as we walk together most days, and enjoy visits with friends. He struggles to understand the scoring for match play in golf as well as for tennis, but he blessed a woman at church with a word from scripture. She was so thankful. Still, his reluctance to connect with other people continues. He resisted telling our homeowner's association president about the bees coming into our house but then brought me a statement he'd written that he could say to him. Apparently fear of not knowing how to convey his thoughts stops him. This was new for him.

October 12 Wayne had a root canal today.

> Lord, my strong husband looked so weakened in that dental chair, so affected by what had been done, and then was so resistant to the steps of care I was told to give him. Please help us navigate this tooth repair process. It made me wonder if this is a foretaste of things to come? Please help us both and lead us in decisions, I pray in your name.

He's been taking an antibiotic, and it has thrown him off. He's not sure when or if he took it or is to take his pills. That confusion remained through yesterday when the antibiotic was finally finished. This morning he asked if he had the right pills ready to take. And now, as we prepare to stay with the Jeff's and Shelly's kids, he's unsure about everything, asking repeatedly about the schedule, pick-up times, dinner menu, and so forth. And that piles up on me, making me feel that I bear the responsibility alone.

We attempted to go to Paw Paw yesterday, but there was dense fog. I know I could have driven in it, but that too would have been too stressful for him. So, we returned. After he'd jogged this morning, I found his socks in the kitchen garbage (he'd thought he was putting them in the laundry hamper).

November 14
I admit, Lord, I fell to fear during the night as I thought about the next stage of Alzheimer's. Lord, I'm not naturally a caregiver, and it scares me. What if I miss stuff and don't think of things to do that would come naturally to someone else? I will need help, Lord. And I remember you will be that for me, for us, just as you always have been. Thank you, faithful Father, and also for your great help to us these years that have remained in the mild stage. Will I know when it changes? And what about further preparing? I read that the mild stage gives people time to prepare for the moderate and severe

stages. Should I research caregiving agencies? get a walk-in shower put it? look at residential care facilities? Father, I am your child; I look to you.

November 16
Father, it's been a hard afternoon. I'd so like to help out in Paw Paw, but I'm getting resistance from Wayne to staying somewhere overnight. I think the enormity of what we live with has hit me, and depressed me. It seems the complaining about having "too much in our schedule," and the preference to staying home will only increase, not resolve in compromise. And as Maria gives up her seminary study for the sake of family needs right now, should I give up getting to our daughters' homes, all so that he can feel more comfortable? Please help me, Lord. Are we already confined? I look to you...

November 28
Thank you for giving him high functioning yet, for keeping him yet in the mild stage. Please keep me alert to his needs and lead and protect us...

Last evening, we each had a small bowl of chicken soup. He removed his empty bowl from the table while I was still eating. Later, I wondered where it was and then forgot about it. This morning I found it put away in the cupboard, remnants of soup now dried and stuck on.

Wayne complained that "no one talked to me about singing on Christmas Eve," sure he had just heard about it. I told him I *had* asked him, as did Maria also, but he'd forgotten that the conversation had taken place. There's so much time given to explaining. Maybe there are too many new things; he's trying to learn how to use the iPhone and its calendar, and now Jeff asked that next year's devotional be on John (changing what had been planned). He's struggling to get it straight. Sunday, he mentioned being so overly tired on Saturday that he thinks we should cut down on activities (and I not play for Christmas

Eve services). Is it changing? AD, that is? Do I need to figure on more time to give to explaining, and so forth? especially regarding schedule?

December 27 I had a dream: I was given the care of a child, a girl about six or seven. Her father took me with her to get a hamburger and to tell me what was expected. Then he was gone. I was alone with her, and it felt all right. But then her baby sister was also brought to me (others had reneged on caring for her). I wondered how long the parents would be gone, how long would I have to provide care. On awakening I remember thinking, "Is my care of Wayne now like caring for a six-year-old?" Probably I feel that it is as I have to give him every step for anything needing to be done.

> So, Lord, if that's now what is or what I sometimes feel it is... is a baby's dependence coming? Soon? Lord God, I am yours and your servant in this assignment also. I know you will equip me for what you assign and I look to

2018

January 1
Father in heaven, it's a new year! What will this year bring? As we have birthdays of twenty-five (Josh), fifty (John), seventy-five (me), also ten (Judah) and forty (Maria), will Alzheimer's take more away? Will I know what to do? But this year too belongs to you – I look to you to lead and equip me, to carry him, to meet us regarding decisions and needs...

January 5
Wayne read some things about Alzheimer's and also heard about someone's struggle with dementia. He felt heavy about it and went to bed that way.

But you met him – thank you – and led him to get up and walk around (he thinks that was perhaps stopping a nightmare?), and you gave him sleep on each return. Lord, it's hard and I know I can stay apart emotionally (in order to avoid falling apart), but then that means I'm not sensitive to him, or in touch with my own losses. So, Lord God my Father, I come to you, and I ask for help to *deal* better, to be better support and not a reactor only, to be better at assuring him (and reassuring). So please help me now to love better and be less intent on what I must do. Teach me yet, I pray…But you, Lord, can help. Help me make good financial choices, as he gets so anxious and fearful about them.

January 10 I assessed our situation somewhat – I think we're still doing really well. He falls asleep often, and tires quickly. He misses the first part of a sentence or communication and then doesn't understand what the second part is referring to, so all must be repeated. He still says he wants to learn to make a latte, and asks me to walk him through it, but each time I must give each step. He enters our monthly check, but has had more uncertainties with it – "something's not right and I don't know how to fix it." Saturday, he tried to put air in the tires, but the pumps were frozen, and he ended up losing air. He went to three or four gas stations; each time, it was the same thing. The cold and the worry about more loss of air on the road kept us from going to church. I knew I shouldn't continue reasoning (a car *can* drive with 30# air pressure), for it made him anxious. Thankfully I was able to stop myself quickly. But at some point, I'll have to insist he trust me and let me make decisions he's afraid of. How will that happen?

January 19
Father, we find ourselves much more aware of *ending*, of the realization that the end of earthly life will come in this season, and having questions about it. What will the doorway that transitions us from here to life without

limits be for each of us? As Wayne often says, should we be doing some things to prepare for the doorway entry, the terminal disease? Should we investigate memory care facilities? I feel pressed to get his devotionals on an external hard drive, to get some of my journal entries transcribed, to reduce stuff in the house, to put in a walk-in shower for down the road... I ask you to help me do these things, to give time and health throughout this preparing...

After not writing his devotional for two days, he was confused about it being from Acts when the daily reading schedule also included Acts. He couldn't figure it out, for they were two different schedules. Sunday night he again dreamed there were animal attackers; he struck out at them, pushing me in the face a couple times. When talking about it Monday, he remembered having become a bit fearful when the three dogs were roughing it up at Jeff's. (And they did knock me over; fortunately, I landed on the couch.)

John Swinton came to speak for the Calvin January Series, and since we'd both read his book (*Dementia: Living in the Memories of God*), we decided to go. He urged people to keep emphasizing the personhood of the dementia sufferer, and to say to each other, "It's good that you are here; I'm glad you exist." We began doing that, but unfortunately, I didn't always remember.

February 9
(Genesis 45) Jacob thought Joseph was dead and now finds he's alive. Lord, we too seem to be in a life-robbing experience, as Alzheimer's slowly takes more away. I ask anew for reversals, for life-promoting to reverse life-robbing.

February 11
Father, you have given us so much. Thank you for such good. I pray you continue to supply the resources

> needed in these declining years. Lord, will we have to pay for nursing home care? I pray you make a way for us both to stay home...Thank you for the ability to watch Elmhurst Church's worship service and for the reminder of how you've used Wayne to plant *New* there, which has grown ever since. ...Lord, I cry for my husband. It seems you used him to accomplish a lot for your church, which he loves. And now we listen to all Elmhurst Church is doing in the Kingdom, grateful to have been a part, yet realizing we sit here alone, apart from it all, mostly because of Alzheimer's. And I don't even know what to ask you...I just say thank you for knowing us, welcoming our offerings in ministry, supplying for life now...

February 14 I had what seemed to be a significant dream: Wayne and I were back in a neighborhood from our past that was familiar to us. As we drove away from a gathering, we discovered that the road that used to go around the corner no longer did. We, therefore, started walking but found the sidewalk also ended; we were on private lawns. A man was working on his landscaping. I apologized for walking through it, saying we remembered when there'd been a road there and that we were trying to get through now. That happened more than once. Then we were on a stone path with side fences. Wayne was up ahead of me when a blanket was thrown from behind me. It was over me and then started to drop on me, beginning to envelope me. I thought, "Wayne will never hear me cry out for help..." Then I awakened.

> Lord, is it telling me my life will be smothered? Or that I'm unconsciously afraid of that, not hearing MRI results yet? or that an enemy force (the landowner did not like our being there) is attempting to rob life. or quality of life?

> **February 15**
> ...It didn't cause fear – does that mean it wasn't life-threatening? It would seem to make sense if it was

Wayne getting covered, kept from moving on. I read yesterday about Persons With Dementia gradually feeling, sensing, realizing they can't keep up with a group's conversation and, therefore, feel they're being removed from society. So, Father, did you give me a picture, an experience of that before reading it, so that I would be more understanding of what he's facing? And the enveloping – no one who keeps walking down the trail ahead will hear the soul cries of the AD sufferer.

O Lord, there's so much more than I'd ever realized. I thought, like most people probably, that AD persons disappear under that "blanket," and don't know it. They're "blissfully ignorant, unaware," people say. But that's not the case, is it? We've made it all about the mind, but there's so much more to the person, and the sufferer feels the blanket gradually descending over him. He knows within that he'll be all alone under it, and people won't hear his cries. He won't even know how to make the cries. And others won't recognize that they are cries. So, Lord, please help me hear today and keep him from loneliness today…

O Lord, what you're teaching me is so good. You're creating in me an empathy that I've not had. I've always kept things at arm's length, I'm afraid – a coping mechanism. So, I marvel at this goodness. You are teaching me to love; you are setting me free from more of my self-protections. How amazing your love.

February 17
(Matthew 16:13–20) You revealed to Peter what was beyond his own knowledge and understanding. You truly are the God who comes near, who reveals things to your children. You showed Peter plain, clear truth, beyond what he could have learned from natural sources. It's information to the mind first, and then you go beyond, and it becomes *knowledge* deep within, with absolute certainty. Father, it's amazing to be led here today when

this is exactly what you did for me in these last days! Through reading Swinton's book, my mind was receiving information about AD, but then you showed it to me in a dream, and that information became experienced knowledge. You went beyond; you revealed deeper understanding. And I lift praise, for I stand amazed. Truly you are able to go beyond, to do so much more than we could think or imagine. I recognize your assignment of loving him, understanding better what AD is like for him. Thank you.

February 19
I sense you taking me beyond how I was viewing our situation; I was letting AD dominate, though unconsciously. You opened my eyes to that, helping me return to having that diagnosis as one of his identities, rather than the only one. I bow anew, and ask you to keep showing me what you see. Thank you, Father.

February 21
(John 21) Lord, I too sense the question, "Do you love me?" (15–17) and it may be that your instruction ("tend my sheep") to me today is to tend my husband in the new assignment you've placed on him. Lord, I so need your help in this. He's again very fearful today – of traveling, driving, being away.

Wayne struggled last night to enter the two monthly checks; it took two hours. I had to sit right there, for he'd write something and then say, "This doesn't look right." He'd written in the wrong places. He has realized things are harder at night than in the morning.

March 1 I had a dream: I was playing keyboard with a band in front of a group. At one point, the drummer asked me to do another song, so I did, but then I was the only one playing. It was a difficult piece, and I was skipping notes, managing to play the chords at least. As it finished, a child stood in my way, blocking the music from view; someone told him to move. When a woman went to close the meeting with prayer, I realized she and the man with her were filled with the Spirit, and I wanted to get to them. (It seems, years later, that the child blocking the view of the music was in fact Wayne. That is what happened in the later stage of AD, as he "blocked" me from participating in the worship music at church. At the time I realized I needed to stay close to the Spirit's flow.)

March 5
Father, I read the book from L____, *Blessed Are Those Who Mourn* (Dennis Maxey), about the pain of losing his wife, of living now with her not there. Lord, it was good, with raw emotion, and was well-said. I find myself wondering about the trek I'm on, one of little by little feeling the loss of the one I'm married to. There are some ways of relating to him that are gone; others are still here, and others are in process of changing. For example, he now checks with me regarding the outfit he's chosen. He never looked to me for fashion advice before AD! But that part of him is starting to leave. A part that's gone is the confidence in his ability to find a destination; he'd never had fear in that and always just headed in its general direction, sure he'd find it. I miss *that* Wayne; I felt secure, knowing he'd figure things out. To me, that's loss, and I grieve. I have to take the responsibility myself. It's not death, but it's partial-death living.

March 7
(Deuteronomy 31:3) "The LORD your God himself will go over before you." Father, I remember how you gave me assurance regarding this move to Zeeland, and again I marvel and thank you.... In the early months here, I felt a strong call to "Get ready!" At the time I thought it was about preparing the house and freezing baked goods for visiting people. It was that, but more. Now, yesterday, I realized it is about getting ready for Alzheimer's next stages. You heard my question regarding a walk-in

shower being constructed and helped me help Wayne accept doing it by urging me again to "Get ready." Thank you so. I stand amazed at your leading, your help, your equipping. So, I pray you provide a builder and show us how to do it.

March 9
Lord, I wonder about the things Wayne thinks he hears at night. Last night again he got up, thinking stones had been thrown at the basement door. (Previous times he'd thought someone was at the front door, or he'd hear voices outside, or someone calling to him.) Is there something here that is revealing? Is the next stage of Alzheimer's at the door? Or are these heavenly voices, meaning he's near...? Or is it from your enemy, suggesting to him he's in danger, when in fact you're with him, keeping him safe? Is it a message to me that his unconscious self is feeling unsure, unsafe, and I need to supply assurance of safety? Help me, I plead, if you have something for me in this.

March 21 Wayne had a dream: I heard him say something, and I asked what he'd said. He said, "Did you see him?" I said, "Who?" He said, "He's standing by your side of the bed." I said, "Who?" He raised himself on an elbow and looked over me at the side of the bed. "He was standing right there; now he's gone."

Lord, my first thought was to wonder if he was seeing an angel? There wasn't any fear in him, or in me, so I didn't think it a demon. Or was it what is known as dementia's hallucinating? I like to think you send comfort, reminders of your very-present care. I know you are with us and give you thanks anew.

March 22
Father on High, LORD God Above, I bow anew... Truly you do lighten my darkness. Yesterday, I was in the

dark, not seeing a way regarding something I'd thought you'd led me to do (putting in a walk-in shower) as part of the "getting ready" needed for life down the road. You broke through and showed me we could recoup the cost in about a year! And then it didn't look so dark! Lord, I'm remembering how firm I was in 2013 in believing you were sending us to Michigan and then specifically to this place, so firm that I didn't even ask the cost before agreeing to it.. And now I have the firm belief that you're telling me to get ready… and this came to mind as one of the things to do. I marvel that you would know me, that you would lead me. O Lord, who am I that you bless me this way also?

March 23
Lord, when I look down the road regarding dementia, I get a little scared. I'm getting ready with this bathroom project, I believe. Please help me get ready also by being more attentive, caring, having less of self at work. I still have so much more to do regarding the command to "deny yourself daily, take up your cross and follow" you. Help me today, I pray, especially in conveying "It is good you're here" to Wayne. We have so much good from you…

I experienced frustration, as I had to explain what I was thinking for Judah's birthday. It was questioned and challenged. I miss the Wayne who would have the idea himself. Now I have to come up with the idea, defend it, and execute it. Since it's not natural to me it can be draining.

March 28
Lord, you have asked me to become a caregiver, something I'm not very good at, and him to accept dependence, something he's not very good at. So, I look to you, as I know he is doing also, knowing you will be there, and you will equip. Help us, Lord, for we "have not walked this way before." (Joshua 3:4) Gone

is the assumption that in this chapter of life we'd be doing what we'd always been doing – assisting in church ministry. Still, we know there's ministry – why should we be surprised that it's to come out of a new struggle?

Wayne brought up the armor of God (Ephesians 6:13–18), asking what comes after the belt of truth? I then realized I haven't seen him putting it on when he gets up in the morning, something he's done, sitting on the edge of the bed, for decades. Why would that go?

April 3
Thank you for providing for me today…I pray you protect us as we move forward with a contractor, guard our nest egg and keep us through the replenishment time. Twice I have been reminded of the replenishment capability, in the first considerations before you and then during last night as fear surfaced and I cried to you. I believe those assurances were from you and I receive. You know our net worth and you know our future and its needs. I have sensed this project to be part of the "getting ready." So please guard our steps, I pray.

April 6
(Psalm 27:13) "I believe that I shall look upon the goodness of the LORD in the land of the living!" Every day there's good from you, including the apparent stability of the Alzheimer's, our health and mobility, and our ability to install a walk-in shower. O Lord, you bring good to us daily – in the land of the living. I bow, overwhelmed again by your good hand being on us, and by your amazing love.

Wayne has put on the armor of God sometimes lately, but last night while praying before sleeping he stumbled with it. He also had another dream: he was kicking at something, suggesting it was under the covers. I said, "Wayne, you're dreaming." He said, "No, I'm not. Don't you see them jumping onto the bed?" "No." Then he resumed sleeping. The dentist visit yesterday revealed there's decay under a crown, at an impossible-to-reach spot. But it made me think: should I be involved in his teeth brushing?

The night before last, I couldn't sleep. Wayne started talking about "them taking dogs back and forth." When asked what he meant, he said, "The men down there (at the garage down the hill) are taking dogs back and forth down there (in the valley behind our house)." He also said, "I'm not sleeping." Later I heard him cry out, but he didn't respond to my checking on him.

There were two changes this week: he wandered in Baker Book Store and had no inclination to look seriously or buy a book. In the past he rarely left a book store without buying a book! And yesterday, he brought his devotional verse, asking me to help him understand it.

TAKING A BREAK
(2)

Some I talked with along this path were surprised that I felt very inadequate being a caregiver, as I've mentioned in these pages. I did learn to care for people in our churches and in the jail; I came alongside them and sought to care by entering their struggle and by attempting to bring the Lord's love and encouragement. But in our family needs, it was Wayne who knew the best way to care for a child's scrapes, bruises, illnesses, and so forth. I just didn't have ideas and felt inadequate in the taking care of health needs.

Similar to that is the fact that he was the idea person in our relationship and family. Ideas for fun, activities, or family devotions came easily to him. He was creative in many areas; I just always seemed to come up empty. Hence, to be the caregiver, to be the one to suggest something to do or some new way of helping was not at all natural to me. I was afraid I'd miss something, something that would come easily to someone else, and was afraid I just wouldn't know what to do and be neglectful. Therefore, I often pleaded for the Lord to supply me with thoughts and ideas; I am still amazed at how he led me.

* * *

May 4 Yesterday started hard; Wayne had the day's schedule in mind and then our daughter-in-law Shelly texted about Izzy's game. Just that small change evoked anxiety – "how am I going to get my walk in?" – on top of the confusion regarding the devotional schedule. He couldn't grasp that the devotional is on a two-month rotation. He also talked again about getting up during the night to walk around and check things. (Does he really do that?) And he said he again heard voices by our neighbor's place (he thinks intruders go in there since she's gone) and down the hill by the garage (one couldn't really hear that far, with all our windows closed?). I said, "Are they angels?" I wondered, "Lord, is this hallucinating? Still, I don't want to dismiss though the possibility of your coming to him."

He needed dental work today. The dentist said there was much decay under a crown and he wasn't sure what could be done until he "got in there to see." Wayne wanted me in the room, not just given a report at the end. I realized my presence was a help to him, and I got understanding of the situation. The Lord answered our prayer for wisdom and made a way to keep the tooth. How good! The Lord was giving me, I sensed, another opportunity, as with the dream, to feel with him. In order to do that I have to *stop* focusing on my lists.

May 22
So, Lord, you took your child P___ home. What a shock, but you spared him great difficulty from "aggressive treatment." I admit I feel a bit "abandoned," as he understood that Alzheimer's sufferers need others who remember who they are. The possibility of that being communicated through him, and of having a friend continue with Wayne, is gone. So, I come to you, acknowledging again that you know and have a way for us.... I rest in you. You have kept Wayne in the mild stage and asked me, I've sensed, to "Get ready..." Lord, am I there? Are we ready after this bathroom is in? But

I thought it was also getting friends in place who'd take him for coffee and engage with him? P___ is no longer available; another didn't respond at all. And we're too far from our church. Is there something else I should do? Who is close by, who remembers who he is for him? Help us, I pray.... (9 pm) George called!

May 25
I pray you continue to make our way. Also, keep me alert to your guidance, as you show me what needs to be done to get ready, and supply what's needed. Thank you for the walk-in shower, for my health and mobility. Help me get at some things: old prayer journals read, storage room stuff reduced, picture albums made for him...

Wayne has taken to slowing way down for a green light, afraid it'll turn red. If he's going full speed, he'd have to make a decision fast and he senses he can't do that. I guess that's the reason, and that is pressure, anxiety-producing. Of course, he responded to my comment by saying, "I'll drive the way I want to."

May 28
Lord, thank you for Wayne's plateau of sorts. Perhaps there's a little deterioration, but mostly, it remains quite even, it seems. Thank you also for talks we can have and for George reminding us to pray for reversals. Lord, that too is good. Thank you for his doing that and for Wayne joining in it. Please lead me, for I don't know what to think. Certainly, I'd want reversal and not have him completely dependent. What does it all mean? Please guide me...and thank you for being merciful to me.

Since he was such a good idea person Wayne usually had trouble doing what wasn't his idea. So, it makes sense in that light that he resists and can get crabby, for almost nothing is his idea anymore. He has to go along with what I put on the schedule. He said this morning, "I'm so sick of tagging along. I'd rather just stay away..." I'm understanding more; it's a gradual losing of autonomy, which feels as if he is losing himself.

June 4 He sat up in bed, saying, "Hi" as though he was glad to see the person. Then he got up and walked towards the door. I asked if he was all right; he said, "I'm getting the light." Then he turned on the ceiling light and stood facing the bed. "Do you see it?" he asked. I asked "What?" "Check under the pillow." I did. Then he said, "Oh..." and went to the bathroom, then to the kitchen area, then crawled back in bed. I lay awake for a while, wondering if this is the hallucinating that dementia patients can have. Is it a sign of greater dementia?

> **June 6**
> (Psalm 69:33) "For the LORD hears the needy and does not despise his own people who are prisoners." You see and hear the cries of your people, including those trapped in some way, such as being captive to dementia, to the prison of self, cut off from all. O Lord, thank you for working in it all, for meeting your child even in a prison, for working good, for being connection to him when all else is cut off.

He's going golfing with a couple guys from one of our churches today (he'll be picked up at 7:15). He spent a lot of time getting things ready last night and was up at 5 this morning. Then there was more concern over what to wear, the clubs, and so forth.

> **June 16**
> (Psalm 77:19) "Your way was through the sea..." How good to be reminded that you take us through what appears to be impossible (a sea) and are so often unseen. I pray you continue to lead us through Alzheimer's realities, parting its normal experiences so that we walk through to the other side.

June 17
My Father, I look to you. It's been a hard morning already, as his resistance kicked in and showed itself. What do I do? Yield to his preferences entirely, which then would eliminate a lot of encounters with people? He thinks about coming things and gets afraid and anxious about it. Please, Lord, lead me. Help me to know if something is good to press him into or if I should back off.

June 18
Father, thank you for carrying us through yesterday, for meeting us in worship (how good!), and in discussing my question. Yes, he agrees there's change, and he doesn't like events back-to-back. So, we need a day or so in between them. Please help me, I pray, to figure it out and to convince him to let me drive when he's tired at the beginning of the day already. Thank you, Father. You know this path you've put us on, and we don't. I look to you and admit I'd been living as though we'd just continue as we were, able to do one or two events a day. Please help me adjust…

June 23
Lord, it's a *down* day. He seems so down, apparently from pain. Please be our strength today and make my strength to be for good rather than harm. I bring you thoughts again that a terminal physical illness would be easier than Alzheimer's. Please, Lord, help me… forgive such selfishness and make new – patience, understanding, and love that's beyond my natural self.

I need to tell the doctor there's pain in his hip and abdomen, which he sometimes says is like a pulled muscle. Other times, he says food doesn't sound good, especially salad or veggies, as though that's what's giving the discomfort, the weight loss. Might that be? His communication is more difficult to follow. (Wayne died two and one half years after this from a bleeding stomach ulcer which had never been discovered. Was this evidence it was already affecting him?)

June 24
O Lord, I wonder why he sleeps so much – is it Alzheimer's, or depression, or something physical? Help me know what's best and what will help...

July 4
(Psalm 88) This describes a really dark experience. The psalmist believes you caused him to be shunned by companions, by his beloved and his friend (8, 18). O Lord, I wonder if Wayne wonders about that – who will shun him, stay away from him because of Alzheimer's? I know I had that capability myself, and I marvel at your mercy in showing me otherwise. So, I desire to be merciful to others, as I see Wayne doing already. This path, this assignment is your choice for him, for me, and I look to you for your help, and also help from others. Thank you again for George moving close by.

Wayne did well on a trip to Door County and while there. He got really tired since there was a lot of activity, and we awakened early each morning. He shared about his disease at Sunday School; Rog said it was clearly spoken, in contrast to the rest of the time when words were hard to find.

We're understanding his wanting to sleep better. After the evening with friends, he was very tired the next morning. It was not only from working to convey thoughts but also from working to follow what's being said. His brain just gets tired.

For several days he's come to me confused between the date (August 10) and the chapter for his devotional (Acts 20). So, I retyped the schedule, repeating the names August and Acts on each day listed. But he was still confused. He's come twice this morning to check what chapter his devotional is on.

August 11
Again, Lord, I ask you to give me enough health and strength to take care of things for our lives and our life together. Put me back on my feet I pray (as you are doing – thank you!) Help me pace my activities so that I don't harm the healing process. (I was dealing with an infected foot ulcer.)

Wayne did really well again with all the visiting in Illinois until returning to Rockford Sunday afternoon. He didn't recognize any of the roads we were taking and kept asking about them. Then it finally clicked. "Oh, we take that way to Sarah," he said, pointing where to turn. I attributed it to great fatigue of keeping up with all the conversations at the friends' gathering.

We talked about what we see happening, realizing that his frequent napping probably comes from the fatigue of conversing, reading, trying to follow what's being said on TV. I told him about seeing the greater cautiousness in driving this last trip. He believes he needs to be cautious so that he can keep driving. I told him I'm willing to drive and not afraid to do it.

September 3
Lord, we have had some challenges this weekend as the treadmill required work and then the fridge quit. So, with that comes *angst* and fussing and worry about money, and more fussing, pressing me to do something. But I don't know what... Thank you for leading regarding the treadmill; please help regarding the fridge... and regarding my responses to him which should be more assuring than scolding. Lord, "the buck stops here" has not been on me like this. There was always someone to help and to talk with about big needs. I'm feeling the weight of it and plead for your mercy, your help to break through to me. Help me know what's best...

> **September 13**
> (Psalm 116:16) "Precious in your sight is the death of your children." O Lord, to us death is an enemy, for it separates with finality and can occur over a span of time (as with AD, or cancer), causing hardship and struggle perhaps. But to you it's a wonderful thing! It ushers your child into your full presence! And that is good! Thank you for such a "benefit" (12) as complete freedom from this life's impurity. Thank you for life today and things to do and see... Please meet us in it all and protect... and Lord, I ask for time yet to do the reading of my past journals and get to reducing stuff in the storage room...
>
> **September 21**
> O Lord, I need help to know how to lead him and not have our lives be led by Alzheimer's or by his discomforts. On the other hand, his discomforts are more pronounced by the AD and call for me to give assurance and security. How? When irrational fears are added in as well (also more pronounced by AD)? What should I do regarding going to Rockford? Please lead me, I pray, to bring good into our lives these days and to give assurance throughout.

We discovered a lump in his abdomen Saturday and saw the doctor last evening. It's a hernia. Wayne prepared all day for the visit, sometimes asking, "What shall we say when telling the doctor?" sometimes rehearsing something himself, asking again what words to use. He also asked what the three words had been from the doctor's dementia test. I told him, and he rehearsed them as well. That was the exact test given then! He got two of the words, and the third one with a clue. So, we 'fessed up to the doctor, who laughed about him "studying for the test!" But then he said it's really good Wayne can remember there *is* a test and that three words were given on it. That shows there isn't "significant dementia" yet.

As Wayne put planned events on his calendar, he indicated he thought it was too much. "We were going to be more careful," he said. We had agreed to have fewer social events and it seemed to me we were accomplishing that. So, I struggled to be understanding. This morning he realized he has an underlying fear – "When is AD going to change something? Will something suddenly happen when I'm involved in one of those events?" But then he also said he doesn't want to drop out of everything and just stay home.

He had difficulty entering the checks in the ledger, needing my help with every step. At one point he said, "I just shouldn't do this anymore." Yesterday he got confused when adding the tip to a restaurant bill. He wrote 250 instead of 2.50. Then he couldn't figure out how to rectify it. He didn't seem bothered that our friends saw it.

October 25
He broke out singing, "There she is..." as I came down the hall and then gave me a tight embrace, saying, "Ah, safety." That's what he looks for from me, and I realize sometimes I'd like it from him. But he did give it all those years.

For some time also he comes to me asking about a name from one of our previous churches, someone he wants to pray for. Almost daily, he asks for M___'s name. This morning he asked the last name of friends in Denver, people he knew so well. Now he's talking with L___ (who called him). The Lord sends him people. Last week it was friends from Lockport, and yesterday at Family Fare a woman who used to work there and whom he stopped to greet and ask about her life told him she now has Parkinson's. So, he told her he's struggling also, and it's with Alzheimer's. She was given encouragement through him. And at church yesterday a man who had come to us drunk in the prayer room some time ago now came up to Wayne saying he's just out of prison and that it was the best help for him. He thanked Wayne for his care.

November 30
Father God, I'd asked you to strengthen me, and I guess I expected it to come supernaturally. I now realize that *has* to be how it comes, for last night was a terrible night, for both of us. We each blame the other. I blame him for waking me up so often and therefore for the heartbeat acceleration I am feeling. He blames me for playing for the concert tonight, keeping him from just staying home. So, here I am, Lord. I said I'd play and do the musical transition each time; did I overstep? Should I be giving this up so he can retreat? O Lord, please help... fill me with strength to make it through (and return home again tonight), to enter the heart of the song, to remember each transition... and fill Wayne with strength for the hanging around, help him to make it through the evening, and especially to bring the whole concert experience into your presence as he opens with prayer. Overcome all attempts to hinder, to steal, to blind...

December 1
Wow! I just keep thinking Wow! Thank you so for overcoming the roadblocks sent to us Thursday night (Wayne's night of great pain, my heart racing and lack of sleep). You prevailed, you gave us both strength from above, you used both of us in the concert, and you blessed our church powerfully. So, so good. Thank you for such a privilege given both of us...

December 12
(Psalm 139:24) "...lead me in the way everlasting." And lead me these days in learning how to love, to give... Lord, what does our future look like? I admit it was hard to read a description of an AD sufferer; what if I can't do this? Please give me enough health, and two legs and feet to take care here (I was still dealing with the infected

foot ulcer). For Lord, do we have enough money for a nursing home? Please lead, show the way, and provide for it, I pray.

(Acts 20:24) "I consider my life worth nothing to me, if only I may finish the race and complete the task the Lord Jesus has given me..." I sense my task is to love my husband, though he has AD and to show it by caring for him, respecting him through it all, to the end. Fill me, I pray, Holy Spirit, and let it flow to him.

We had such a good time last night with friends. Wayne could throw the dice for Bunko, but couldn't tally the score. Others kept his score, and he seemed okay with that. As we left, one friend said to me, "Take good care of this guy."

Wayne asked me about the positions on a football team – running back, right and left tackle, and others. He couldn't come up with the terms. And last night, climbing bleachers for a school concert was really hard for him. He told me later that his depth perception is off, plus he can see two bleacher rows rather than one and wondered which to aim for. This morning when we prayed, he told the Lord he realizes he's not learning very well and asked for the ability to learn. (Yes, Lord.) Two days ago he napped a lot in the chair. On waking up he said, "Look at those bugs!" I couldn't see anything. I figured his deep sleep was still affecting him. But several minutes later he got up and started hitting the wall in the living room. He said, "Come see all these orange bugs." Still, there was nothing there. He gradually just walked away.

December 24 We're in Paw Paw for the weekend. We came Saturday for two rehearsals, I played three services Sunday morning, and we stayed so we could be part of the Christmas Eve service worship team. We learned Saturday that my brother-in-law John had died. Adding the visitation and funeral to these days' schedule totally confused Wayne. He kept mixing the funeral and the Christmas Eve service; it threw everything off last night. He was very confused about clothing, and also got up several times during the night. He put on a T-shirt at one point, inside out and backwards. He knew he was confused and apologized.

> Lord, lead me from here "in the way I should go" – should I stop playing? Is the long morning too much for him now? Should we always stay home and not be in other (increasingly unfamiliar) places overnight? But wouldn't he deteriorate also if only at home?

It was still new for me to pick out his clothes. Now I had to find the whole outfit for the funeral. I suggested a sweater vest, which he found, but he kept bringing flannel shirts. Once I found a shirt, he knew which pants.

December 29
> Lord, another funeral has me thinking even more about funeral services and my desire to put order to this house and especially to the prayer journals. I pray you give me health and strength to do it. An article I read today was about being relentless in faith in moving toward the finish line, having a "finisher's anointing." I ask for that, for the ability to overcome whatever your enemy sends our way, and for Wayne to be a "relentless conqueror," as the article called it, as he too finishes rather than quits.

There's great confusion today because he's finished both the devotional and reading schedules, and the new ones start tomorrow. He just couldn't figure it out. Yesterday he slept all afternoon, waking up after two hours to use the bathroom, then went back to sleep. I awakened him for supper and then he slept all evening also. The Christmas and funeral services really took a toll on him.

December 31
Lord, as I look ahead, I wonder – I read yesterday that "some Alzheimer's would be reversed (cured)." But as I see greater confusion and realize he slept all day yesterday, I question myself: do I want it reversed? Or do I like the capability you've been building in me as you've responded to my cries for help? I admit, I like some of it, and I think it would not have happened without AD. So, Lord, I come to you; you know this already and I know you receive me. Reversing AD would be so very good for him and, yes, for me. And I give to you my self-concern and continued self-seeking. If reversed, would I be "learning to love," or would I return to responding to love? or will competing be there? I seem so complicated. But you know the way. Please meet me, reveal to me your will, I pray, and forgive my selfishness again... Am I learning to love because I finally see him needing me, needing help, when he actually did before but I was too focused on self? Lord Jesus, please carry me today and into a new year.

2019

The outside Christmas light timer got messed up and Wayne couldn't sleep. He worried that it would cause a fire. He got up several times to check and finally asked me if he could pull the plug. After that he slept a while. I woke up at five and saw him sleeping in the recliner, the TV on. (He'd already put out the garbage.)

Sunday was also hard for him. Once a month Wayne sang and I played keyboard in our church which is pastored by our daughter and her husband in Paw Paw. Since we were on the schedule yesterday, we needed to get up early. The alarm was set for 5:40, but he was up before 5. He came in making noise and was all anxious, so I was then also awake. I drove to Paw Paw in the dark; he slept. He also slept during the sermon in each of the three services, got two naps in the car as I drove home, and slept two hours in the afternoon (as did I). He also slept off and on during the evening. Doing this kind of thing makes him so anxious — afraid of AD causing something unexpected, and uncontrollable? — that he does a lot of sleeping. But he still enjoys singing on the team, and the fact that he does it is appreciated by many.

Hernia surgery has added to Wayne's confusion. He couldn't figure out the difference between pjs and the next morning's clothes, or how to make coffee. But that is now better. Still, he gets terribly confused regarding the devotional schedule; he can't figure out the difference between the date number and the chapter number.

> **January 13**
> Lord, these added struggles showed me that confusion could become our "normal." He'd then be even more dependent, even unable to be left alone. Will that be what we experience down the road? If so, what things should be in place? What comes to mind are the projects around here that I want to accomplish: pictures sorted, stuff reduced and disposed of, memorial services planned, prayer journals sorted, housecleaning done –- things that should be done before needing to give more time to him. Should I be investigating the home help options?

I asked yesterday if he thought he's slipped in entering our income checks. He said, "Yes," and we talked about it being a month between each time so there's lots of time to forget. That led to getting simple math workbooks for him.

January 25 As he hears about financial things (as at the bank this morning) fear rises, and he jumps to believing "they're out to get our money," and things like that. Still, thank you, Lord, for providing for us there.

Every morning now I help him get started in his journal and help him find the Bible passage.

> **February 1**
> (Psalm 9) "The LORD is a stronghold to the oppressed... in times of trouble." Lord God, you are a stronghold to Wayne, oppressed by AD, and to me, in this time of "trouble..." He's always been good at sensing things, and that has increased. It's just that what he senses now is much more fear than he'd ever had. So, I need to give assurance, rather than use logic, and I need help in this, for logic is my approach! Will our living get to the point of being run by what he fears? Probably? "But the LORD sits enthroned forever..." (7)

February 5 I had a dream: I was with a family and saw that the oldest child (an eleven-year-old girl) was taking care of everything. Wayne, who was the father, had AD. Several times she asked him to get something from the kitchen, and he kept bringing different objects. She was getting more and more frustrated. I said to her, "He doesn't remember what you ask for." Later, I was telling some others about it, saying, "An eleven-year-old is responsible for the household!" I felt bad for her.

> Lord, as I awakened, I sensed I can be that eleven-year-old; I can forget that he forgets and get frustrated. I need to keep before me the truth of his condition. I should, for I'm an adult, not an eleven-year-old!

> **February 6**
> Father God, grumpiness came out again today. "Going to three events a week is too much," he's saying, and that leaves me needing to ascertain if that's indeed what AD is doing – is it making him fearful of encounters with people so that he wants to reduce the number of times? It leaves me – hurt, that he can want to skip family opportunities; confused, wondering if an AD experience

needs my help; angry, that he verbally jabs me and blames me for having to do something he doesn't want to do. So – what now? I feel dominated by it. Father, please help, and turn my thoughts; show me how to proceed. AD has required me to take the lead; perhaps that's what's bothering him.

O Lord, am I also jealous, as I feel alone? I see a couple dealing with cancer, and they had tons of responses to their Facebook plea for prayer. I get none. We have to retreat in silence to our corner, and within that corner he gives me the message that he doesn't want family contact, forcing me to be alone. I guess that's jealousy. What they have (cancer) isn't something to be shunned. "Be gracious to me, O LORD!" (Psalm 9:13) I need your help. We used to shoulder everything together, and now I'm feeling that shift.

February 7
Father, thank you for your awesome care. You gave Wayne understanding of why he was resisting. One thing was that "it all mounts up and looks like too much; therefore, I wonder if I can do it?" I talked about AD robbing space and time differences; that then robs the ability to see things separately, to realize they can be taken one at a time. I need to remember that also. Secondly, he loves our home, but being in this area reminds him of all that's *lost* because of AD. We can't do the things we used to do – he had autonomy, he ministered to and served people when he chose to, and separated when he wanted or needed to. He doesn't have that control anymore. All that loss hits periodically. Thank you, Father, for giving this ability to express what's going on inside. Someday, I suppose, that'll be gone, and then I'll need to do whatever it takes to calm fears. I think part of my reaction yesterday came out of this question: have we arrived at that point? So, Father, please keep me alert to your leading. Help me to know. Equip me, I pray.

He's very confused. He'd decided to take Sundays off from his devotional writing so there was no passage listed behind today's date. That totally confused him. Also, the numbers continue to confuse: today is the 17th and he kept saying, "There's no I Corinthians 17; something's wrong."

February 21 He suggested we should start throwing away sermons. We got the boxes out and I opened files. But I couldn't get rid of everything; it was too good! I kept the sermon itself and the bulletin, getting rid of notes and handouts. After two days of that, he admitted it was really hard to watch. Yesterday was check entering day. He did some of it, coming to me several times to have his work checked or to get help with a step. Finally, unable to understand my explanation of what was needed, he had to quit. It was early afternoon. Since he'd been at a ministers' prayer group in the morning, his mind was perhaps too tired.

> Lord, you're showing me further decline. I need to stay at getting ready for the next stage. Please prepare him for a talk about driving, and Jeff also.

February 23 We discussed having him drive with Jeff. He was quite disturbed. "I'm not there!" that is, he didn't yet have to stop driving. But finally, after a while, he settled into having Jeff check it out. He had taken it as accusation. I tried to convince him it wasn't that and that I was just trying to be responsible regarding AD's effects.

> Thank you, Father for helping me, us, to have the conversation and helping us get out the feelings that were also involved. He had felt accused, hurt by thinking I'd go off without him. I had felt responsible, needing to be aware of AD's progression. I hope I convinced him that I was not trying to be accusatory. Also, I'd so like him to understand that he took care of many things for me all those years, and that I now hope he'll receive

from me. Lord, thank you so for watching over us, for leading us in this journey. Please continue to alert me to steps I should be aware of, take...

The drive with Jeff went pretty well. Jeff and we talked together afterwards. The mental strain of being tested like that made Wayne very tired, so he slept three hours that afternoon. During the night he awakened me, asking me if I saw all the bugs flying above us. I said "No, I don't." He said he didn't either anymore. But then he kicked at them. This morning he said that he'd gotten up during the night, that he'd seen a swarm outside, that he heard someone say, "Good morning," and that he saw our neighbor feeding a deer. He added that he was fully awake for it all. I knew none of this was in fact true.

March 4
(Psalm 18:31) Lord, you have met me in the midst of hard things, renewed me, carried me on. You are my rock, my strength, my hope, my life. Thank you for such great love, such great care. Now, Lord, I plead for your care to fill me and then to flow out to Wayne, who's need for information to be repeated seems to grow. Is there going to be a sudden turn? Will he forget how to stop the car or how to get home? Please, Lord, protect him, me and other cars' passengers from harm if that happens and give me and our kids alerts and the ability to guide him. Help me make the most of this time of "high functioning." And I pray I'd have time to go through files, my teachings, my journals...

Buying a new car brought truth home – they were dealing with me, not him. That was hard, but he said he knew it was reality. He agreed to do it and then afterwards, we both realized that the change was too much, too new for him. He jumped to believing all concerning driving had changed. But he's been working at it, thinking he's made progress. Yesterday it was on his mind all day, so he practiced several times. After several days of practicing in a church parking lot, the starting, shifting, and stopping is making more sense to him. He really likes the car.

March 25
(Psalm 23:4) Lord God, my shepherd, I may be in the last turn toward "the valley of the shadow of death," with however long before I get there known to you, planned by you, and today at least, "I fear no evil." I could experience fear of AD's demands on me, fear because I don't know how... But even there, "You are with me, your rod [to fight wild 'animals'] and staff [to lead] are with me, [truly] they comfort me." Ah, Sovereign Lord, so very good you are to your children. I praise... I thank... I look to you to equip me for today and to lead me on your path.

All Monday afternoon we conversed with my sister and her husband and yesterday we talked for over two hours with Michaela. This morning he thought of skipping the ministers' gathering since he was so very tired mentally. I saw him fade from the conversation with Michaela. Two in a row is too much.

April 11
...Lord, I feel the weight of our current assignment. Before AD he would have taken hold (of income tax filing, for example), making the calls needed for it. Now it's all on me, plus there's his worrying. It feels very alone. I plead for your help in this....and in helping him navigate things. I need to do a better job of providing safety and assurance; please come and help...

April 21
It's the Day of Life (Easter), yet I saw death yesterday at work in Wayne, taking more life from his mind as he struggled to remember what to do in entering the checks. I admit I was frustrated because he kept interrupting my reading (I'd offered to sit with him for the process, but

he said he wanted to do it.) Finally, I think I realized the loss and felt for him. Then we did it together. Lord God of Life, please watch over us in this process and alert me, help me see more quickly. Conquering Lord, you have the way...

I was in bed all day yesterday with no strength; I slept almost the entire time. He worried and slept a lot also. That made him more confused. This morning he was very tired, confused and not able to get a devotional written. Later, we attended Isabel's soccer game; he couldn't follow what was going on. With each score, he asked who got it. Each time a save was cheered he asked if someone scored. It's so different for one who's always loved sports.

April 29
(Psalm 30:9-10) "What profit is there in my death...Will the dust praise you...Hear, O LORD, and be merciful to me! O LORD, be my helper!" Lord God Above, I too reach out to you for more time with physical health here, so I can be helper to him and bless him on his downhill slide – is he there? Has it begun? O Lord, please protect my heart health and circulation, please keep me walking and standing, able to continue working at house order, I pray. I will praise you and tell of your faithfulness (9).

His driving now is often more like a fifteen-year-old's. He's unsure what lane to be in, he asks often, "Should I....?" or receives from me, "Now do this, and so forth.

May 3
It seems, Lord, from old-age perspective, that if one isn't an initiator with other people, she will just be forgotten and perhaps more so because of AD. People are unsure if conversation is possible, perhaps, and therefore stay away. I also realize they miss a blessing that way. So,

I look to you and ask you to help me with the initiating, scheduling, and keeping contacts for him.

He's more confused this morning. He couldn't get the coffee making right, made a mess which he cleaned up, so to speak, and then got me out of bed. His entries in his journal were just scribblings.

May 6
(Psalm 38:11) "My friends and companions stand aloof from my plague…" Lord, sometimes it feels as though AD has brought this to us. I must remember the contacts you give, that you arrange and that are so good. As I see Facebook posts and pictures of our friends' travels, I think, "no one wants to see pictures of our journey, our 'travel' deeper into AD." That is reality here, but *reality* is with you, from you. You are here, and you do preserve his, my life. That is good. And I lift praise.

Now there are times Wayne can't read the clock and tell what time it is. This morning, he mentioned he was confused as he woke up, also saying he's "sick of it." I asked if he was referring to what AD is doing. He said yes.

May 14
Lord God my Father, you are *life*, you are my Life, forever. Father, Death has come near (several we know just died), and Wayne has lost more inches – he had no idea this morning how to begin in his journal. Yet the world in front of me is teeming with the life of spring! New green and more of it each day. You hold life in your hand. Yours was the decision to take them home; yours is the decision to take life from Wayne inch by inch, even the life of the word – how can it be, Lord? But you know, and you work good, for you are good.

May 16
He said he wasn't feeling well (it wasn't a physical thing) from the beginning of the day. Nevertheless, he wanted to enter the checks. He needed help and direction, however, each step. I told him what to do, he'd do it, though sometimes he was not able to subtract because the "borrowing became too hard to remember." A few times, it clicked, almost automatically, and then was gone again.

May 26
Lord Jesus, I ask you to lead me regarding the changes in Wayne. Are there things with which I could occupy him in these hours when he can't come up with something to do himself? Please lead me, give me ideas, help me know… And I ask for others to help – who? Please provide.

Yesterday, apart from church, he mostly just sat, slept, watched a little TV. He did no reading, no exercise, no Bible reading. He didn't feel like playing a game or riding to the lake.

June 1
Lord, please counsel me regarding Wayne and driving. It seems it shouldn't be done anymore, except perhaps around town here. But saying that would be so hurtful. If it's right, please prepare him and overcome all possible shame, I ask in your name.

CHAPTER THREE
Bigger Downward Steps

Yesterday was Wayne's six-month checkup with the doctor. I noticed he didn't bring up the three words ahead of time, only once a couple of weeks ago. He struggled to come up with his birth date for the nurse (though he'd written it at check in, or did I help?). Perhaps because of that the nurse did not give him the memory test, none of it. The doctor seemed to know there'd been change. He advised him to keep using the brain, read, do word games, and so forth.

June 8
Lord, it's a new day, a day of realizing Stage II is definitely here. I wonder about the ramifications of that – regarding keeping him going, keeping him participating in activities, yet without overloading him. Lord, you'll "never let me down" nor leave us to do this alone. And I thank you. Please help me to help him honorably...

June 15
I pray you lead me to know what I should be doing for him – how can I keep him active but not pressured? And how do I honor him as my equal even as I take over for him? Please lead, I pray...

Changes keep happening. We had a good trip to Rockford, then to Dubuque, and back to Rockford. He kept voicing a desire to shorten it all, however. We were gone five days total. He accepted me doing the driving and did pretty well overall, though he was quieter. This Sunday he insisted he'd drive to Douglas but then backed off and let me do it. Last night he put away some of his folded laundry, then brought the T-shirts, asking where they go. He also admitted he was uneasy about me being gone three hours today to have lunch in Grand Rapids with high school friends. Neither did he want someone (I'd suggested our granddaughter Michaela) coming to be with him. So, I cancelled going. This morning he brought his pill box to me, asking which he should take. I helped him write the date and reference in his journal and showed him where to start in his Bible and where to end. It took a few times of showing him before it clicked for him. (He hadn't done it for a week because of our trip; apparently, he lost some ground in that week.)

He got gas in the car yesterday. He needed to go in and ask for help because he couldn't get the credit card to work – he was using his driver's license. In the morning I had to deal with the internet being out, again. I couldn't get it to work and said I'd have to call. He apologized, feeling very bad that he was no help to me. I admit, I'd had a similar thought. It'd be so nice if he could take care of something. Yesterday we tried the check entering again. It just didn't make sense to him. He wants another crack at it this morning; he keeps reviewing the steps. Yesterday we grieved together.

June 22
Lord, I also sense that life on earth includes loss all along the way, and we are just seeing it now as AD robs more again. Yesterday you helped me to see, to feel, and not just move on to the next thing to do – thank you! Even as the robber takes, you give, and I praise you. I look to you and plead for you to open me more and more, to let care preempt doing (caring for). Lord, I

am so weak here. Thank you for your graciousness that, in this late season of life, still offers newness. Open my eyes today, I pray...

Wayne told me about all the bugs he sees when he gets up and showed me the toilet bowl, the light fixture above the mirror, the bedroom light fixture – all covered with bugs, he said. I cleaned the one from the bedroom. Hallucinations?

June 29
(Psalm 37:7) "...fret not yourself over the one who prospers in his way..." Lord God, I come... and realize I can see prosperity not in all that money lets people our age experience, but in the fact that they can do things together, both fully cognizant and both able to take responsibility. I see that and I feel the loss. I admit I would have liked that (and liked to have been taken care of at times). I come anew and bow before you. You are my Lord, you have chosen my path, you are working for good in it, and I thank you. I know I'm carrying responsibility only in the help you give. Thank you so for all you supply. I look to you today; please show me how to be blessing to him...

June 30
Father, these days have been hard since putting AC on. There's wondering and inability to understand how the thermostat works, fearing and worrying about doing it wrong and therefore spending too much money, fearing when it starts running and when it stops. O Lord, such helplessness, and such fear, and such inability to trust me with it. Please help us, help me... and what about driving today? Please protect, I pray.

Yesterday he came to me asking, "Where is your woman book?" It took a while, but then I realized he meant *The Apostolic Woman* (Linda Heidler, with Chuck Pierce). This morning I remembered the question, and we laughed together.

It was really good to laugh. Last night I asked him if he'd like to make his secret sauce, the one he had always made for brats and burgers. So, he did. When I looked at it, it was thick and lumpy; he'd put stuffing in it. I reacted, he defended, "Well, the liquids I'd used aren't here." It was too awful to eat. Later he said, "I guess I've moved past doing that."

July 5
O Lord, I've walked outside two days now! (I'd been struggling with hip pain.) And it's so good to have that again – thank you! And thank you for carrying us in this season of AD, for your mercy to me when I react badly – O Lord, forgive, I pray. And fill me with your Spirit today to love and honor… Please protect us and meet us, I pray…

July 8
(Psalm 37:39) "He is their stronghold in the time of trouble." Lord, it's not necessarily "trouble" I'm facing, but it is a pressure, and I feel alone in it. There's this decision regarding cataracts for him – do I spend the extra to get the best help? Or recognize AD is shortening the time it's needed? I so wish someone could help me know what to do. I feel very alone. Still, you are in there with me, and I know you know and have given some thoughts. If we do the traditional, am I skimping? cheating him out of the best? Or is it the best given our AD component? Maybe it would prolong his ability to read? It seems I should go for any possible help, no matter how short its duration.

July 9
O Lord, how you provided yesterday and led – so very good! Just when I was thinking that B_____ hadn't come as he'd said he would, there he was! And promising more. You…led me regarding the cataract surgeries, and then you provided a person to join us in this decision-making. I bow in awe and thank you. (He affirmed the

decision I'd come to by sharing what he'd chosen for his wife, even though she was gone five months later.)

Yesterday we headed to our friends' home and then on to Calvin with them. Wayne offered that I drive there but said he'd then drive home. I declined, knowing he should not drive home for he'd be too tired. So, he drove there. At one point the car ahead slowed way down. Wayne was not doing anything about it, so I cried out and then had to do so again. Afterwards, I said, "What were you doing?" He said, "My finger (meaning foot) was on the brake but it didn't work." I realized his brain didn't tell him to press down. Then we got to Hudsonville where he again got confused. I told him we were to make a hard right, but he couldn't understand and went straight in the middle of the intersection, at an angle, with a pickup coming at us. Somehow we got out of the intersection safely. I then directed him to a parking lot so that I could take over driving. He was glad to have me do it, saying, "I should quit." This morning, however, he returned to saying he could drive some because he doesn't follow as close as others do. I said we have AD to figure in.

July 11
Thank you for being with us as we discussed the driving and yesterday's episodes. Please continue to free him from the shame of not driving and enable him to accept the change, I pray. Keep us from harm; thank you for doing so all these years.

July 12
(Psalm 38:9) "O LORD, all my longing is before you; my sighing is not hidden from you." My Lord, thank you. I know this is true for me also. Sometimes there are heavy decisions to make, and then something else goes, like the internet, and it adds on to all the things I have to take responsibility for, by myself. Sometimes there's added pressure from him, even though it's actually that he's trying to help. I think I stopped yesterday and even

dozed, for I felt the weight of it all (especially the driving mishaps). (v. 15) "But for you, O LORD, do I wait; it is you, O LORD my God, who will answer." Yes, I know this. Each time I feel the weight, the pressure, you provide help, you meet me, you carry me through. I bow in awe, in praise, in thanks. Whom have I but Thee... Thank you for our discussion regarding driving; he backtracked from Wednesday's thought but seems more ready again to let it go. Please meet him, help him, and remove all sense of shame from it, I pray.

Then it changed. He insisted on driving to Paw Paw, though I tried to stop it. We had another bad experience. Beginning a left turn from M40, he drove *into* the oncoming traffic, focusing on the road he was turning into. He didn't see cars coming straight for us. I cried out to stay in the lane; he turned back but was still over the center line and the cars had to move onto the shoulder to miss us. I got upset and told him I was done with him driving. This morning he apologized and told me to carry on.

July 13
Even as I say "Help me, please help me," I remember all the help you gave this week, and I marvel anew that you kept us safe on the road as we experienced dangerous choices or inability to act three times. Thank you for revealing his loss again yesterday, for he seemed to need that third time in order to accept my decision. You kept us from harm yet showed him he can no longer do it. Thank you for protection for us, for others, for our car—so very gracious. You answered my prayer to have it made clear and to keep all safe. O Lord, your help is so good, so timely – regarding driving, regarding financial decisions, regarding attending events – Thank you...

July 14
O Lord my God, how good to be yours, to be helped by you. Thank you for meeting me also in this decision to

stop his driving, and for giving me a strong sense that I must do this, despite his anger, his accusation that I'm condemning him, his plea that I trust him the way he trusts me and let him take care of me (he worries about my leg, for example). Friday, I gave in and let him prevail; yesterday I didn't, and it feels right. O Lord, again I marvel that you showed me it was time without our having an accident and getting hurt. Please give him increasing peace about it and give me strength for it all, and alertness on the road...

July 15
(Psalm 40) O Lord, I know you hear my cries and respond, lifting me up (1) repeatedly. I plead for you to lift Wayne today "out of the miry bog" (2) and "set his feet on a rock" again. You know how hard it's been, how totally lacking is his understanding of what I'm saying, how acceptance comes and then in the morning depression and anger return. We've never been separated before like this, nor has his strong insistence ever been overridden by me – it's new territory for us. I feel alone in it. He must also, so I plead for you to "incline to" both of us and "hear our [hearts'] cries." (1) Please "make the way" through this also (Isaiah 43:16, 19) and help him "remember not the former things" (18), not only in cognitive forgetting but also in accepting their being finished. Enable him to accept the "new thing" you're doing – making a way in the AD wilderness. Yes, it's new, and we need your help, your protection, your leading, your equipping. Thank you, thank you, my Lord, my God.

His anger at driving being taken from him so abruptly (it seemed to him) returned Saturday, Sunday and yesterday. Sunday night we talked it out with Jeff, who spoke wisely to him. It came up again this morning, including, "There's a lot of drivers around here that are worse than I."

July 16
(Psalm 40:17) "As for me, I am poor and needy, but the LORD takes thought for me…" Yes, Lord, yes. Whom have I but you? I am poor and needy in this new assignment, feeling alone, but you are taking thought. You see and you know the way you designed for me, for us, regarding AD and caretaking. O Lord, am I getting this wrong, as he says? Did I make assumptions about signs, maybe because I wanted to? Lord, we're not together anymore as we always were, and it's shaky. Still, I sense the responsibility of it. AD has taken another step, and it's ugly. Please protect us, and please lead me so that I'm firm but honoring.

Today I feel less separated from him as I again saw his own frustration with AD. He has four name and address cards, one of which he takes with him when he walks. He could find none this morning. I remembered seeing one in the car and then found all four there. He had no idea why they were there and said, "I'm so sick of this stuff; I want to quit."

July 17
O Lord, thank you for meeting us in this adjustment time, for helping us feel more together again with fewer digs about it. But then during the night I felt the weight of all the driving and all the responsibility and couldn't sleep for a while. O Lord, I need your help, I'm not cut out for this. But you know exactly who and what I am, and assigned it. You are my maker, my redeemer, my helper, and I give you praise. Please supply for today…

Wayne's focus has been on the cataract surgery so he isn't scolding about driving anymore. But he can't remember anything. He's asking all the time about what should be done for his eyes, and then he tried again to enter the pension check, but it made no sense. He left it, came back again, and it still made no sense, so he gave it up. A few minutes later he said, "This won't take long." I probed his meaning: the takeover of AD will escalate, and it won't be long till he's nonfunctioning. I asked later if that was a sense given him or a frustrated grieving. He thought it was the latter. It seems I could write something every day now, something indicating more loss. There's more struggle to understand, more fear dictating thoughts, more accusation of me for not agreeing and succumbing...

July 22
Father Above, thank you...for bringing us back together again through yet another challenge to my decisions. Does it come from being sidelined (which he claims, though I'd told him my thoughts and asked his opinion), realizing we used to do things the way he preferred them done? I try to involve him and find he doesn't understand my explanation. Or does it come from fear, fear because of the unknown, unknowable, therefore uncontrollable, that is growing?

July 26
(Psalm 43:3) "Send out your light and your truth, let them lead me...to your holy hill... your dwelling!" Yes, Lord, yes. Lead me through this lonely place of making a major decision by myself with which he disagrees strongly and which he uses to attack me. Lead me... I still sense it is right, and I got confirmation from good friends, but our kids are being careful about what they say. I don't feel afraid of his attack, so I take that as some confirmation. He can't understand the reasoning and has forgotten the incidents that led to this. But you, you are here, providing for us both. You have honor for him, and it must come from me and those who love him, know him. So, lead me, Lord, in truth and in grace. Lead me to find things that he'd enjoy and be blessed by.

July 31
Lord, I start the day feeling really down, though I'd looked forward to hosting these friends today. His independence returned – he went out to walk before I got up and didn't tell me. He said later he thought I was leaving for a breakfast (I'm not; I don't leave him anymore) so he would just do his own thing. What is going on? Is that a return to his normal (independent) self, or a deepening into AD? I guess that on top of trying to figure out how to host people here tonight and get everything ready for them, this action just gave a heavier load than I'd expected, and I'm having trouble. Thank you for meeting me so quickly – I see him more confused than usual about his devotional passage. So, my Father I look to you for help, for leading, for strength today to help him and to prepare for dinner guests…

TAKING A BREAK
(3)

It may be good to pause and reflect a bit about how Wayne and I related together in making decisions. Because Wayne's likes and dislikes were well-defined and well-known to him, it sometimes seemed they dominated our choices. A lot of those decisions didn't matter to me; for example, he was much more in tune with what kind of food he wanted to eat than I was, and when he had something in mind, that was it. Usually, I didn't care. We were used to accommodating his stronger preferences in several areas of life.

    I recall learning something about leading and being led when I played for preschool programs in one of our churches. Sometimes the little ones' singing would drag and I would lead them along. At other times, I followed the leading of the teacher. I didn't consciously realize this until a grandfather in attendance one day came to talk to me. He complimented me on my doing this, explaining what he had observed. He too was a pianist and an accompanist and knew of what he spoke. Sometimes a pianist leads, as when playing for group singing; sometimes she has to follow, as when accompanying a performance. I realized how right he was and that I did in fact use both in my playing, depending on the occasion. Since then, I've often thought of this as a metaphor for living in the marriage relationship. At times one leads, and at times one follows the lead of the other; both are necessary. I believe

Wayne and I functioned that way, with the flow between the two for me being as natural and unconsciously done as my work at the piano in a preschool program. But into it at times came Wayne's strong, very apparent preferences which occasionally felt dominating to me, and my prayer journal excerpts in these pages reflect that feeling.

When facing bigger decisions we usually talked it through and spent time praying about it. I knew he was in tune with the Lord's leading, and I trusted that. I also knew the Lord would bring me to the same conclusion. On occasion, I wouldn't have any sense of the answer and would agree to trust Wayne's sense of it, but that was rare.

AD brought change to this understanding of each other. Let me illustrate. Each time we moved, it was because Wayne had received a call from another church. We would talk together about it, pray together and separately. He would sense from the Lord that we were to move and each time then the Lord graciously confirmed that within me. It was different however after retiring in 2013. We had always expected to scale back in ministry (we were at the jail at the time) but not stop altogether. The Lord, however, showed Wayne clearly that we were to make a complete break, and when he shared that I knew within me immediately that that was right (though I didn't know at the time the reason would be AD). Then as we sought the Lord about our future, the thought started coming to me that we were to move. I began to sense strongly that we were to do so, and then, also a strong sense, that it was to be near our son. Wayne, however, was terrified of the idea at times ("we'll lose all our money," and that kind of thing). But at the same time, he believed I was hearing from the Lord so he knew he couldn't object. We both sensed he was not his normal self. He settled down, so to speak, and trusted the Lord was leading this. Still, he was not able to take hold of any of it. Besides moving to a new city, we had moved into a new place in the decision-making process.

Throughout our marriage we had had each other and had

known we could always look to and lean on the other. This AD path gradually changed that as I felt the ability to lean on him slip away. At times it would hit me hard that I'd have to make decisions without him understanding what was going on; then without his agreement, then with his great opposition, even anger, then with his accusation of my wrongdoing. As I saw these coming and then in fact happening, I felt fear and had to bring that to the Lord. There, each time with him, I received the strength and courage needed. I found him able to "supply every need of [mine]..." (Philippians 4:19).

* * *

August 2
Father God, I bow in awe of you, of your goodness, your mercy to me, us, again yesterday. You led us in conversing, though he didn't have complete understanding; still, he quit fighting, again, and we returned to loving each other. O Lord, thank you for such good, and for the leading he still does in such situations. Thank you for B___'s visit, for the confirmation I could get from him, as he reminded Wayne that his brain is dying. You do know what we experience, and you do have the way for us to go. I continue to look to you.

At a neighboring church this morning we were invited to the front for communion. As Wayne watched people, he had questions about what to do. Afterwards he said he missed the grape juice. I think he meant he was afraid of getting the wafer too wet and was trying to just dip the end but missed. He just went on. Returning home, he (from the passenger side) said, "How do you get out of here?" He forgot how to open the car door.

He had his second cataract surgery yesterday. Again, he was more confused than usual but is doing better today. Still, he's really struggling to find words for what he wants to say.

August 7
I'm sensing I have to plan less (host less) so that I have less on my plate that I must do and more time to give him. Please help me with that, with making good decisions. And Lord, I'd like to accomplish the Romans project for our family Christmas gifts, get a photo album ready for Wayne, get back to reading my prayer journals, further reduce amount of stuff here – I ask for time and health to do this, in your name.

August 9 I asked him the questions, from *Being Mortal* (Atul Gawande), regarding what he'd like his life to look like as AD progressed. He had trouble with them, but the overriding thought he conveyed was wanting to "live with dignity and integrity in my own home." He also expressed a desire that the robbing of AD be "over." I said, "Then we'll ask the Lord for that."

> Lord, please continue making a way for us as we navigate AD; help me promote dignity and integrity each day, the two things he values highly. And Lord, he expressed he'd like to finish this race in his own home, so I plead for that for him, for me. Please be merciful and grant peace through it all.

We're back from visiting friends in Illinois. He came to me feeling bad – "We're just back and I can't come up with their names."

August 22
Lord, he still lectures me regarding driving –- he wants to "give me a break," believing he can. Maybe so, now yet, but each day it seems there's further erosion of understanding. I sense it would be wrong of me to back down. Lord, please counsel me, help me, lead me...

He still brings up his driving, saying it's unthinkable that I do it all without any break, and he "certainly can take a section of it." I feel no pressure to give in, however, and he then accepts. After a few days, he said he was "okay about not driving." I was touched. But then he proceeded to say he wanted me to know how much it hurt him and that he believes I'm totally wrong. I don't know what to say anymore, so I don't say anything. Nothing will give him understanding, so we go on, separately. And, is he depressed? Every event he balks about. But if there's no contact scheduled, he feels alone and left out. I try to space out contacts, but he'll still say, "There's too much." It seems he can't be pleased.

> **September 3**
> Father, I'm not any good yet at loving. "Did you learn to love?" still comes to me. And now it feels that we're so separated from each other because of his hurt regarding not driving, and because I withdraw into self as I've always done. Forgive, I pray, my great self-protection and help me today.

> **September 4**
> Thank you so for helping yesterday, for enabling me to reach for him, and him to return and to apologize. Thank you! You're a good, good Father…and I'm loved by you…

Wayne admitted as a movie ended that he did not understand about the two people ending up with each other, saying, "It's just too complex." Little by little there's more evidence of decline. I've been helping him start his prayer journal each morning, and it seems it's harder for him to grasp the verses he'll be using, harder to grasp the reference and then to stick to that section in the Bible. I get called back to help, sometimes repeatedly. Early Tuesday morning we have to get the car out of here and put it over on a different street (for the driveway to be resurfaced). He's confused as he worries – what does that mean here? Will the washer still work? with more questions like that. He's becoming less certain about taking meds and wants me to okay what he takes. He also wondered again yesterday about how to get out of the car; he was not remembering what opens the door.

September 16
Job had prosperity and esteem but is now being mocked, robbed of dignity, health (Ch. 29-30). Lord, it's similar for Wayne – in a sense prosperous in ministry, experiencing esteem, dignity and health. But I saw kids mocking him at Captain Sundae's last night. To them he was just an old man who drools and drops ice cream out of his cone. Esteem is gone; dignity is slipping away. Job got it all back, but Wayne won't. Both are chosen, assigned by you. We look to you...

September 23
Lord, I sense my ability to be in charge of my schedule being taken from me. I knew it would come someday, but I realize it's shaking me a bit. I guess it means I can't plan much. Certainly, I spend more time helping Wayne. I know you know the schedule of deterioration and ask you to alert me, to keep me from missing him because I'm focused on something that must be done. Please help me remember what needs to be done around here and to be able to plan it, to space it out. Thank you so for meeting me yesterday in worship, for assuring me, reminding me you are God – always.

September 25
(Psalm 57:2,3) "I cry out to God Most High...who fulfills his purpose for me. He will send from heaven...will send out his steadfast love and his faithfulness." Yes, Lord God, my Savior, my help anew. Lord, it's been a shaky day so far, but you remain steady, for you are The Rock, and I am on It. Thank you for helping me navigate, for protecting him, for meeting me...please bring safety and love to him through me today.

I fell apart last night. It seems I spend all my time with Wayne listening carefully, working hard to grasp what he's actually wanting to say. Then, added to that were three hours listening at the board meeting (of our condo association), figuring out what was for the minutes and what wasn't (there was a lot of extraneous talk!). Afterwards Wayne misinterpreted something I'd said and got ticked off and accusatory. I had to try to figure out what assumptions he'd made and why he was jumping to wrong conclusions. I was totally drained, however, and started crying. I said, "I can't figure out anymore." Then he just held me.

Yesterday we sang hymns with friends from seminary days. He sometimes had trouble finding the number chosen, not knowing whether to turn back or forward. And, at times, the same happens with scripture passages. Today he was also confused about the things he puts in the prayer journal – why write that? What do I do with it?

We made applesauce this week. It was cooling off on the table when he said, "Did you try it?" I said I only taste-tested as I made it. A few minutes later he came to me carrying a piece of toast on which he'd put applesauce! "Here, try it." But I declined, "Not on toast!" He left, somewhat disturbed with me, and ate the toast. I thought he confused it with our making jam together. Later that evening he mentioned changes in his condition, so I spoke of the toast episode. He defended it, saying his grandma had done that. But a few minutes later he wondered about it too. For me, it was either confusing the two or living in a very distant past, jumping back over all the decades in between. In fifty plus years I've never seen him put applesauce on toast.

October 7
Father…help me get needed things done before AD gets worse and to be ready for that time, to be patient with and safe for him today…

October 9 I had a dream: We were visiting, or had heard report of, a jail ministry. Then we prepared to return home. I went to get donuts and then headed to a coffee shop. As I left that building, it was raining hard. I was under someone's umbrella for a while but then went alone to the car. Once inside, it seemed more like a room. I was trying to place the coffee cups when suddenly Wayne appeared. I exclaimed, "How did you get here?" (For I was about to go back to the jail to pick him up.) He said, "I came to help." Then I realized the rain had switched to snow, and I felt tremendous relief and gratitude that he was there to help me in that situation. On awakening, I realized it was Wayne without AD, the one I relied on for help in difficult situations.

> Is it that person that pleads to drive every time he sees me as weakened? As one he'd always helped? But I no longer have that same response, no longer can I feel: "Ah, he'll take care of it." Instead, I try to find a way to say, "No," and be nice at the same time.
>
> Lord, I grieve that loss, that feeling of being taken care of. And I thank you so for giving me that experience all those years. He was so good to me. How can I honor him for it, while also protecting him from AD's results? It seems I should let him "take care of me" in order to preserve his self-identity, but how...?
>
> **October 16**
> Lord, I admit I can look for others. I feel bad and disappointed that family doesn't come when free, that I have no one to take care of me as I live with pain (my husband wants to, but can't). So, I grieve and end up feeling sorry for myself. And I come and plead for your help; help me take care of him and myself. I plead for your hand to heal the hip and the foot ulcer and for you to forgive me for demanding more, for feeling alone when countless others have had this same experience,

and I didn't think twice about them. You only are my rock, my salvation, my fortress, my help, my supply, my strength; I receive for today...

There's been confusion this week regarding how to dress. We got out long underwear (for soccer games), and he then planned to wear it for his walk but had no pants on. I asked what pants he planned to wear, and he pointed to the long underwear. We went back and forth a few times before he realized he had to wear something over it. (I think he confused it with sweat pants.) Then yesterday he came out ready to walk, wearing long underwear under walking shorts, and a long-sleeved underwear shirt over a short-sleeved polo shirt. He had one gray sock over the underwear and one under it. Again, I said no to it. He kept the top as it was, took off the thermal bottom, but still wore the gray socks with tennis shoes. He's also having some difficulty with telling time, saying, "When the hand gets here, that's when we leave?" as he points to the place on the clock.

October 30 I had a dream: I was in the living room recliner reading my Bible during the night when I heard someone in the kitchen. As is usual in dreams, I tried to call out but struggled to get words out; finally, I was able to say, "Who's there?" At that moment I awakened and saw Wayne walking from the kitchen towards the hallway. Then the nightlight came on. I told him in the morning that he was up about 3 am, but he didn't remember it.

> Was the dream alerting me to his "wandering?" Is the fact that I actually am sleeping in that recliner (I had too much pain in my foot to lie flat) enabling me to learn of this development in AD? For if I had been in the bed, it's likely I would not have caught it. O Lord, thank you for being watchful of us, for showing me this last night, for hearing my cry to be alerted and helped in caregiving. Please keep showing me and help me help him feel

safe (he's objecting to going anywhere in rain now, for he's afraid).

October 31
My Father in heaven, I come with thanks for health and mobility this morning, but I'm oh so tired for it was a night of constant, great pain. Lord, what does it mean? Is it worsening to the point of possibly losing my leg? Or was I just too sedentary yesterday, with the shoes rubbing, aggravating the vulnerable skin? Father, I plead for your help to stay able to care for him and our life together...

I find things in strange places: a table knife stuck into the steak knife holder, a strainer with thawing blueberries placed in the freezer, a wastebasket put into the trash bag instead of being emptied into it. Wayne's devotional (and prayers) are more and more just religious words, though they're his religious words. It's a vague stringing together of phrases. This morning his devotional had nothing to do with the verse he'd chosen. I asked him what it was he'd wanted to convey, and then I made it tie into the verse.

Last evening Wayne told me he sometimes sees a man, dressed in suit coat and tie, who's just behind him, to one side. When Wayne turns to look at him, he disappears. Also, when Wayne walks into the kitchen, the man is standing by the fridge, looking toward the window and "then he leaves." Later in the evening, as we were sitting in the living room, he got up and walked into the kitchen. He came back saying, "So, it's just the two of us here?" I affirmed that it was, and he said that was good. Then I remembered that he's asked similar things several times, sometimes sure there'd been more here beside us. At the time, I thought it was from dreaming.

PART II
The Steep Descent

CHAPTER ONE
The Slide

It was early morning, the day after Thanksgiving, when I had a dream about Wayne and me being somewhere together, but then I realized he was gone. Though I searched for him for a couple of days I could not find him and awakened without having found him. I got busy with the day and forgot the dream. At one point I saw that the Christmas tree, put up and decorated the day before by Maria and Asher, was too close to the sliding door. So, I got down to move the stand, trying to be careful. But one leg of the stand broke. I asked Wayne to hold it up so I could find something to put under that side of the stand. I did, but it didn't work. So I was under the tree, holding it up, wondering about something else to use for bracing, telling Wayne where to hold it as well. But he couldn't grasp what I was saying. Getting frustrated I kept telling him to hold the middle section of the tree. He said, "Here?" as he grabbed the top portion, making the bottom two sections topple over, sending decorations flying. I was extremely upset; he was extremely confused. And then I remembered the dream.

November 22
Ah, Lord, you were warning me. The Wayne I knew, the one who would understand what was happening here and be able to help, cannot be found.

More confusions followed. Last night he tried the garbage disposal; there was nothing in it, so the sound was different. He concluded it wasn't working and decided to try the toaster to see if it worked. At first, he thought it didn't. He called me in to check it all; he was believing the two were connected somehow.

Many evenings he'll say, "Are we the only two here?" The other day I asked if he believed there were others, and he said he saw three persons walking alongside him. One handed him something.

He's very unsure this morning. At seven I was aware of him looking for something. He kept saying "glasses." He found his wallet and phone. I helped him get clothes and toiletries together, and then I heard the old shower. (We'd had a walk-in shower built and had been using it exclusively.) After dressing, he came with his car keys, which was what he'd meant by "glasses." He also told me he'd seen two late-teen boys looking for things in our bedroom, hence his urgency to find his valuables.

December 7
Lord, the dream – here's another demonstration that the Wayne he was is not around anymore. Thank you so for warning me.

This morning was better, with less confusion than yesterday. He made coffee and got his own breakfast. After yesterday morning's confusion about morning routine, I set up all his toiletries in the new bathroom, all in one place. He likes the idea.

It seems at some point each day he comments, questions: "We're the only ones here?" Yesterday he added, "When did they all leave?"

Last night I awakened as he was asking if he'd done something wrong. I probed his thought. Because of a dream, he thought he was to be removed from our home, and he thought it was because of having done something wrong. He started to cry, saying "I didn't do anything!" I tried to reassure him; I felt so bad for him. It seemed he did not go back to sleep, but showered, put on the clothes we planned for this evening's program, made coffee, but didn't eat because he thought he was going to the doctor (which is tomorrow). When I got coffee at 7:30, it was already lukewarm; it had been off at least half an hour by then. So, he'd made it before five.

We were heading out and he was ready to go three hours before leave time. He kept putting on his jacket, then taking it off when I told him it wasn't yet time. Time is a problem now; he checks the clock, but doesn't always get it right. Saying we'll leave in fifteen minutes doesn't seem to compute.

He told me he'd seen children behind our house when he got up. He decided they must be our neighbor's grandchildren, here with their dad who works at her place. After one nap, he said, "Chris, come see kids playing out front; it's really neat." When we got to the window, he said, "They're gone! They must have gone that way," pointing right. Then after another nap, he got up, looked through the pass-through and out the kitchen window, saying, "They're on skates." I said, "Skates?" He got frustrated with me, and said sarcastically, "Yeah, skates; what you put on your feet." We went to the window, for he was still seeing them, but then he said, "Oh, they're gone. They must have gone that way." Again, he pointed to the right. Later that evening, he said, "There's people playing outside [between our condo and the one next door]." Last night he wanted me to go to bed before he did so he could check outside without me there.

When I got up this morning, he was full of questions regarding what the people who were here during the night had said to him. They had apparently thought this was their place, till it dawned on Wayne that it's his. They spoke of going to a "show," so he was somewhat agitated about it all. I asked if he thought it was a dream; he said, "No, not at all; they were here." He also said there was no fear in him.

When I said good morning to him the next day, he whispered, "Are we alone here?" and then greeted me.

December 16
Lord, in the first months we were here in Zeeland I sensed a strong "Get ready" from you. So, I prepared estate-planning folders for the kids and got the house prepared for guests. Later, I educated myself regarding AD and made changes in the house, now also in my use of time, in taking more responsibility for what he wears, and things like that. I made copies of my paraphrased books of the Bible; I cleaned out our study files – I am aware of more culling to do and ask your help and supply for it, I made picture albums for his remembering. Am I ready for a complete stage two, then three? Can one be emotionally ready?

Lord, he says he asked you for five more years. I admit I recoiled a bit – what would that look like? I'm sorry, for I find I still look for what's easier. So, I plead for your help, your readying of me. I see changes daily now, it seems. And it seems that will escalate rather than plateau. But, it's in your hands, and your good purposes are at work. I again look to you for further readying, for your supply for the assignment. Please minister comfort to his spirit, his soul, as he feels the slipping...

He said this morning, "We need to call that guy and tell him this isn't working; it's leaking," as he pointed to his neck and just below. "You get all wet." I realized he was talking about the drooling that occurs as he sleeps in his chair and that he expected our doctor should be able to fix it.

There was great confusion last evening, all night, and this morning. He was sure other people were in the house, even hearing a voice during the night. He also thought we were somewhere else, and would be leaving to "go home." When I asked this morning about making coffee, he said, "I'll do it if I can find the kitchen." I helped with coffee and then helped him shower. He wanted me to walk through the house, which we did, into every room upstairs and down. Then he realized it was familiar to him. Still, he thought we'd moved to Paw Paw. I think my talk the last days of staying overnight at Maria's raised fears within him about being able to know where he was, where things were, and so forth. That probably led to believing we had gone to someone else's place.

> **December 19**
> Father, what am I looking for? (I'd found notes from an Advent sermon series Wayne gave in 1988 called, "What Are We Looking for This Christmas" and was using them in my quiet times.) I guess I'm looking for the *new normal* I'd known was coming, with the "Wayne I'd known" not being found any more (as in the dream). The talk of various trips to Paw Paw and an overnight stay there so confused him that he thought all night and this morning that we were actually there. So, Lord, I plead for actual normalcy as I play for Sunday services and Christmas Eve in Paw Paw...please give him enough settledness to spend that amount of time there, I pray. And meet him with peace...

He's very confused. I helped with clothes and food, but he's wondering where are his children and God's children. He wept several times, then broke into prayer for covering. He seems unfamiliar with our home here; he doesn't think it's ours and says "When did you get here?" to me, both last night and this morning. Does *home* now mean a childhood place, with different furniture, lay-out, and of course, no *me* there? He asks where to go for clothes and for food. He also asked me if I'm "ready," and it seemed to come from the Lord to me – ready for the next stage.

December 20
Lord, I realize I can be an "Assessor of the Situation" rather than "One who Meets him in the Moment." I guess I wasn't ready; I need help emotionally entering, so that I don't just stay disengaged. Please set me free from my natural responses and break through with empathy, I pray.

He was confused about my playing with the band, thinking it had happened when it's still two days away. But then he gave a word, and I knew it was from the Lord:

"I realize there are things I can no longer do, but you can, and I will tell people, 'Go to her, for I can't do it.' You are equipped to do them, and I release them to you. The equipping has come not just in the last year but in all these years. There are times he will call you to give a rebuke; you must give it for you are equipped. And you need the full armor of God."

Later he said he wondered if the Lord is testing him to see if he'll continue "to receive the word in the hiding place." We went out for lunch and then to the lake, walking out to it; we had an awesome time of real connection.

I sensed the next stage had come. There was so much confusion: "Whose house is this…who's to be here…what day is it…are we moving…we must bring Jesus to people needing him…how will it work at church tomorrow…whose church is it…is another church using it…is Maria in the next bedroom," and on and on. He asked if he was going to be moved out of here, and wondered if he'd done something wrong. Then he said, "Where are my children…why can't I see my children… did I do something wrong?" He can't grasp the answers, so he just keeps asking. He's so contrite at times, worried that he's hurting me, or others.

December 21
Ready me, Lord, to do this, to give him safety and security, to have strength for all the issues raised (it takes a lot to

figure out what exactly is being said), and for all the work to be done, to be alerted to more that I now need to cover (for example, check whether he took his meds), and to check out home care agencies…anything else?….You're a good, good Father, it's who you are (Chris Tomlin)… and you are watching, always, for good, with good, and I trust you. Please equip me in spirit as well as in mind and body. Should I look into an anti-anxiety med so he can calm down in the evenings? Or will this pass?

December 22 No, it won't pass. I *know* the next stage has come and will not leave. Restlessness and wandering, confusion about the things in our home and how I got here are daily occurrences. Still, at four am, he said something very clear, which I sensed to be from the Lord: "Don't be afraid; you are protected. You must say what I give you to say, people are listening…" On the 20th, it seemed, he released to me the things he used to do for me, for us. Today, it seems, he released his assignment to protect me. And he seemed to bless me to take to others what the Lord would give me. I marveled and wondered...

December 23
Lord, on Friday the 20th, we enjoyed a time of connecting, and on Saturday the 21st, he told George he realized he has had greater loss due to AD, but on Sunday the 22nd, he retreated from such understanding, insisting on telling no one, talking with no one about his AD. So, I feel assigned by him to carry this alone since he isn't carrying it with me, nor is anyone else. Yet, I am not alone, you will go before me… I praise you anew and look to you for your supply…. And Lord, he reads my impatience and frustration as anger, perhaps because he so greatly needs assurance as he feels himself losing hold.

Some honesty returned as he expressed his desire for someone to explain what was happening to him. I told him about the illustration of a bookcase getting shaken so that the top shelf books (most recent memories) fall off, then those on the next shelf fall, and on down the falling goes. He took that. He asked again about this place we're living in. I said, "We bought it." "When did that happen...how come nobody talked to me about it?" I said we had, but he forgot it.

December 24 At three am he turned on the bedroom light, walked purposefully to the end of the bed and began speaking to me. First, he said, "I've been watching with the Lord." Then he said things like, "You are blessed; rest now, the Lord knows you're tired. He got tired too..." and things about making sure people hear about Jesus. Then, getting into bed, he said, "Rest now, you are protected." Then he said something about "Chris...," which startled me.

In the morning he had a question about cords on his desk, saying, "Chris knows about them..." I said, "I'm Chris." He said, a bit sheepishly, "Of course." But then later he launched into things about our church, then about our marriage: "I have one marriage..." (suggesting he's feeling something off here?), and "I don't know who's stirring you up; someone is feeding you this stuff."

> I couldn't get from him what he meant. Lord, is it fear others will learn from me that his AD has deteriorated? What fear is it, Lord? Fear that others will now see him as shameful? Fear of losing even more control? Fear of being disrespected?
>
> Lord, the words spoken during the night sometimes sound religious – am I wrong? His spirit has always been tuned to you; can AD allow foreign entrance? He has spoken more recently of needing the Armor (of God), of being aware of battling. I pray you protect him even more, since he can't do it himself....Please cover, I pray.

We had a wonderful time at our church participating in a rehearsal and two services. Wayne enjoyed it all. But as we drove home, he got increasingly agitated, then terrified that we couldn't stay in our condo, "someone else's place," or that we'd suddenly have to come up with a huge amount of money for it. He kept pressing me to call someone to check it out. When we got home, it all continued. He pressed me to call the kids. I said, "It's Christmas Eve; they're with their families." Still, he kept pressing, pressing, finally saying, " Then I'll call Jeff." And immediately the thought came to me, "Good, then Jeff will finally know things have changed." Jeff didn't answer so Wayne called Maria. She started to counter the falsehood about us not owning this place but then quickly realized his AD change and just spoke reassuringly to him. Then Jeff returned the call and heard it as well. That was enough for Wayne to settle for the night.

> **December 24**
> It was good to have it shared! and to have the hold of fear broken. Thank you, Lord.

Wayne felt better in the morning, though he still had questions about whose house this is. Sarah called, which meant our three children had had a conference call the previous night.

> **December 25**
> And now they all know, and I feel helped and less alone.
> O Lord, you are with us; you are Emmanuel, and I lift praise and thanks…

Two days later, at 3 am, he awakened me asking if he was going to be moved. He was crying and saying he's never known such fear. I tried to reassure him, love him. After a while he prayed, and then slept.

He's now regularly seeing other people here. That's

Delirium. For some time already he's believed someone is coming to steal his valuables. That's Delusion.

He was clear at one point, and a word for our kids came:

"Maria – she's getting ready to serve the Lord beyond whatever anyone in this room has seen. Jeff too, and he must learn more from his mother, whom he loves. Sarah – I see there's purpose the Lord has created in her for the Lord's children. She will be blessed in conversations that she will not be afraid to look for. She'll call loving attention to those needing help. I can't wait to talk to her; what comes from her rates high with me. God is using her; if he wanted someone to do what Corrie Ten Boom did, Sarah could."

He also said his love for the Lord is so great, it's even deepened in the AD experience. "I don't yet love him as he deserves, but am learning to know Jesus better. I'm surprised at how small I am, which I'd known only in theory. I know that what I'm about to go through is a privilege. My Christianity is related to the people who were in Door County in those early years." (He was referring to the friends of his parents who joined them on vacations in Door County, who had robust discussions together about Christianity and about living responsibly before the Lord.) I marveled and thanked the Lord for these moments of clarity, moments with no searching for words…

But two days later, he showered at four am, afterwards asking me what my husband's name is. I said, "Wayne." "From around here?" "From Sheboygan." "Oh, like me…" Then he told me several times that he loved me. About 6:30 he came into the bedroom, put the light on, and was looking around. I asked what he was looking for. "For the front door. "Why?" "So, I can go out and see where downtown is." That scared me and told me to change the locks, or get something to keep him in. Shelly found door alarms and Jeff put them on the front door and the door leading into the garage.

We had a good time going to church, despite his now thinking of me as two people, sometimes Wife Chris, sometimes

Helper Chris. He was looking for her to go with us to church. On the way he talked to me about her and the help she's giving – "she told me I should not be driving; she knows a lot about this [AD]." He was disappointed that she didn't show up in church.

We spent New Year's Eve Day together for our family Christmas celebration, also taking an hour for a family meeting regarding this new development of AD. I had asked for this, and I was so thankful our kids came prepared with options for next steps in care. It was obvious they are now talking together and are intent on helping us navigate this journey. I felt blessed.

*　*　*

2020

January 1
Good, good Father, thank you for making me yours, for giving rest and protecting health, for showing us that you know us, our situation and that you have a way for us, for using our kids in that way – please help me in tackling it, for meeting me last night with the song "I Am Not Alone" (Kari Jobe), for the help grandkids were giving also, for the sun shining on a new day and new year. Father, I lift my praise and I bow in gratitude. I ask you to give me courage to take steps needed, steps outlined by the kids yesterday. You know my fears, but I'm no longer a slave to them, and neither am I alone! Thank you.

January 3
(Matthew 2:12) "...being warned in a dream..." You, Lord God Almighty, knew all and chose to reveal to people things that would be helpful. And you still do; you showed me in a dream the night after Thanksgiving that I'd no longer "find Wayne," and that is certainly the case....I bow anew in gratitude... (I realized later, in reviewing all my notes, that the Lord had given me

such a dream already in March of 2017. How greatly he prepared me.)

Lord, as I read descriptions of what our future will probably be, I admit I can slip into denial – "not us! We won't have that!" I know it's out of fear and self-protection. Please forgive and be merciful to me... and to him regarding the prolonged debilitation. Be merciful, I plead...

January 4
Lord, I have had a half-conscious thought of what I'll do with my life when Wayne is no longer here. O Lord, it's so not right, so self-centered, so selfish, and yet it is me. And you saw it, knew it, and met me with forgiveness before I even acknowledged it. The first song that played on my playlist was "Jesus Paid It All!" Again the "It is finished for Chris Leys" message came through. O Lord, you see me, *everything* is known to you, yet you forgive, receive in mercy, cover anew... It's so good, with so much grace, and I stand in awe...

Wayne was angry when I got up, suspecting that other people were leading me. He said to just let him be for six months to a year, and then he'd be gone. I asked the Lord, "Is that depression, a deep wish to be let out of what he's experiencing, or a knowledge given by you?" (It turned out to be the gift of knowledge, for the Lord took him home to heaven a year from then.) Apparently, he too wanted our life back, and both of us are feeling controlled by AD – he by others because of AD, I by his needs. He accused me of not praying about these things: "You were always a person who went to the Lord for leading and guiding," and now, he said, I'm "listening to others."

He's sometimes bothered about "the other woman" (that is, Helper me) and says things like, "I've never had a thought for any other woman." But then he would wonder where she was or talk to me as if I were she. Again I turned to the Lord – "Lord, how do I handle these references to another woman? It seems I should go along with it, but it stymies me. What can I say?"

He's more and more seeing me as the other woman; he asks me "get-to-know-you" questions: "Did you always live around here? Do you have family? Do you have siblings? Have you met my brother Ken? When? Where?" At times he gets upset about her apparently being around, saying, "I just can't be part of it." I probed that and realized he was afraid he'd have an illicit affair with this other woman (because "she's really very nice").

He gathered his desk stuff believing there would be a move; I said, not yet. He asked how we'd know when. I said, "When the Lord shows us."

> **January 7**
> Lord God, this is all happening so fast, it seems. Will there be a plateau? Or just continued falling? Please equip me for today and prepare me for talking with the doctor...

In the evening, he said, "Sometimes you need a little season of renewal."

January 9 We saw his doctor, something we'd asked for due to the changes. Maria heard Wayne's anger and then the nurse did as well. But the doctor's calm soothed him. Wayne told him he'd trust him. The doctor started him on a low dose of Sertraline for anxiety.

He's all worried again about someone else owning our house. He said I was being "sheistered by them." Maria and Ben have offered to add on to their house in Paw Paw for us. It looked good to both of us.

> **January 13**
> Lord, I'm in a fog and feeling pressed, even angry maybe? I'm realizing "they" have no understanding of who I am in you and are instructing me according to

our society's assumptions and prescriptions, telling me that I need to go to a support group and telling me that Wayne needs to go to AD day care. They do not see who we are before and in you. And that's making me angry. I know there's fear also. I am an introvert, one who doesn't initiate stuff, and I also fear Wayne's reaction to day care. All this is manifesting as anger. So, Lord God, my Father, my helper, my strength, my light, I come, carrying this stuff, asking you to meet me, to open my eyes to your way for us. I had to make the driving decision alone – this one too? Please help me.

January 14
How good is your help to me. I came to peace about just making the decision myself… (regarding a possible move to Paw Paw.)

January 15
I experienced deep sorrow. Wayne didn't know me as Wife all day, and I felt the loss of the possibility of moving to Maria's, then the loss of sleeping in the same bed as my husband. He said he couldn't have "the other woman" in his bed, so I was on the couch. It seemed I needed to honor his sensibilities. I only got a couple of hours of sleep.

I slept again on the couch the next night, but at four am Wayne invited me in, as he recognized me! Later I texted Maria about it all. She offered to buy a bed, but then talked with Jeff who offered one of theirs which was not being used. Ben and Maria came to carry the bookcases down to make room for the bed in the office. Jeff, Shelly, Josh and Alyssa brought it over and set it up.

January 16
I bow in awe of your great love, your minute care… And then I didn't need the bed! He's known me since yesterday afternoon! Amazing! Yet, I sense it was a right

step to take, for I expect it will be needed. However, I am so grateful for the reconnection. It was so hard to be treated as someone else, and I missed him so much, feeling so alone. So, thank you for this day and what we have now...

January 18 We went into different rooms last night, deciding that was the right thing to do. After starting that way, though, he invited me back but then said, "This isn't right; it's over." So, I went back to the office. Yesterday he'd said we need to face the fact that the day will come when he's not here. He admitted knowing he's in and out of reality. He commented that AD is going faster than we'd realized.

January 19 He showered at 2:30 am, then wandered and dozed intermittently the rest of the night. He definitely has hallucinations. He told me there were two kids downstairs and motioned for me to go with him and to stay quiet. When we got there, he didn't see them and said they must have gone.

January 20
Lord, I'm again pleading for your mercy for him in this disease progression. Will mercy keep us on the present step (of the AD staircase) for a long time, or will it be a continuous move down, ending without a prolonged slide? And I admit, I'd like a normal life. So, dear Lord, I bring these questions to you, seeking mercy from you anew. Please forgive my selfishness in it and release your love through me today. And Lord, we together asked you to allow him to stay here all the way. I again ask that of you, even as I also bring my fear of carrying a heavy care load. So, Lord, please be merciful to both of us. If it is your plan to institutionalize him, prepare us both and prepare a very good place, I plead.

January 21
My Lord, my help, my strength, my supply...I remember he told me on December 22 that I don't have to fear, for I am protected. That's so good now as I have had the thought on the bed in the office that I don't feel safe there. But I am!

He knew me as his wife, and I could sleep next to him! He also felt so good about it and could admit he's confused at other times. We're going to check the Day Center; he wondered what we'd talk about there. I said, "Alzheimer's." He said, "I'm okay; I realize I have limited time and that's okay." He had peace about it, though seeing people sitting in chairs doing exercises bothered him. "I don't need to go somewhere to exercise!" But he wasn't angry or upset.

Tom and Lor came, and then Wayne recognized me! saying to me, "Where've you been? How'd you get here? Did you drive?" He felt free to describe to them his struggle regarding the other woman and his great turmoil about it. They saw, they understood, they grieved.

January 25
Lord, I cried out for mercy, and you gave me a whole day and night of him knowing me! But at breakfast, I was other woman again...And Lord, who's gone ahead, show us the way of mercy you've chosen...and please provide for him so he can keep his dignity, providing a way that's in keeping with who he is.

January 26
Father God, I come, and ask you to meet me, to overcome all the clamor and the fear. You are God – "When I am afraid, I will put my trust in you..." – I must do the *putting*, so I turn and lift to you my thoughts. Should I get ready to move (to Paw Paw – we were wondering about it again)? Will physical deterioration happen as fast as this last month's cognitive fall? How do I manage that? And will I get sick?

I sensed from the Lord that since my time wasn't being given to meeting his physical needs yet, I should put together picture albums of his childhood and cull stuff in the house.

January 29
Good morning, Father...please counsel me regarding how to respond to his belief "three of us" are here together – he, I, and Helper me. Help me know what to say; it seems he mainly needs assurance... I felt deep mourning as he went back and forth between Wife me and Helper me.

One day he came, asking me in a whispering voice, if he and I could go to the office to talk. He thought others were around, so he closed the door. In a long rambling speech, he talked to Helper me, saying he was stopping the relationship. Several times I mentioned being both wife and helper and reminding him of AD's confusions, but he kept saying the same thing. I finally took down his dictation of a letter to her and then typed it. He wanted us to pray, me first. I cried, so sad for what AD was doing. He then went downstairs to use the treadmill. When I went to give him the typed letter, I realized he'd already forgotten about it.

January 30
Lord, thank you for this outlet (my prayer journal); somehow, I need to tell someone, and it's so good to be able to do it here. You told me years ago to "Get ready," and I've done a lot, read a lot...so I wasn't surprised about him not knowing me as his spouse. But I was not ready to handle the in-and-out recognition; I didn't know that would happen. The question of who I am in any given moment is always there, and then a decision must be made – do I go along with it or tell him I'm both women and AD is messing with him? I find I do both. So, I come anew, pleading for your new mercies this morning to us both...

* * *

I started reading *The 36-Hour Day* (Nancy L. Mace, Peter V. Rabins), finding many good and helpful suggestions there to consider.

After getting in bed last night, Wayne got upset, and started implying I and the kids were conspiring against him, making plans for him. He pleaded that we "just let him be." I realized he couldn't follow or understand what was being said as I talked with Maria and later with Jeff and Shelly, so he got suspicious.

"And those women – I don't want any part of that." It bothered him to have someone else (Helper me) around, along with the women he thinks he sees who apparently are on the helper's team.

He keeps asking to put together a ministry group, to have people come, have coffee cake, and ask them what they see God doing and "What do you need him to do?"

February 5 I realized we had a new normal – I was Helper me most of the time, but then he would recognize me when we were with family members or friends.

> Lord, has he separated me because he doesn't want to get this much help from his wife, for he's supposed to be her helper? It's interesting. So, I ask you to help today. Maybe I should be working to help him remember me? I think I avoid that (and say it's okay he doesn't know me) to reduce confusion and therefore his being troubled. What should I do? Lord, how do I show him love when he thinks it should be that of a friend only?

Later in the afternoon he was very confused. I found him trying to put underwear on his feet, though he had jeans on. What he'd wanted was socks. He also struggled to get out of the recliner, falling back numerous times. He said his thigh or hip area hurt and that was the reason. It seemed to me he doesn't have enough strength in his legs.

February 8
Lord, thank you for meeting me so powerfully yesterday while Wayne was with Jeff, for unlocking the grief that lodged deep and then graciously sending a text from Sarah regarding her coming right after it! How wonderful! How marvelous! is my Savior's love... you see me, you hear me – my inner, words-lacking cries. I know you're with me and will lead me through these waters. I put my trust in you.

Sunday was a pretty awful day. Helper Me drove to church where, on seeing Maria, he recognized me as wife, asking when I'd come. He said he misses me. He kept pressing with questions, so I again explained the two-person thing. He said, "You mean you were in the house all night? That's sick; I want no part of that..." He got angry and stayed that way. When we got home, he accused me of trying to get him to do wrong things, saying also that "they" were manipulating our lives and I should get rid of them all. But then he broke, saying, "I can't do this without you; don't you realize I'm scared?"

February 12
Father, thank you for a new day... Please give me strength to continue the course, for, Father, I feel like bailing this morning. I'm still tired – from a cold? – and I think there's unsettling within – from grief? + How long, O Lord? + what steps will we be taking? + more?? So, I come...

Sarah came. He displayed his increased fear regarding what is happening to him. He also expressed his anger to her about people making decisions without him and made accusation of me – I'm sinning – and he does not have AD. He doesn't understand things so he draws wrong conclusions.

Wayne, Jeff, Sarah, Maria and I met with a consultant from Evergreen Commons. Wayne was okay in it all, and we had a really good time as a family.

February 15
(Matthew 16:24) "...deny self and take up his cross." This verse has impacted me in my life more than any other and continues to speak. My cross is where I put my attempts for self to death; your cross is where I receive atonement for them. How did I miss so much? The cross-life is the "it's not about me" life, and I ask for your filling for it today. Please protect the tent, my body, and keep it functioning; help me put self on the cross today...

I went into the bedroom to take a nap (at his encouragement) and was there over an hour. When I got up, he asked where I'd been, indicating he'd looked all over for me but didn't dare look in the bedroom because he knew she, the other woman, was in there napping. He went into a long speech about being upset having her around and wondering how I could allow such a thing. Later Jeff and Shelly came but their presence did not trigger recognition of me.

As I was dressing after my shower, he called me on my phone, asking, "Where are you?" That led to another talk about AD and the two women.

February 18
So, Lord, I too plead for help today. We've always lived such a connected life, and to now have this kind of separation is really hard. Please forgive me when I unconsciously say, "Enough Already!" Please pour out patience and ideas for distracting him and for being honoring of him.

Later, sitting in the living room, I heard what sounded like water pouring down. Twice I got up to check. It was the washer, but it seemed to be a sound I hadn't heard before. Then I remembered I'd asked the Lord to "pour out patience," and I realized he wanted me to know he was doing that.

Last night Wayne had known me as his wife so I could

sleep next to him. But in the morning, I was Helper. He asked, "Where did you sleep?" I spoke truth, "When you know I'm your wife, I sleep with you; when you think I'm your helper, I sleep in the office." That puzzled him, but he didn't get disturbed.

It was a day with many discussions, starting with a reprimand for Wife me for not being with him, to fluctuating between my identities, to a serious look at my being in his bed. He wanted that but decided he just couldn't do it, saying, "It hurts." At bedtime, however, he wanted me there; I asked if he saw me as wife, and he said he did. So, I stayed. But in the morning, he again said it should end and said he was sorry.

There's now a general acceptance that we won't be together at night. And again, there was talk about the other woman being around – "it needs to stop, it isn't right, it's divisive." (He apparently believes she's trying to get him to be unfaithful to his wife, and he feels that powerfully.) In the evening he asked if I was going to sleep with him, so I asked who I was to him. He said he was working on it and then launched into prayer for his "friend here." Then he gave me a blessing. But after that he said I was Wife, and I said, "Then I'll join you." He was pleased, seeming even settled.

Again, he talked long to me as Helper, saying people are blaming AD for everything and are meeting at City on A Hill Ministries to plan how to put him away. He got more and more angry and shut out any explanation I tried. He's angry about being led, being driven around, having no say.

February 24
Lord, I know there's no possibility of understanding so explanations are futile. What should I do instead? What can I suggest or offer that would bring some relief to him? He wants to be done with "the other people," "to just be us, as we were..." Lead me, Father, and be merciful to him, to us. Others have experienced this. I have no right to ask that this stage be shortened, so I ask for mercy and for help today to provide for him.

February 25
Lord, I just want to cry – it's so close. I'd like to have nothing to take care of, face, deal with for a while. But it isn't possible, I know, so I come, seeking your strengthening, your help, your encouragement...

Daily, long speeches continue: rebuking Wife me, pleading with Helper me to get his wife, and so forth. He acknowledged (when knowing Wife me) that he fears what he'll wake up to in the morning – will she be in our bed? I told him I wake up fearing him not knowing me as wife again.

February 26
Father, there's mounting tears in me. It was so hard to listen, trying to figure out what he's saying, for an hour. All the while he was seeing me as Helper me.... All these speeches are so hard to follow, to respond to, and it's hard trying to bring him reassurance and peace again. But that's what AD persons live with, isn't it? Inner struggle to understand, difficulty in expressing the question, uncertainty, fear. My assignment is to give reassurance, safety, and I'm so bad at that. O Lord, please help me today – lead me, show me...

I asked the Lord if I was in a holding pattern, just waiting for and expecting the next stage to appear any moment. And then we were given a whole day of recognition! No questioning, no reprimands, no accusations. What a reprieve. He wondered if she (the helper) herself has AD, for "she knows a lot about it and has times of disappearing." I said it's something to think about.

* * *

An interesting thing occurred today. I suggested to him that we ride out to the lake; he agreed. A few minutes later he called me on my phone saying the other Chris had asked him if she could go along. He'd gone downstairs to make the call so she wouldn't hear it.

The night was hard. He fussed a lot about where his wife was, and this morning he was very distraught about it, wanting to call the police to find her. I finally got him to call Jeff instead, who came over. That triggered recognition of me. But it left Wayne disturbed (even afraid?), believing the other woman is out there and will return. We both decided to yield the whole thing to the Lord and give up trying to figure things out regarding "those people" or "the Body." (He talks a lot about the church, the Body of Christ, and what it should be about.) Peace came for the moment and for the day.

It seems he's accepted there's two of me. I just assured him that I'll be with him. As with all mornings, he knows me as Helper but is all right with it now at least. We started a higher dose of Sertraline.

It was again a hard night – there was so much confusion. He cried for his wife and pleaded with me to find her. I told him Alzheimer's was causing this confusion regarding me, making it impossible for me to find her. We both cried, prayed together, and then separated (since Helper me couldn't be in his bed). Neither of us slept much. At one point I heard him walking, so I also got up, and suddenly he recognized me! Again, I cried, and we clung to each other. We still struggled to sleep, for he kept wanting to make sure I was still there. In the morning, however, I was again Helper me. This was the first evening of him crying for his wife.

March 8
So, Lord, thank you for answering my prayer for mercy. Mercifully you gave us a wonderful window of knowing, loving, clinging to each other. Thank you for it.

March 9
I wonder if I'm finally learning to love. Lord, I realize I'm a *doer* rather than a *feeler* in this, like Tevye in "Fiddler..."

> O Lord, I'm starting to see. Has my caring all been self-protection, a careful shell? Thank you for beginnings of that breaking...please be merciful to me...

When Wayne again got angry about not finding his wife, the Lord gave me love for him. Though I couldn't produce her, he accepted the love (even while saying we couldn't be together in bed) and got to feeling peaceful. So good!

He was troubled this morning. I suspect it was connected to his hearing the discussion at the lawyer's office about finances and his future care. He was disquieted all day yesterday after that meeting. He talked about "them" coming to take over the house, sending us somewhere; about not being home but at a place where we work; about being sick of his wife not being here, and on and on. I wrestled with the question of "playing the game," entering his reality, or providing distractions.

March 14
> O Lord, I've never been good at puns or games like this. I have no creativity that would come up with alternatives quickly, so I plead for you to provide, to show me what to offer instead. Lead, I pray...

When Jeff came over, Wayne recognized me as wife again. At times of recognition, it seems he's also now aware that loss of recognition could come again, for he'll say, "Stay with me!" or "You're still here!"

He had a bowel accident in the afternoon.

Tonight, was the first evening of having to call Jeff over to help settle him. He was so hurt that his wife had left (as he believed) and became suspicious of "that group and its board" who are making decisions about his life. Through Jeff's coming Wayne recognized me but then harshly scolded me for upsetting the marriage covenant, for defiling his family.

March 17
(Matt. 26:56) They all "left him," left Jesus to the soldiers, leaving, they hoped, what could happen also to them. Lord, I have *left* an amputee, that is, struggled to look at the person, and I know it's from a deep fear that that could happen to me. As people stay away from AD, perhaps it's also because of fear, fear of not knowing how to relate... and perhaps, fear that it might happen to them? Oh Lord, you who forgave the disciples, forgive me for avoiding a person because of fear. And in your strength, I forgive those who've already shown this avoidance of AD. Thank you...

March 19 Jeff has had to come over almost every night now as sundowning affects Wayne, keeping him from settling. Last night Jeff's presence didn't trigger recognition of me as Wayne bounced back and forth, regarding me as helper and wife. But he calmed down anyway, and that enabled rest. Jeff suggested Wayne gets to thinking he's being cared for in a facility and wants his wife to take him home.

I had a dream about us being at our church with a lot of people. I became aware of Wayne not being with me, so I looked for him but didn't find him. This is now the second such dream since Thanksgiving. I went to the Lord: "He's 'leaving' more and more, Lord. Thank you for the moments of togetherness we are yet given and for the peace and acceptance he's having more also – how good."

I realize that in December he started drooling as he napped, so much so that he'd have to change his shirt. Now I am seeing it occur a lot even when he's up and functioning.

March 20
Father...thank you for the breakthrough of recognition a few minutes ago – what peace that gives him. O Lord, I'd so like for him to have peace, but it seems AD will rob that piece by piece. So again, I pray for you to be merciful to him, to us...is it possible to handle what's

coming here? Father, please grant his desire to be home, but I'm puzzled, for he doesn't recognize this as home. Lord, sometimes it seems he has a lot of time yet ahead, and sometimes it seems he doesn't. You are the one who knows and has decided. I pray that it won't be like his aunt (lying in a fetal position for months). (We had been praying this prayer together for some time, asking for the Lord to be merciful to him, to us, and to shorten the AD life.) Please, Lord, we just ask for merciful dealing...

He determined he was going to drive and actually got the car backed out. I heard it and ran to the garage. When he saw me, he stopped, then yielded to my saying no (but then couldn't remember how to put it in drive to come forward again).

March 22 Jeff couldn't come, as he wondered if Josh had COVID-19; that hit hard. I cried to the Lord, "Lord, with the shutdown and Jeff not being able to help, I feel very alone in dealing with the confusions - all day, all alone (and phone calls just stay superficial). BUT you are here, and you knew this was coming... Please help...

March 24
Josh has no fever! "O Lord, thank you!"

Wayne accepted a substitute car key fob (from Maria) and continues to make sure his four valuables are in sight: car key, wallet, phone, pocket notebooks. He admitted it had felt good to get in the driver's seat, but then he felt bad realizing he couldn't do it.

He brought up marriage, saying the helper wanted him to marry her. He decided to tell her no; it was very troubling to him. I wondered if he realized down deep that he *is* connected to me and doesn't want separation?

At supper he wondered where his wife was and kept looking for her. I decided to "play the game," to "enter his reality," as the books say, and suggested she'd gone out for a while. That was a big mistake. He spent the whole evening looking out the window or front door, in the basement, in the car. He left the door unlocked for her and the front light on till 10:30. Even after that he got up frequently to check; I heard him many times throughout the night. He showered at 4:10.

He knew me the next morning. He said he'd been ticked that I'd left and that he'd thought I'd gone to get married. He said there was a gang of people in the neighboring condo all night, that he had sent one of his professors to check it, that he'd seen Jeff who made faces at him, that he saw people in our house, that he was scared.

> **March 28**
> (He thinks he's in spiritual battle.)
> Lord, please show me how to battle also and how to help him feel assured and loved. Help us both weather this complete isolation. Phone calls and conversations really fall short; still, they indicate we're thought of and probably prayed for – thank you! Also, for Jeff's family stopping last night to greet us from the lawn...for your presence with us, your very present help in this time of trouble: increased AD with mandatory isolation...

He thinks again we'll have to leave this facility (our home) but then has moments when he says, "This is good; it's familiar; this is my house." He's restless though, checking always for people or his valuables.

> **March 31**
> Thank you for connection all night (though it left in the morning), and for the moments we get. They might be disappearing. O Lord, I pray you give him peace in the times when he thinks I'm gone... Please help me *deal* as Jeff leaves town for nine days – how can this be?... Please be merciful to us all through this time – thirty more days of isolation! Can I make it with the in

and out recognition and resulting mood changes and accusations? But you are here. You know the situation and what's called for better than I, and you have the way for me, for him, for us. Please be merciful to him (and to me), I pray, and keep him from a prolonged last stage…

* * *

April 1
…Lord, I plead for help: to overcome this head cold and be kept free from the virus (CORONA), to carry the AD-affected load of listening, listening, seeking to assure, trying to figure out what he's saying, trying to get grocery items, and such things. Help me, O Lord, as he mourns his wife's "disappearance." Please, Lord, be merciful to us and refrain from giving me especially what I deserve. I plead for health, and ask you to take him past mourning or accusing and give him peace. O my Lord, I bow and accept your way for me, for you are God.

It was an easier day, for he knew me all day. The Lord heard my plea, and I felt assured I'd make it while Jeff was away for the week.

Recognition of me was in and out, disappearing again about 8:45 this evening, even though we'd talked with Jeff by FaceTime. It took me by surprise, therefore, and I was disappointed. However, he did not get anxious about it, neither then nor the next morning.

In the evening he called me into the office for one of his discussions. He talked about "church participation," and such things. It was quite mixed up so he agreed to drop it. I asked him if he'd like to sing. He said, "No, not without Chris. Who'd play?" I said I would, but he didn't like that at first. He agreed later to "do a couple." We did several songs, and he really enjoyed it. Jeff called, but it brought no recognition of me.

April 6
Lord, as I read about AD, I realize there's more to come. I pray you equip me (to respond rightly to him today, to know, from you, when to take him to a day center), and ready him for these steps also, I pray.

Right after I wrote the above prayer, deep mourning and anger hit him. I could do nothing except embrace him, and then I suggested a ride to the lake. He loved being there but continued to feel bad. Jeff FaceTimed from Gulf Shores, and Wayne told him about his wife being gone, but then Shelly joined and it got dropped. After hanging up, Wayne said, "She was in there! Did you see her?" He meant me; he saw me on the FaceTime screen. He told the other woman (me, sitting next to him) that he'd seen his wife! The rest of the evening was hard as he talked and talked about being the church.

He seemed to know me most of the time today but at one point got very restless. He was sure "they" were coming to talk with him about marriage. He felt so pressured that he wept. I assured him he didn't have to get married and that I'd take his side in it. Later, I playfully asked if he'd like to marry me again. He responded with great relief, saying he'd wants that so much.

April 9
Lord, my husband came to tell me he's leaving, saying he told "representatives of the leaders here" that also. "This is a good church, but he's an evangelist and must be about that, so could he talk with his wife?" (It was interrupted by my struggle with email...) So, Lord, it's shaken me, probably because the weight of carrying all feels even heavier when a link to the outside (email) doesn't work and I can't fix it. I know it's a small thing, but I plead for you to help, to restore, to equip me to help Wayne. Thank you. You are my help, my strength, my supply.

That help was given! Recognition finally broke through. Wayne was so relieved, saying he could now stay. And thankfully, Josh helped me resolve the email glitch.

April 10 It was Good Friday, and I was recalling the great good the Lord has also given in this journey. But that perspective got severely challenged even as I was writing. Wayne got very restless, looking questioningly at me several times as we talked with Maria on speaker phone. After hanging up, I reiterated what she'd said about scholarships for the coming school year. He got very angry, saying, "It's *my* dad, I mean daughter!" He was seeing me as the helper who had no right to talk with *his* daughter like that. Maria had picked up the anger and suggested a Zoom visit. Wayne continued giving me a verbal lashing, not understanding either about Zoom. When he saw Maria and Ben on the screen, he continued talking angrily. Gradually it simmered down. Maria suggested praying together and asked him to start. He confessed getting confused and angry. Maria also prayed. It was good and we ended up enjoying each other. Later Wayne apologized to me.

The next evening the meltdown came. Wanting his wife, he was upset and said he was leaving to go home. I said that we couldn't go back to the way things were and that we needed to stay here. (I had read that "home" can be used to refer to the way things were before memory loss started and not necessarily to a particular place nor a particular time frame.) But he insisted, saying I could stay but he was leaving. I asked where he'd go (by walking). He said he'd use what's in his billfold to find a place to sleep. Then he pressed, "Can't you just take me home?" So, I suggested we drive in the car and look for what he was thinking of. He agreed, and took his Bible. We ended up driving around Zeeland. He said at one point, "I know this place! I brought people to Christ here," and then was disgusted, angry, wanting to "just go home." I said I'd take him to a place where we could get rest for the night and that he should trust me. We came here, he was quiet, and then asked where he could sleep. I showed him our room and got things ready. He asked, "Why do you do this?" I said, "Because I love you," and hugged him. That broke the belligerence.

He had talked a lot before the meltdown about doing ministry here, gathering people who need help, who need Jesus but said it all depends on me for he is limited. After the meltdown, he said, "We can't do ministry here for you aren't ready..."

He showered and shaved at 3:30 am and then said he'd sit in his recliner. I heard him looking in drawers and asked what he needed. "My Bible." So, I found it, got him settled, and slept a couple hours. In the morning, he apologized, saying he was grateful for me (though he thinks I'm a helper).

Easter was a wonderful day. Maria's family brought dinner, and Jeff came in the evening. That stopped the accusations of my leaving, abandoning and being underhanded. Even when he thinks I'm someone else, he shows he must have some belief that I'm his wife because he asks how my legs are doing. (I've had circulation challenges in one leg all my life.)

April 14
Father, I come...I feel so weak, yet I'm trying to steel myself for when the shoe will drop. Thank you for sleep for us both. I was surprised last night when his endless talk seemed designed to send me out of the bedroom, for I had thought it was possible he knew me. But he thanked me for being all I am, saying he'd seen Jesus, and it was I. Thank you for peace there and for rest, and for the opportunity to see the huge waves on Lake Michigan...Such good... Lord, please help me know what actions I should take when the shutdown is over - should I have him go to the day center? or should I make a schedule of people to spend time with him? or should I hire someone to do that? Please lead, I pray...and I plead for your mercy to us both, sparing him a long last stage...

I was grateful the other shoe hadn't dropped, and we'd had a couple of good days, though he occasionally asked for his wife and asked Maria on the phone if she (his wife) was there.

But it finally did. He recognized me, and the verbal lashing exploded. "Why do you leave? Why don't you stay with me?" and on and on. I kept countering with truth and mentioning AD's affects, which didn't make any difference to him. Finally, I just asked his forgiveness, and he gave it. I kept my arm around him, and he mourned but not with anger anymore. We eventually came to a stalemate, deciding to just enjoy each other. We had coffee and coffee cake, did some of his grooming tasks, sat in quiet, even dosing a bit. But then recognition started slipping away, and again it was gone.

April 16
So, Lord, here I am again. I was drained by it all and could not move for a few hours. Is this how we are to manage the journey of AD? Being mostly alone, proceeding, awaiting recognition and meltdown, then doing nothing in order to recover from it? I long for someone else to do the work of listening to and figuring out his thoughts.... So, Lord, I bring this whole journey to you again, and my sore back, and my sense of injustice when falsely accused, my demanding cries that we be spared its worst ugliness, my desire for someone else to bear what I've been given to carry, my longing to be carried...here I am. Am I able to relinquish these to you? I don't even know...and my dread at having this lockdown go on and on and on, with no help, no socialization or stimulation for him. Merciful God, I know you carry me, you watch over me for good, you are making the way for me, and I praise you and look to you and with as much as I'm aware, I say: Whatever, Lord; whatever you choose for me...

April 17
Good morning, Father – how good to be yours, to be cared for and carried through the night, given health and

a little improvement in my back. How good to see in the steady though slight snowfall your steady, little by little, provision falling to me, us...

Recognition came and went. I was uncertain during the rest of the day which identity I bore. In the evening, Jeff came right in the middle of Wayne's talking about feeling pressed again to marry Helper me and being troubled by that. He really wanted to do it but didn't feel right about it. Jeff's appearance brought recognition of me, ending the marriage talk, but I was again Helper me by bedtime. That makes five consecutive nights in the office bed.

April 19
Father, I am angry. He made me turn off the news, help him pull up Psalm 92 on his phone, and then sit there as he read it. It seemed so religious. And dominating. All night was dominated by him, by his restlessness, sleeplessness, anxiousness, carrying on about the group we're starting ("You sleep here because you're in this prayer group. And Chris will join us too; where is she?" Then there was the comical scene of catching sight of me in the mirror, thinking I was standing in the office, as though the mirror was a doorway.) I decided to sleep in his bed, and I'm glad I did, for it helped me keep some track of him through the night. This stage turns sleep habits upside down...I've pleaded with you to grant me good sleep, but again, why should I have a different experience than other AD couples? Why should I be given an easier road? I think I really want to have some life without AD, a normal life for a while after AD, and I don't want it to so weaken me now that I'll die too. There, that's it, isn't it? How selfish it sounds; how selfish it is. So yes, I'm angry, watching my desire be taken from me, little by little. I know I must lay it down, and it's so hard... But I want to be clear with you, so Lord Jesus, Father, Counselor, I bring my desire to have life apart, after AD, and if it's your plan that this journey

also cause my death, I accept; to die is gain, and I should prepare for that also. Please help me to give this completely – your will, my Lord, your will...

April 20
Father...your mercy is so great. You received me yesterday and lifted me out of anger and gave a peaceful and good night of sleep. And it was *with* him – please make him comfortable with that going forward. It would show him he's not alone and would help me keep better track of him...

I then told him I wanted to be in his bed with him, to be of help finding the bathroom, and to assure him he's not alone. He liked that.

It was a hard evening, and I lost it, getting frustrated and angry. Then all I could do was apologize over and over. It showed me I do need breaks from it all and someone else to do the work of listening at times. But it's COVID Shutdown... there's no one else...

April 24 He called Jeff just now "to tell him where he was." Later Tom called, and Wayne told him he was in "a facility run by the police." Tom asked what he could see out the window (he was expecting to hear "trees, birds, and so forth"). But Wayne said he saw people getting booked and asked him to "call Chris." I asked the Lord, "Is COVID making him feel imprisoned? Is he feeling AD is closing in more?"

He doesn't know anymore which phone is his and has started taking my phone now to a "safe" place and then I can't find it.

April 25 I realized the Lord was giving me the idea to form a prayer team for me in this assignment. I sensed him saying, "You're going to need help in this," and five names came to mind. I felt scared, anxious as I texted each one about it, for it's not my nature to initiate such things. But each heartily agreed to do it. Then I sent a group text. There was enormous release as it went – I wailed and sobbed... "I am not alone..."

April 26 I said to the Lord, "I'm surrounded...I am in awe. I had no idea there would be such encouragement and blessing poured out like that." My first request was that they pray for me to avoid losing control, for when I do Wayne remembers it emotionally, not cognitively. (He had asked me if I still wanted to kill him. I at first thought he was joking, but he was serious. That's how he *felt* when I'd gotten so frustrated with not being able to get him to understand my explanation.)

April 28 (Psalm 125:2) "As the mountains surround Jerusalem, so the LORD surrounds his people..." I'm surrounded! There were many, many friends and family members praying for us, which we knew and felt deeply. I in no way want to minimize the help they gave us by praying for us, nor suggest they weren't being led by the Lord. I can't explain why he gave me these five in this way, I just received the gift. I could send a group text at any and all times of the day and they prayed, sending scriptural encouragement. They were an Aaron and Hur to me, keeping my arms held up and steady. (Exodus 17:12) They were like the Roman shield that wraps around, surrounding much of a person, so I called them my Prayer Shield.

* * *

May 2
It looks awful: another month at least of shutdown isolation. O Lord, make the way for America, I pray, and also for Wayne and me, for me, looking at another month...of *dealing* by ourselves.

May 3 I realize I haven't updated his AD this whole week! It's been quite peaceful, though with some times of great confusion, some mourning for his wife, times of not knowing where the kitchen or bathroom was. Last evening, when I directed him to the bedroom, he said, "This is really nice; thank you for getting it." He slept all night!!

May 4 All peace left. Wayne got very angry at Wife me for not being around, then at Helper me for usurping her place. (Some time earlier I'd mentioned to him that the Holy Spirit is called Helper in John 14:16, 16:7, so I was okay with that name. I reiterated that analogy when needed.) At one point he asked, "Who are the theologians in your life?" I said, "Charles Greenfield (my father) and Wayne Leys." That made him angrier, accusing me of using these names, of trying to pass myself off as his wife. But then he talked and talked — about theologians, about Lew Smedes, about not allowing biblical error in his life (suggesting I was doing that), about funny things he and his friends had done. I tried a diversion, suggesting we go buy geraniums, which we did. He was friendly, even loving. I later fell into a nap, awakening to him looking for keys, pressing, pressing me about locking "the office," (which he says is down the street). I broke, and cried. So, he hugged me. But I was shaking inside as if spiritually hit.

> O Lord, is there such stuff here? Stuff that comes from him without his having welcomed it in? In your name, Lord Jesus, I reject his accusations of being unbiblical, deceptive, manipulative. I am not a usurper, and I declare truth: I am a Child of God, I am Wayne Leys' wife, I have every right to be here, I am caring for him, not manipulating him.

Later, we had a wonderful time walking at Helder Park. We both enjoyed it. On the way home, he asked where the group went, the one he often sees. At home he looked over the whole house for them. He got very disturbed when I couldn't answer his questions about them. "That's no way to treat people!" He went into the bedroom, closed the door for a while but then came out in a better mood. He'd gotten very discouraged as he tried to figure things out. But he saw I was also trying, trying to understand who he was talking about. He appreciated it, saying he'd understand if I wanted to just leave, divorce him – "You deserve better."

This morning he wondered if the group that's making decisions about us are CRC powers-that-be. (CRC represents the Christian Reformed Church, the denomination in which he served as a pastor and as president of its board of trustees.) He again expressed the worry that we're not going to be able to stay in this home, along with, "How are we going to move our stuff?"

May 7
Lord, is he thinking, sensing moving to heaven? Should I, instead of saying "no, we're not moving," talk about preparing to die? For example, should I ask, "What would you like to get rid of? or to give to someone?"

When at the beach, he didn't make it to the bathroom in time. That was a first.

May 9
It's now been three weeks that I've slept in our bed, even though he thinks I'm Helper me. He seems to accept the fact that he loves her and deeply admires and respects her.

Thank you, Lord, for peace about it, this measure anyway, and for the doctor understanding that the hallucinations could evoke anger and being disturbed. (He therefore offered to increase the Sertraline, which I accepted.) Father, is this shutdown, with the possibility of a day center experience probably many months away yet, your answer to my cry about not wanting him to have to go to one? Thank you. Could we set up something here in our house?

The doctor also confirmed my suspicion that the drooling could indicate the brain isn't telling the throat muscles to swallow.

In the evening, we enjoyed a walk down the hill here. I asked then if he minded me watching an hour episode of Pride and Prejudice. He said fine. But during it I became aware of him wandering around, looking, looking: in the car, in the basement, all around the house. Then I heard him talking with someone, but I didn't know who. He told me "they" don't know where we are. I went to him, trying to figure out what he was getting at. He showed me his phone, wanting help to call someone. I saw he'd already called B____ from church. He talked about needing to leave, pleading with me to get hold of his wife, whom I shouldn't blame because "she's doing a wonderful job." I showed him our bedroom and he agreed that that's where he spends the night. I asked him to sit with me, but he couldn't do it for more than a couple of minutes. Then I saw that Jeff had texted. He didn't wait for an answer, however, but came over, thankfully. B____ had gotten worried about Wayne's call and called Maria, who called Jeff. Wayne then recognized Wife me and asked why I hadn't been there. But he backed off from going further into accusation, and said I should just shake him when he gets like that, tell him what's real. Jeff and I both said I *do* do that, and it makes no difference. Calm, settledness returned, though there was no logic that did it, no answer to anything.

> Lord, such times will not only continue but grow and increase in frequency - right? My presence doesn't stop the escalation, and I expect the time will come when Jeff's won't either. So, Father, thank you for meeting us again, for carrying us through another episode. Please keep providing what I need to help him through. I wonder if this worsening is your answer to my plea that you spare him the last stage? Thank you for having the plan, for working it out, for working good in the midst, for being merciful to us.

We were awake very early. I checked on him, finding that he'd opened the front door because he said a man had called him, and Wayne thought he was coming for him. He didn't shower because he said someone told him not to. In the evening he focused on finding a particular place he had in mind, so we went looking in the car. He directed me all around Holland but never saw what he was looking for. At home he got discouraged. He called Maria, asking her to come over, saying he couldn't find me. I texted her, telling her also about the front door episode. We FaceTimed with Tom and Lor; Wayne spoke a word to Tom, but he stayed "down." Afterwards, I decided to play the piano and worship. He was angry, but after a while he came, humming, then singing in the Spirit. Then Jeff and Shelly came, and he was back.

However, he got up several times during the night. At 1:20 he stood at the foot of the bed saying, "It's 1 + 20." I said "too early," so he came back to bed. I found him at 3:20, dressed and sleeping in the recliner, lights and TV on. I urged him to come to bed, which he did. This morning I asked him to take meds, but they were missing. Apparently, he'd taken them at 1:20. So I told him I would take charge of them. He agreed.

All evening he pressed me about starting a ministry group, about being on the planning committee for it. He asked if I was "getting it down," so I finally took pen and paper and wrote down the things I could understand.

May 12
I bring my budding anger.... I'm seeing that I have to give up all sense of my time (last night I couldn't watch an hour program). I have almost no "my time," it seems. But that is a good picture of life with you. You, however don't dominate, or control but want me to see that everything is yours. I only have what you give. Thank you. I "lay me down" anew... and put myself in your hands. Forgive, I pray, my desire to have something my way and the anger that comes...

Wayne was very *down*, despondent, disturbed, angry, accusatory of me, saying I was passing myself off as his wife, and that's sinful. He talked and talked and talked, but then we separated (since I couldn't do anything to appease him). Later, he came wanting to reconnect. It all seems to drain him, for he sleeps a lot.

It was a beautiful day, but I just felt like crying. I sensed I was grieving Wayne being this far gone, grieving the loss of understanding what he says and the changes in how we live here.

May 16
Lord Jesus, I come to the altar once again and plead for your help, your renewal of my mind. My life is in you, not in self. I lay it before you and seek anew to die – I am not my own, I belong to my faithful Savior. I was bought with a price. I bow, I receive, I stand in awe. And Lord, I grieve R___'s death; both he and P___ were pastoral to me. They communicated care and awareness of what I'm experiencing, and it felt good. Thank you for that and for his great release now. Perhaps this loss reminds me of daily loss with Wayne and stirs me within. Perhaps it makes me wonder if there's any pastoral care for me? Or is that also a loss? It also seems true I never had it, and it is a reminder of being left to myself always in all we went through in churches… Still, I am yours, I am cared for by The Shepherd. I lift praise and gratitude. You are so, so good.

I really got angry. I found Wayne in the recliner, fully dressed at 1:15 am. He then messed around in the kitchen, finally coming out with cereal and milk in a cup, then did more messing around, looking, looking for his valuables. I found them, so he finally sat down and fell asleep in the office recliner. I, however, couldn't sleep, so I read in *The Great Divorce* (C.S. Lewis) and finally slept a bit. I realized my anger was due to worry about getting sick from lack of sleep. In the morning, he didn't remember the night's events but did remember there'd been anger. He said, "Are you angry with me too?" These last days he's mentioned "wedding" several times. I asked if he thinks he's getting married. "No!! It's the entrance into the Kingdom."

> **May 17**
> Lord, is he still having confused thoughts about needing to be married to Helper me since he really likes her and wants to be with her? Or is there revelation to his spirit that his final entrance to the Kingdom is imminent? Help me, I pray, to encourage, to assure...

He showered at 2 am. I tried to stop it, but he insisted, saying, "This is what he told me to do; it's not me. He said it." I got upset. We talked about his being up much of the night, but he didn't remember the events. He did remember being led by a strong male. He asked me why I didn't just overrule him when this happens. I said I'd tried, but he was belligerent in resisting me. He was disturbed by that.

It was a hard afternoon. It started when he asked me for a key. I wondered what it was for. He took me to look out the front door and pointed to the right, saying, "It's just over there." Apparently, he was thinking of the Elmhurst set up where his office was located in the church next door to our house. I said we had moved everything from that office to this place. He got upset, "That's not right. How could you do such a thing without asking me?" I said we did, but AD caused forgetting. On and on he talked and cried. He was disturbed, thinking I and others were undermining him, doing things behind his back. "We need to get your lawyer and mine to meet and figure out who's right here." I texted Jeff to come; that helped. Later, Wayne felt bad about it all and apologized.

May 20
Lord, countering with objective truth isn't the best way anymore, it seems. Books say to "enter his reality" or to distract him. What should I do? I'm not an idea person!

At 2 am, he started it again. I said I was too tired to talk about it. He lay awake, whispering, gesturing. After a while he said, "Chris, just ask the Lord to save you..."

All morning he thought we were being put out of here. "____ owns the building, and there's tension with him..." I said we'd been able to buy this part of the building and everything in it. He accepted that but also said, "Stay alert..."

I was seeing belligerence, insistence on doing things his way, and derision of my suggestions. For example, at 9:30 last evening I suggested getting pjs on rather than different clothes. Instead, he changed several times, wondering if he looked okay for church, for the Ascension Day service. "I should gather these people (the ones he was seeing here) and tell them what the Ascension is because they don't know what it is. Do you play golf? We can organize a group and play..." He changed clothes several times, then searched the house for something he couldn't identify. He finally lay on the bed, fully clothed, slept some, awakened several times, got up... He's always looking, looking, looking. In the morning he tried to put salad dressing in his coffee. I protested, but I finally just let him do it.

May 22
So, Lord, thank you for letting me use this venue to "tell someone." Somehow it helps, for it seems I'd be totally alone if I couldn't somehow tell. But Lord, I felt dislike for him through it all, but also great pity. And some anger at losing all that sleep. How, Lord, how do I do this and stay in health? Only by your giving it, for my natural course would be to get sick. I plead for some sleep today and for your protection of health... I think you showed me to just let him spend the night in his clothes, but that I should stay awake and available. Thank you. Please continue

to supply my way. (I sent a request to the Prayer Shield about this this morning and got immediate, wonderful responses. At the same time the sun broke through, on a day the weather app showed no sun!) O Lord, you are good. I am yours. I am not alone. You go beside me; you never leave me... and I lift praise...

Wayne admitted he's discouraged and asked me several times yesterday and again today, if I'd been notified that someone died. So, I asked if he was wondering or sensing his own death. He said, "Probably." He was discouraged, probably aware he'd done really strange things all night. He later told Jeff he'd met with an undertaker. There'd also been anger and determination. At one point he took his Bible and a book and walked out. I asked where he was going, and he responded sarcastically, "Where do you think I'm going?" I suggested it was to the church office. He just mumbled and left, standing in the driveway a bit, then returning.

When Sarah came, Wayne was in and out of seeing her as Sarah or his sister Ruth. After supper at Jeff's house, he went to her, shook her hand, saying. "Hi! We sat at the same table. Have we ever met?" He asked her to pray about being part of his newly-formed ministry group. She later advised me to take steps regarding care, saying, "The AD personality is beating you down beyond what your person should take." She also said I should guard against stress and emotional strain affecting me physically. Then she, Maria, Jeff and Shelly met with us, talking about next steps.

At supper, Wayne said, "I'm thinking about my dad. I think it might be a time for me to go to a place [a care facility]." I asked if he thought that placing Dad had been a good thing for him. He said, "Absolutely!" Maria sent the link for Grand Brook Memory Care, a facility being built in Wyoming, MI. It looked to be a really good fit for him.

May 27
And then I saw myself. I wanted the end of this and got eager for it, and I felt guilty about putting him somewhere earlier than absolutely necessary. Not a pretty sight - my soul. It wasn't news to you, however.... Lord, I think I've been learning to love these years. At least there's been more than there was. But now there are times (like now when he robbed me of sleep, made me get up, and then went to sleep in the chair!) when I don't like him. Yes, it's when sleep has been taken away from me, when it should have been a right (it's nighttime, after all!). So, I come and plead for you to help me, even though my goal may still be to look good. O Lord, I'm pathetic; but you've paid for that, and it is finished.

Wayne wanted Wife me to go to a meeting with him where people were making decisions about this place (our home).

I'd made brownies, and they were still warm and gooey. I heard him in the kitchen, and finally I asked what he was doing. He came out carrying a spatula covered in chocolate; his mouth, his chin and his hands were covered with gooey chocolate. He said, "Did you do this?"

A woman we'd worked with sent a picture of a GED graduation (taken in the jail) that included both of us. I asked him if he could find me. He could not. I pointed to myself, but he didn't believe it. Still, he remembered others as I named them.

We had a wonderful walk together and then at De Boer's Southside we got coffee and donuts, which we took to Kollen Park. He spoke angrily, and I finally understood he was angry that I, his caregiver, had paid for gas and for the coffee cake. I countered it somehow, but when we got home, he wanted to talk: "There were two women beating up on me, not like this (he tapped my leg) but like this (he swung and hit me pretty hard)." I wondered if he was thinking of both Chris's, Wife and Helper.

May 29
Lord God, Father, I come, feeling foggy, tired, tired of it, and selfish for having so little tolerance. Please, Lord, help today... Thank you for loving mercy; each morning it's there... and I praise and stand in awe and receive anew. Thank you for this sanctuary – my swing in the woods (on our patio), where I can hear birds, see the sunlight on leaves and feel the wind blowing through – so, so good. Thank you.

In the evening, he pleaded to go someplace. I gathered it was for a ministry group. He wanted his brother in Wisconsin or sister to help him since I was hesitant. I suggested we sing, which we did for quite a while. Later he talked of having the group, saying to me, "Do you play?" I said, "I just did." "That was you? You're really good."

When he couldn't figure out how to change into pjs, he said I'd have to help. I had to walk him through each step. (That's totally new for someone who'd always wanted complete privacy.)

I realized from reading *A Grief Observed* by C. S. Lewis that I've been in a waiting room, continually grieving losing him to AD, just waiting for this to end, not planning, not starting anything...

May 30
How long will we be on this step, when will we drop to another; how long till I can't do it anymore? These kinds of questions are keeping me from planning get-togethers and trips. It seems I'm just waiting for his timeline? "And grief still feels like fear. Perhaps, more strictly, like suspense. Or like waiting; just hanging about waiting for something to happen. It gives life a permanently provisional feeling. It doesn't seem worth starting anything. I can't settle down." (*A Grief Observed*, C. S. Lewis, p. 33 Harper Collins Paperback Edition, 1994)

May 31
Lord, I've been thinking about Lewis' comment regarding the waiting room experience. Not only have I been in it because of the COVID shutdown but also perhaps because of AD –- not planning anything because I'm just waiting for the next manifestation of decline or maybe even for it to be over. Consequently, I don't actively bless or love him. I just take care of things (his messes and needs). Thank you for his expressions of wanting groups here to fellowship with, to share the word and sing together. Help me actually do that. Thank you! (I tried finding things to do that would bless him, hoping that would help me get out of the waiting room. I knew Wayne wanted groups here so I invited Jeff's family over to sing.)

* * *

Wayne spent a lot of time planning his new group and wanted to go invite people. But not being able to drive to do it frustrated him. He was also frustrated regarding his clothes. He couldn't figure out how to put on pjs and didn't want my help, so he finally put his shirt back on (though inside out) and his shorts and slept that way.

June 2
O Lord...you had told me to move here to Zeeland, I believe, and then when here, to "Get ready." I did work at that, not knowing what for. It turned out to be AD. And it turned out you prepared me also and equipped me. Now I believe you've told me to get out of the waiting room and do life with him. At the same time, I believe you're urging me to begin preparing for next steps. So, I believe you will show me what to do, what is needed, and will help me decide.... And Lord, are you preparing me to bring things to others regarding AD, down the road when I'm not caregiving? Will there be such a time, a time to collect, and then somehow convey all that

you've shown me, all that you've had me learn? I ask you to fulfill that also, for that thought has been in me for a few years already.

He was sure someone was coming to pick us up or to tell us whether or not we could stay here. He wasn't sure which it was. I brought supper to the porch, but he wouldn't leave the front window, being sure this person was coming. He got mad that I went ahead and ate.

The next morning, he continued thinking someone was coming, so he stayed where he could see the front of the house. He wouldn't go for a walk or to the lake because, "I told them I'd be here." When Tom called Wayne told him that we were waiting for those who would transition us. Wayne suggested he get the details from me and handed me the phone. He was very down all morning because nothing happened. Finally, he gave up, napped, walked with me, and stayed with me, but belligerence returned at bedtime – "leave me alone; stop trying to run my life." I did and went to bed. He came to say he was going to sleep (in the recliner, I assumed). I told him he usually sleeps in the bed, also saying I'd only been trying to help him. That softened him. He took shoes off, lay down, and went to sleep.

He returned to the idea of being moved, saying, "Sometime today, I suppose, a truck will come." He's expecting "them" to transition us out of here.

I couldn't figure out what he was trying to convey in a devotional. We had tried Psalms, but it made no sense and then Luke, again no sense. I suggested he dictate and I type; again, no sense. He kept pressing, pressing. "It's important stuff, people need it," he said. Finally, he agreed it didn't have to go out. I practically cried, being released from his great pressing on me. I said, "Let's get out of here." We got coffee and almond sticks at De Boer's and went to the lake. He was concerned about me (he'd seen me very close to tears) and treated me with friendliness and the get-to-know-you questions he asks Helper me.

June 5
Thank you for helping me with all that. He's still talking about people coming to get him. Lord, are you preparing him for a move to full-time care? If so, please show me, please make it abundantly clear to me, for right now doesn't seem to be the time – not for quite a while, unless there's more great change. And Lord, if it is to happen, could it be that new place in Wyoming? Or is there something similar closer? Or something closer that would be just fine for us?

I spent the time he hiked with Jeff redoing his devotional to send out and searching for car keys. Thankfully I found them. The devotional was the generic gospel message he's been giving for some time. I organized it and sent it with an explanatory note. He's still thinking of stuff to take along when we leave this place.

We had another talk session of accusation, sorrow, hurt. Then he said he was going to take his Bible and things and go to "his office." He asked me to take him when he remembered he wasn't supposed to drive. We got in the car, and then he changed his mind. After a long time of being down, he said he still praised the Lord though. I thought of "The Goodness of God" (Bethel Music) and played it on my phone. We both worshiped; it was so good.

> (7:25 pm) He asked me to join his group, which I wondered about. He indicated he'd gathered a group in the living room, including kids, so I moved there. He welcomed everyone, turned to Isaiah 49, prayed, preached, instructed, testified, prayed, invited others' thoughts. Then he blessed them and promised to pray for them each day at 5:45.

At bedtime, he said he had something to say. He whispered, "The Spirit of God is working. You do not have to be afraid. Help hurting people and be sure to talk about Jesus."

At 2:15 am he said, "Can I ask a question? Do the kids have a way of communicating with Mom and Dad?" I assured him they do. "So, they can communicate with Dad?" Was he worrying about being cut off from them when taken from here, which he kept expecting to happen?

I had a dream that I had to replay music at the finish of a program of some sort, but I couldn't get the pages in order fast enough and everybody left. I also noticed my purse missing. I was then in a car, wondering how to get home and get what I needed without cash or credit card.

June 7
Lord, is there something here for me? Am I worried about not having the "music," whatever is needed for the assigned task of AD caregiving? Or not having money needed to get him help? I look to you anew; please give me the tools I need for this AD assignment and help me with the financing of things, I pray.

In the evening it all started. He wanted to talk with the office of the agency he thinks is working here about financial misdealing. I asked why he thought that. He said he knew that was happening because his billfold was empty. I asked him to show me. "I can't without an attorney present." He admitted he doesn't trust me, saying he trusted Chris and would check things with her. Anger, accusation followed – "This is not the way Jesus would do things." He wanted me to get hold of a guy from Denver whose finances are connected to his and to pray for the relationship between the four of us: he and Wife Chris, Helper Chris and her husband. Then it was back to finances. He said he'd take it downtown to be looked at. He said downtown was in Atlanta, Georgia.

He wanted to have another group meeting. He studied

for it, pressed me to say when we could do it, and then said, "It's NOW, I'm ready." He walked into the porch to talk with kids, staying aware of the adults in the living room also. He preached, then offered others opportunity to give a word, prayed, and then said, "Now we'll sing." (I ran to the piano and found songs.) After singing, he gave a benediction and said, "Thank you for coming. You don't have to leave. You can stick around if you'd like."

> **June 9**
> Lord, I again broke under that pressure last night (retreating to a backroom – an old tactic of mine). So, I plead for strength for today and for a very clear answer regarding Grand Brook.

The talking about being moved from here continues, now with some bitterness and a lot of sadness.

I felt pressed. I was trying to make a lunch for Jeff and Maria, to get the house ready for the Comfort Keepers consultant, and he was needing attention. I realized I would feel less pressed if I had nothing to get ready for myself, or for guests, and just allowed his needs to be my complete focus.

> **June 10**
> Lord, you are here, you are in me, you have a way for me, you know the plan you made before Wayne and I were born, and you are carrying it out. I will praise and give you thanks. I marvel, even as I grieve, I think. Wayne is changing continually. When awakening this morning, he not only asked if it was time to shower but also asked where it was. Now he just came to say, "I don't know how this works for you, but can we have lunch together sometime?"

But then he came in saying we need to leave here. We can't do all the things the group wants anymore. We can take our things one by one, starting now (Wednesday) and finish on

Saturday. "I worry about you. I don't want my wife in this. It's a growing men's group that has different partners each night." He asked if I've been solicited since being here. I reacted strongly, and he responded, "It's the filthiest language I know; it's really bad here."

At the meeting with the Comfort Keepers representative, he was first funny, friendly, but then angry, giving expression to it. Jeff and Maria responded well, Jeff telling him that he (Wayne) had told them to take care of Mom and that's what this is about (something Jeff told him often after this). After lunch and a nap, he felt better, saying this could be good.

I learned that the kids all think he'll be ready for residential care when Grand Brook opens in August (it didn't open until November; COVID delayed it); I was surprised.

> Lord, I'd like to know their reasons, wondering if it's because I've complained. O Lord, I need your help here. I have very mixed feelings; I realize I'd like to be done and then I feel guilty – isn't this my assignment? This new place would offer him more time with people, more stimulation than I can come up with – would it actually be better for him? Would I be abrogating my responsibility? And am I wanting to avoid people's judgment? I know that's in there. So, I come, Lord, and plead. I asked you to show me, and I do see increasing confusion and unsteadiness...

He wanted to talk. There'd been four to five people who'd hurt him badly. He cried and cried. They'd had a meeting – they're people with whom one can laugh and pray. They talked about him, even with accusation. (He was referring unconsciously to the meeting we'd had with the Comfort Keepers representative. He couldn't process its meaning and felt its impact instead.)

June 11
Lord, we are separating more, little by little. I could not protect him from such hurt nor even explain why it was

a necessary thing to do and what benefits could come from it. I find with separating going on that I tend then to just detach emotionally (to protect self). Please help me here. Help me choose attachment instead. I'm still needing to "learn to love" and end the cycle of waiting to be loved. I am yours!

This morning after our walk I told Wayne I was going to shower, which I did. When finished, I found him in the kitchen extremely distraught, almost in tears: "Where were you?!" He had his phone in hand, but he seemed unsure what to do with it. He was so frightened. I just tried to reassure him. Later this evening, he wanted to remove his dirty shirt, so I gave him his pj shirt. He wanted me to leave so he could change further. I did. On then checking, I found him putting shoes on, jeans still on, with tomorrow's shirt on over the pj shirt. He got ticked when I reacted. Again, he wanted me to leave so I did. Then I found him putting on different shoes with a different shirt and dress belt. I said something. Again, he got mad, saying, "Jesus had to endure this too." He then sat on the porch for a while with a book. I got the place ready for nighttime and got into bed. He came, saying he'd sit in the bedroom chair. As I reclined in bed, he said he'd leave to sleep somewhere. I said, "You sleep here." So, he lay down, fully clothed, including shoes, and immediately fell asleep. About 1:45 am he removed the belt and the shirt. I asked if he wanted pj bottoms. He said he did. It took a long time figuring out how to remove the jeans and put on pjs.

Jeff came twice today, and each time Wayne recognized me as wife. He was so pleased, he hugged and kissed me. But in the evening, he asked what time I leave. I said I stay because I'm your wife. He said, "I don't think so," with sadness.

He seemed lost, looking and looking, but he didn't know what he was looking for. After my shower, he said "Can we talk?" He talked about a group meeting where he'd been hurt. It came to me that he'd been so hurt that he couldn't participate in the open mic session at the memorial lunch the day before.

He knew people had been really nice. They hadn't prevented him – AD had. But he couldn't process nor even articulate it.

Friends had the kids and us over to listen to the ECRC Farewell tape. Wayne seemed lost most of the time. His eyes were fixed on me a lot - his anchor in the confusion?

He came to me on the porch. "So, this means we can't talk?" I invited him to sit with me. With tears filling his eyes, he said, "Must I be looking for a job?" I was surprised and questioned what he was worried about. "They told me I have to be out of here by Tuesday night." I countered that strongly. He believed me and felt better.

A friend from Colorado called and must have said something about my helping with the devotionals. That made Wayne thank me for doing so. He then seemed to say I would be doing things (in ministry?) "beyond him," without him it seemed, and should expect it. It seemed to be a blessing of me.

He fell today getting into the shower. Later he was talking about making plans for a group and thinking something should happen. He opened his phone, wondering where Josh, his "son," was. (Josh is our grandson.) I pointed to Jeff in the Favorites. He called him, telling him we were all right, that we were across the street and other confusing things. Then he said he was going to his office, pointing next door. I was trying to distract him when Jeff walked in with three sundaes! I cried. It was good to release the building pressure.

He didn't shower nor brush teeth. I'd stopped his shaving at 3:30 am and he accepted that. At 6:30 I found him in the kitchen spreading jam on a piece of paper towel as though it were toast. I helped him get a shower started before bed, for I realized he didn't remember what to do.

He awakened me, looking for clothes (I'd forgotten to put them in the bathroom the night before). He took them into the bathroom, and it was quiet a long time. I finally checked. He'd done nothing, admitting now he didn't remember how (he'd tried to put underpants on though he hadn't removed the pjs).

June 19 Friends were coming for coffee, and I was busy getting ready for it. He didn't like it that I wasn't fully available for him. I'd had to help him with teeth brushing and the shower water – I'll need to be more available. "Lord, may I have an AD-free life when this is finished? Or are you planning that I, my life here, retreat also? You are my Father, my Maker, my Savior, the One who knows me and has the plan regarding me all made, and I submit anew to you. (And would you make it possible for Sarah's family to get here? Wayne was working to come up with her kids' names yesterday: Emmie, Colin – pronouncing it with a long o vowel sound.)

Wayne went with Jeff to Calvin and said, as came home, that "they" had given him nothing to do. So, he was depressed. He slept for two hours in the bedroom, came out, slept by me on the couch for another hour (I slept too). Then there was more group planning; I suggested he write the thoughts down, keeping the tablet. He loved that and worked at his desk quite a while.

June 21
Lord, I bring to you again the AD progression. I know you have mapped its course, and I plead for your mercy in it. Spare him a prolonged "fetal position" last stage and make clear our steps along the way. Please prepare him to receive the hired caregiver and provide a man, or woman he can be comfortable with. And Father, I bring also again my desire to have some life without AD – only you know... So, I give this to you and accept again the AD life today and tomorrow and the next... I am yours – do with and for me what brings glory to you. As I got up this morning, I had these words in my mind: "Take my life and let it be All for you and for your glory, Take my Life and let it be yours... I sing 'Glory to God...'" (Steve Fee, Vicky Beeching).

He was eager to go to church and had a good time there. Afterwards he wanted to hurry out to the car and leave. I said we were staying for a Father's Day lunch (which he forgotten about). He got angry and wasn't very friendly throughout lunch. He slept going home, and when getting out of the car at home he said, "I can't do this." Questioning him, I realized he meant that the long morning, the riding an hour each way weakened him. He felt it in his legs.

At Jeff's home later, he sat down in a lawn chair, but not squarely, and fell backwards. Amazingly, he didn't get hurt.

He talked to me for two hours. Then he badly needed a bathroom but struggled to get up, to get steady. I finally got him up, and, and with him leaning on a walker (which he usually refused to use), I pulled him to the bathroom. He wasn't sure where it was. He went in but couldn't get his jeans undone in time. He told me the toilet had leaked, but he let me help him get his clothes changed.

I told him about signing with the care agency. He got angry, saying he was deeply hurt. He cried, saying I was betraying our marriage commitment. He said he never expected something like this and told me I was sinning and this isn't the Lord's way. He was too upset to work on a devotional. Maria came and he continued, though not with the same anger. He had said I shouldn't listen to the kids, for they have no business speaking into our lives. I'd told him they'd suggested this step, saying, "They're afraid I'll wear out." "No, you won't. You'll be fine." Maria calmed and reassured him, taking him for almond sticks. When I realized he wanted to make sure I wasn't disturbed with him after she left, I suggested we go out together. We decided to take a walk at Helder Park. On the way there he was pressing again, pressing, pressing. I couldn't understand and suggested we just enjoy the moment. He said, "So you want me to stop?" "Yes." "Then I'm leaving."

June 25 The next day I felt really pressed; there was NOTHING he'd written that could be sent as a devotional. Although we spent hours trying, he just gave religious-sounding phrases and then told me to just write it.

> Lord, I feel I could break; he's mad at me for not using what he gave me. He says he gave a lot of thoughts. I said, "They don't connect to Psalm 128." He said, "Make it!" Lord, I really need help to be help today, for I really want out, to get away, away, away…. He goes through my stuff – I feel he's taking everything away from me. As I give permission (that is, let go my right to things, time, for example), he seems to go for more, taking me into his demented world and extinguishing me also bit by bit. Do I keep giving more permission? Is that what the cross life is calling me to experience? It will be taken whether I permit or not. O Lord, I just need mercy, and help in this…

He announced he was taking a walk. I tried to stop him but couldn't. I quickly checked to see if he had his phone. He did. I followed him down over the foot bridge, down Paw Paw Road, and then he turned back. I was relieved.

He didn't shower again this morning. I also read yesterday that Persons With Dementia "rummage." That helps me understand about him going through my things.

When he asked me if I knew his name, I laughingly said I did and asked if he knew my name. He said, "You're C… C… Chris." Later, after our walk, he did the same. So, then I said, "Tell me your name!" He couldn't. I asked what name was given when he was baptized but he could think of nothing. So, I said, "I know who you are! You're William Wayne Leys!" "Yah, that's what the trouble was – William." Apparently, he was remembering the problems he had all his life because of going by his middle name. Or was he actually starting to forget his first name William since he was always called Wayne?

June 30
O Lord, today we start with Comfort Keepers. I know it's right, but I have some dread regarding what he'll then do to me. Please fortify me and give me the ability to respond with respect and assurance. Lord Jesus,

Waymaker, show me the path you've arranged, and equip me for steps to take. (It had been a night of interruptions, confusion about where the bathroom is, and I'd had to stop him from putting toothpaste on the razor about four am.)

He got very angry about Vee (not her real name, a Caregiver from Comfort Keepers Home Care) being there. She told me to leave, saying she had a lot of experience. I did. I had resolve and no fear of him. (But I checked with the Lord, "Did I just disengage and walk away, Lord? No, I didn't, not like before at least, for I burst into tears as I drove away.")

L___ called as I was driving home from the Comfort Keeper break. He was very confirming of the choice to hire someone and to take breaks, but we both cried. He said it seemed there'd been quite a decline in the last six months. He knew! His last phone call with Wayne had shown him even more decline. There was no ability to carry on a conversation anymore.

Later, Wayne said something about a coming move, adding, "But I don't really want to leave Wisconsin." (He'd grown up in Wisconsin.) I asked if he thought a move was coming; soberly, he said yes. I asked if it was scary. "Yes."

* * *

I was extremely tired, napping a bit, even though he was wandering around. Later he dictated thoughts regarding a group meeting, and after supper we had the group. He asked about walking with Jesus, he shared, prayed, then dismissed all. I started reading, so he said each could do what he or she wanted. He continued to interact with some. Then he got down on the floor near the porch and started talking with a group there, softly; I heard "school," so maybe he was with kids, giving a "children's sermon" (which he always did, getting down on the floor with them each Sunday).

We struggled to sleep. We'd awaken after drifting off, one time because he'd had a dream that something fell between us, breaking. He told me to stay away as he looked for the pieces. I finally lay on my good ear, so I wouldn't hear him, but then I missed his getting up. When I awakened about seven, he was finished in the bathroom but he hadn't showered, though he insisted he had. After we walked, I suggested we try something: I could help him shower. He was a bit reluctant but then agreed; we made it fun. I realized through that process how much he feared falling there and that that emotional memory was leading him to avoid showers.

He talks and talks; in the midst I heard that something was "the most hurtful of all." It seemed to relate to Comfort Keepers. Then it was something about him "not being around anymore" and the usual suspicions about people trying to get our money or our house. We got a diversion from it all by Jeff inviting us to see their packed camper. So we went, and also prayed with them for their trip.

July 3
So, Lord, please meet me – I don't know… I admit I again have times of wanting to be done, along with other times of thinking AD's not really that bad yet. (But some things are harder.) Lead me, especially without the help from Jeff this week…

Wayne slept a lot, then involved me in group planning. He spent time at the dining room table studying for it. He let me clean his eyelids and shave him. He had showered but didn't shave or brush teeth.

July 4
(Luke 8:15) Good soil people "bear fruit with patience." Patience – allowing time, giving the time needed for something or someone other than self to accomplish something. It's the natural development of fruit that

comes as the tree or vine submits to the process. For me today it's spiritualized fruit – character – that comes naturally as I submit to the Spirit's process, and don't try to manufacture fruit myself. Again, *self* must get out of the way, and yield…

July 5
"You are the God who sees me." (Gen. 16:13) O Lord God, how can it be? That you, my God, would love me, would take me in, would see me, and watch over me. O my God, how can it be? But it is true, and I again receive…

He didn't shower, and I let it go. In the afternoon he announced he was going to take a walk by himself. Though I said No, he insisted. When I asked if he had his phone, I discovered he did not. So, I ran to get it and his ID card, only to hear the front door. I ran after him with the items, insisting he take them. Then he changed his mind and came back in. It shook me, maybe because Jeff is gone. Who would help me if I couldn't find him?

He accepted Vee's coming better today. He's been struggling to come up with my name, once saying, "C…C…Chris;" but today it was, "C…C…Cliff." Three times last night he had to use the bathroom, each time struggling to stand steady enough to pee. He had an accident but refused help in the bathroom, even as he stumbled around in there. On getting up in the morning however, he did all right, even remembering to shower, saying he hadn't done it yesterday.

I felt love for him in returning after Comfort Keepers yesterday. Unfortunately, loving is usually in the doing: jumping for needs, cleaning up clothes and bathroom (he got there too late yesterday), taking care of everything. I was so thankful to be able to feel.

These have been hard nights. Many times he gets up and is unsteady. And I had the start of a bladder infection, but didn't realize then what it was.

July 11 I got over four hours of uninterrupted sleep!! "Lord, I am so grateful! You heard my cry for sleep…"

> **July 12**
> Come, Lord Jesus, come… please carry me through preparations for his siblings' visit. Help me, I plead… Have I been displaying or feeling an "I can do this" attitude? Probably, and now I feel I can't. But "I can do all things through [Christ] who strengthens me." (Philippians 4:13) "And my God will supply every need of [mine] according to his riches in glory in Christ Jesus." (v.19) You are my supply…. O Lord, thank you for knowing me as you do, even better than I do, and for still receiving and loving me.

Jeff, Shelly and family got back on the 11th but didn't come over thinking they needed to quarantine. I had to go to the Lord: "Lord, I admit I was disappointed. Perhaps you're reminding me that it is indeed only you who can always be available. Thank you. I look to you and stand in awe…"

July 14-15 Wayne's siblings came to visit, and we had a really good time. He thoroughly enjoyed it and believes it's the last such time. During the night he had a bowel explosion in the new bathroom. It was everywhere. I think all the rich foods they'd brought affected him. It took a while to get it, and him, all cleaned up. When we were back in bed, I put my hand on his shoulder, wanting to say, "It's okay." He took it, asking, "Who is this?" "I'm Chris, your wife." "I'll believe you."

It was hard on all to say goodbye. Some of them said there are hard decisions ahead, perhaps just a few months away.

> **July 16**
> Lord, it reminds me of reading about the "Finishing Anointing" the other day. I put this decision and the time frame in your hands and plead with you for the "Finishing Anointing," so that I don't quit and fall short. So please let me know when or if this present assignment is finished, I pray in Jesus' name.

I asked the Lord for a Grand Brook kind of place. Would it actually help him to be in such community? (Apparently some family members think so.) Is it possible to make a transition plan?

I moved his toiletries back to the old bathroom. The sink is too small in the new one and he spills over it. He's confused about which bathroom to use anyway. It had worked really well for two years.

July 18
He's steadier on his feet than he had been, and he showered and shaved without me hearing anything. I wonder if that is a result of having more stimulation from his family being here? I asked the Lord, "Does it mean, as I initially thought, that we are indeed still able to be here and that I should stop moving him in my mind? I should stop that anyway...thank you for that."

I got a good nap while George was here with Wayne.

July 19
Thank you for excellent sleep – the best night in a long time! What a provision, what a gift! Thank you also for calmness from him, for his acceptance, for his not fighting me regarding shower and clothes.

July 20
...Lord, please help me live today *with* him and not be looking down the road. Still, I ask you to prepare the place for down the road, whether here or some other home.

He fell during the night on my side of the bed, falling backwards towards the closet. I called out, "Wayne!" He said, "Get out of here!" As I put the light on, he indicated he thought there was someone around who was a danger to me. We got up and looked everywhere, and then he settled.

He was planning a wedding a few nights ago and wanted my help. I asked "Who's?" He said, "Yours." I was surprised, so he got a bit sheepish but then offered to meet with me and my groom. Somehow my vagueness was able to divert him and get him into bedtime stuff. But the next morning he returned to it.

When I returned from the lake (where I go while Vee is here, taking my prayer journal with me), he met me in the garage, looking terrible, asking, "Where's my wife!" He introduced Vee to me and then started to lash out at me. She started to leave, so he took her hand, apologized, prayed for her, and then she left. He then recognized me and started letting me have it: "How could you walk out on me? I never would do that!" There was crying, anger, then sarcasm about my control over everything. He wouldn't let me touch him. Then I wasn't Wife me anymore. This all took me by surprise, for his getting disturbed about me as helper *and* wife hadn't happened for a while. After he settled a bit, he said quietly, "I need you." So, we just sat together.

He hasn't written a devotional for over a week. After family left last week, he wanted to reflect from John, starting with chapter 16. He brought me his scribblings but there was nothing to use. That continues each morning. Today I typed his dictation and then said I'd think about it.

He said, "he said to..." a couple of times, referring to someone directing him. Who?

Last night he had one of those nightmares where he would attack me thinking he was attacking a ferocious animal, and by doing that he'd be protecting me. In the past, I'd cry out as he started to hit me and he would awaken. Then he'd feel bad about it. This time, however, he did hit me and I cried out, "Wayne, don't hit me! Don't hit me!" Then he stopped but never awakened. I got up, not feeling safe; after a while I went back, lying alertly. At one point, he turned towards me and asked, "Who's there?" or "Who is this?" I said, "I'm Chris, your wife." He said, "I know." I put my hand on him, and we slept.

July 23
So, Lord, naturally I'm asking if this is a sign for change of living? Or does it mean I sleep in the office again? But then I can't be aware of his movements, his possible stumblings, his confusion about time to shower. So that doesn't seem to be an option to me. Lord, forgive me for wanting a sign, for wanting it over, for wanting my life... and I bring it again to you. I realize he's had that nightmare, and swung at the animal before but not actually hitting me. This time he hit me. Is AD the animal? Please, Lord, protect us both... and lead me to know.

We had lunch with friends at a restaurant. Wayne ordered a sandwich which I knew would confuse him. I tried to help by picking it up and handing it to him, showing him he could eat it by holding it in his hands. But he put it down and used knife and fork instead. I decided to let it be.

George came to stay with him as I met a friend for coffee. It disturbed Wayne that I did that. He suspected me of doing something behind his back. "Why can't I go to these meetings? We used to do these things together. I don't need George here; I'm still the head of this house!" Somehow, we got through it.

July 24 His rambling speeches can sound religious. He said something like, "There was another woman there when we walked. Where is she now?" "I didn't see her." "If you're in Christ or looking at people in Christ, you'd see them..." I react to religious-sounding talk, and I didn't like the veiled accusation, nor what seemed like his using of the Lord. So, I reacted, "Don't lecture me." He responded with something I couldn't understand, then went into the office, closing the door.

In the evening we had the COVID-delayed Chicago Cubs opener on TV. His eyes indicated he wanted to say something. So, I muted it. He started whispering, and I asked him to talk. He said, "Be quiet, they're worshiping." He was looking out for the people he sees here.

(Luke 12:35f) "...awake and ready." O Lord, please ready me for what's next in AD care. I desire to be your servant, to keep "dressed for action" until you end the assignment. Please, Lord, make it clear...

In the evening, I was finishing the supper dishes when he came with his Bible and asked if I was going with him. I asked "Where?" "Just over there." I said I'd have to finish but would follow. He walked down the street to the roundabout, and then stopped. He turned around, saw me, and came back. At home, he started talking about the makeup of the groups he imagined ministering to and what he'd do with them. I invited him to sing and we did. Then he returned to talking about the groups. He said he was having them "right there," pointing next door to Unit #6. I began to wilt under the press, and told him I was exhausted. He said he'd leave; so, I asked, "Where?" "To find my wife." I tried to tell him who I was. He said he knew my tactics and went looking for his wife throughout the house. He called her on the phone; I answered in front of him, which upset him. He then called Jeff saying, "This is Wayne." He told him about a guy wanting something. He said it "was hard on Chris," and told about the group forming. Shelly texted to see if they should come; I said yes. Meanwhile he talked again about wanting his wife. I showed him the sheet I'd made explaining that I'm both Helper and Wife; he said it was bad theology. We parted and I went to the piano. I played, "In the Midst," a song the Lord had given me years ago. He then came and sang it with me. It was powerful; then he prayed. When Jeff and Shelly walked in with sundaes, he dropped his anger, though seeing me still as helper.

July 25
Lord, I felt exhausted from it. I just wanted to scream, "Stop!" This week felt like a relapse instead of the disease progressing. He hadn't been upset about his wife in several weeks, and all of a sudden, there it was again. So, he wasn't yet into the "blissful ignorance"

stage as I'd been unconsciously assuming. He was angry that Jeff came to stay with him while I went for a mammogram. "We always did that together." It was easier when he was more oblivious. I'm just so tired, weakened from the demand that I listen, join, take part in his planning sessions and then endure accusation, sorrow and anger when I tire out. Lord, what's right in this? Please help me, please lead me. Renew my strength to cope, to help, to love.

We went to our church in Paw Paw. As we entered, he said to me, "How'd you get here?" As we sat down, he said, "Who did you ride with?" He was angry, for recognition of me as wife had come there. Driving home, he said, "So you're saying we rode together going to church? And I was sitting here?" He talked to Wife me for the hour ride. It was rambling and confusing, but as I listened, I gathered he was saying that what we were together is gone. We don't just talk together anymore. He says he's been shoved aside. I struggled to respond and was pretty quiet. Finally, I told him it hurts me too that things have changed so much, and I talked of AD. He rejected that explanation.

The morning was hard with much restlessness, lashing out in anger, accusation, sorrow. In a calmer moment, he said "They will be moving me." I questioned what he was thinking. He said, "I told you there'd be a different wind, a different breath, and you must follow it; it's going to be hard." I told him I was sorry that I can't fix these things, and suggested we go grocery shopping. That went well. After lunch I asked for help from the Prayer Shield. Peace came! He felt it, saying he received it from Jesus. "We're going to make adjustments... They'll come, it's going to go quickly..."

In the evening sorrow returned but without anger or accusation. I suggested singing; he said he couldn't and was so despondent. When I asked if he minded me playing the piano he said okay. I did, and he sat in his chair, worshiping. Then he cried, and we clung to each other. "I feel like I'm being torn..." he said. We prayed. He agreed he could trust the Lord and he asked if some men could show him his room. I said I'd do it. (Earlier in the evening he'd been intent on leaving, with Bible and journal in hand, going to the place where he could go to bed.)

July 27
Lord, is this separation coming, the physical one? The mental one is here – he thinks I'm from a facility or agency. He doesn't know me. O Lord, the cruelty of this disease is awful. I can look at him and see my loving, fun, lovable husband, and my heart reaches out. But he's having fun with, and being friendly to, his caregiver (me!) in those moments. So, so wrong, so separate already.

At bedtime, he pleaded with me to call _____ (I couldn't understand who), to "let him know where I am." I wondered if he's afraid family and friends won't know where he is when he's in a facility.

Jeff, Maria and I toured the yet unfinished Grand Brook Memory Care Facility. We got a really good impression of it. Wayne was very upset about my leaving. He starting looking for me already before 3 pm (Vee came from one to four). He really let me have it when I got back. I listened and tried to assure him for a while but then just walked away. All of a sudden, he walked out! I checked to see if he had his phone. He did, so I changed shoes and walked after him. He went down Paw Paw Drive and continued down 104th. I came back for the car and got to him in Haven Church parking lot, but he was angry and wouldn't get in. I drove to Lee Street, where he reacted the same. I then watched to make sure he turned the right way on Main. I had texted Jeff about it. As Wayne (walking) and I (driving) got back home, we found Jeff already there. Jeff did a good job talking it through with him, avoiding accusation of him, but he also saw Wayne's anger. Wayne was more peaceful for the evening. (He'd walked his old route, which takes an hour, and thankfully, he made all the turns automatically.)

He needed help with every step of getting cleaned up and dressed. When I'd told him we were going to the bank, he got very upset: "They're going to take stuff; I don't have any money... I don't have anyone who can help me... no one tells me where we are on this campus..." He was more at peace after the appointment. He reluctantly agreed to go to the lake but did enjoy it. In the evening, questions started again, but he accepted things.

He was grateful for all I (Helper) do. He also said he was grateful for the length of the trail at Helder Park. "It's just enough for me, not too long like that other" (which I figured meant the old jogging route he'd insisted on walking Tuesday afternoon).

Later he came to me asking, "Where have you been!?" Thankfully, it didn't escalate. He didn't understand my explanation, but he seemed willing to trust me. He keeps asking if today is the day a truck is coming to move him? Or tomorrow? Jeff now fully believes he'll have to go to a facility – just when?

> **July 30**
> Father, again I bring the question of putting him in a facility. We'd asked that he be able to be home the whole time. Is that now answered with a "No" because he doesn't have a home sense about this place anymore? I believe you give Jeff discernment, and he fully believes a facility will become necessary. The question is *when*, the *why* being to keep me from deteriorating further. Is that right? It seems failure on my part, especially if I quit early. Last Saturday night I thought I was going to break under the pressure, but you supplied help from Jeff and Shelly. ...O Lord, you have led, you will lead...

He allowed me to do some grooming: shaving, eyelid washing and fingernail trimming.

I didn't hear him get up. He showered but without shampooing his hair or shaving. Last night he put toothpaste on his razor. I got some groceries while Vee was here, and when I returned, he again said he didn't like it that I did that without him. "You don't know what that does to a man." "That's all I'm going to say about it."

TAKING A BREAK
(4)

I pause again on this path to offer some thoughts of an explanatory nature.

During early 2020, because we were seeing so much deterioration in the disease, one of the options for care was the possibility, offered by Maria and Ben, of adding to their home to make a place for us. Maria researched it from many angles, including what's allowed in their county and envisioned what some call a mother-in-law suite on their property. As mentioned in the preceding pages, the idea of that looked good to Wayne and me. To have family that close seemed ideal. But further discussions, along with others' counsel, led me to accept that it was probably too late for Wayne. Such a move could increase his confusions considerably. So, we gave it up and, as I already expressed, I grieved the loss.

My journal entries sometimes referred to a religiousness from Wayne to which I reacted. By that, I mean expressing religious words in an empty way, reciting familiar phrases without acknowledging their import. Wayne and I had learned that such empty use of the Lord and his truths can come from his enemy, and we fought such influence in our faith journeys. We were aware that though Jesus achieved victory on the cross, his enemy still comes to steal, rob and destroy by tempting, accusing and deceiving. Our faith walk included seeking to be alert to those activities and to be made ready to battle against them by his Spirit in his name. But in the AD experience I found Wayne sometimes using words or phrases and referring to the Lord in what seemed inappropriate ways.

So, I had to plead for the Lord to clarify what it was about. Perhaps the Wayne he became with AD was repeating old tapes, words that had at one time been full of meaning and helpful for him and which he now used as he tried to hold on to the person he'd been. I also realized much later that with AD he didn't know how to express his dislike with or disagreement about something and resorted to words that came most easily. Looking back, I really think this had a lot to do with it. Perhaps another reason these religious words came easily was because they reflected his relationship with the Lord. His spirit was dependent, childlike, as he leaned on him. And now in his childlike mental capacity Wayne's "go to" was that realm. But I didn't realize any of that in the moment and questioned it.

CHAPTER TWO

The Slide Continues

I realize I need to watch where his valuables (phone, wallet, car keys, pocket notebooks) are put at night, for he can't find them in the morning. He hates it if I find something for him and tell him *he* had put them there. So, this morning I said maybe one of the people who've been around did it. He thanked me, saying it meant a lot.

When he rummaged through my corner of the office and came out with the condo association secretary's binder, I got upset. Later he said, "I really do love you," but then rebuked me for something I'd apparently done, telling me I need to get clear with the Lord.

He told me I should call someone because the roads are slippery and we should cancel things. He also said he had four men in jail: the first is Paul of Tarsus and the second is Christ.

About 8:30 pm, he came putting on a long sleeve dress shirt over his T-shirt. I said it was almost bedtime, but he said he doesn't go to bed this early. He asked me to help with buttons, so I did. Then he changed his shorts into jeans.

> (9:30 pm) I thought he was reading in the office recliner, but he was sleeping. He refused to change into pjs or brush teeth or come to bed. About 11:45, I was awakened by a noise; I thought it was the chair he was in, so I ran

in there. My coming awakened him, and then he knew me as wife! He was glad to see me.

Sarah's family came to spend some time with us. Sarah too believes he'll need a facility. She mentioned markers: Activities for Daily Living (ADLs), cognitive ability, and relational ability. He definitely needs help with those ADL activities, definitely has lost cognitively, and now relates to others only in a dependent way (there's no sharing, nor any hearing of what another is actually saying).

He did well with Vee but then really scolded me when I returned, accusing me of dishonoring our marriage by doing something by myself. Then he broke down, sobbing, repeatedly pleading for me not to leave. I held him, and he held on. I sensed he feels unsafe, insecure when I'm not around and can't process feelings.

August 4
Lord, I remember our first retirement years. He'd say, "I'm going to Ace to get such and such," and go. But if I said, "I'm going to Ace," he'd say, "I'll go with you." Was the insecurity caused by AD there already then? I sense you reminding me that in his prison of sorts, he can't wrap his mind around anything (of my explanations), so all he has is how something makes him feel. And he feels unsafe and insecure when I'm gone. It has to be so hard when a mind can't process things. Thank you for helping me again. I had first thought, in seeing his anger when I returned, that taking a break isn't worth it. I should just stay and not have her come. But I realize again that doing so is right. I just need to be ready to renew assurance. Thank you! And thank you for the reminder from the Prayer Shield about the airline rule of putting one's own mask on before helping someone else....O Lord, how good and faithful you are. You are leading me and you will show me if facility care will be needed. I lift praise. You are so worthy.

Recognition of me as wife suddenly broke through; joy followed at first, then sorrow, sobbing, wondering why I don't stay with him. Finally, he asked, "How could you go to another man?" I countered that and then prayed for the armor of God to protect us both. As he grieved, he acknowledged AD was affecting him, saying in effect that the frequency of his recognizing me would decrease: "It's going to get worse." After a while, his recognition disappeared, and he admitted he was angry.

August 8
How awful to live inside those walls, knowing at times they're closing in. Please, Lord, meet him there, fill the place with your presence, your peace. Would it be merciful to take him past these times of recognition and awareness that simply bring sorrow? Lord, I plead for your mercy to fall on us both. Please, Lord, continue to supply, for I'm so tired...and renew strength...map out the next days, weeks, months, I plead. (Should I add *years* also to add to that prayer?)

It finally clicked in my thinking that getting help for an AD sufferer is for his benefit also, not just for mine. The doctor said it (on the tenth), Sarah has said it, and now notes from Rog came saying it as well. Still, Wayne was very angry when I left him with Vee.

Sundowning started about 8 pm and he pleaded with me to take him to his wife, to let him go home, to get him to his kids, and things like that. I texted Jeff and he and Shelly came with sundaes. That always settles Wayne. Jeff makes him laugh which Wayne had always loved to do. He's then willing to go to bed here, with me here. Before and after their coming he talked and talked, making church plans and assignments for me. In bed, I finally told him to stop.

August 13
Lord, I feel I'm more ready for outside help for him. The episodes like last night now make me feel really weak, pressed into a corner, shrinking, shrinking, shrinking, and I contact Jeff more quickly than before. Lord, please help me navigate things today and to *know* regarding Grand Brook...

Wayne told me he's very thankful for me, even loves me, but he was missing his wife on their anniversary. He talked of "them moving him to a place of care." He rejected my saying it was *our* anniversary just about all day. He treated me as though I was an imposter. When we went to the cottage that Maria's family was renting, he was not happy. He was actually mournful. On the way home he talked and talked about having a group session to plan mission and vision, trying to make me responsible for it. Jeff came to watch the Chicago Cubs for a while and when I could, I told him Dad denied it was *our* anniversary. As Jeff left he said, "Take good care of Mom." "She's not here." "Yes, she is," pointing to me. Then recognition came, and he was joyous and loving! It lasted all night but was gone in the morning. And during the night he fell out of bed.

A friend, whose wife was also diagnosed with AD, called to talk with him. Wayne came to tell me about it: "He's in jail along with his wife." That was his feeling of what it's like to live with AD, indicating this was a prison for the AD sufferer but also for the caregiver. The next morning, he took a shower in the therapy tub, forgetting about the walk-in shower we'd had built and also forgetting to shampoo his hair. I had to help him out of the tub, the sides being quite tall. I'm going to have to remember to tell him where to shower if he does it by himself.

Last night he was confused and could not understand my saying, "It's bedtime." He finally put pjs on, though keeping shoes on also. He said, "What now?" I said, "Lie down and we'll read a Psalm." He liked that. We did and prayed. After a while he said, "Where are we? What is this place?" He was so restless I couldn't sleep, so I read until 11:30. Starting at 3:30 am he got up several times, thinking it was time to start the day. Each time I pleaded with him to return to bed and he did. We got up about 6 and got cleaned up, but then he fell asleep in the chair.

I had asked Jeff to take Wayne to church so I could have a personal quiet and worship time (I'd had no break all week). He was getting ready when he realized I wasn't planning to go. He cried and got very upset about what I was doing to our marriage so I told Jeff not to come. Wayne got angrier and angrier. He continued to get dressed and then expected me to take him to church. I refused, saying we weren't in any condition to worship. He changed his shirt and then walked out. I took the car, asking him to get in, but he refused. I watched from Ace parking lot, then the Baptist Church lot, then met him on Pine Street. This time he agreed to get in. We didn't say much for a while until he said he'd been trying to clear his head. I said that had been why I'd wanted to stay home from church. I think that penetrated a bit. I suggested we take cinnamon bread and coffee to the lake. There he became apologetic, talking a lot, even speaking of his being jealous. I've picked up that he is sometimes jealous of my ability to function normally, and since he can't process it, he just gets angry.

A whole week with no break taught me I really, really need it. He seems afraid of further separating and doesn't like it if I have my quiet time on the porch when he's in the office. Once he came to the porch and I asked if he was okay. "No!! My wife isn't here! I follow Yahweh. When promises are made, they're supposed to be kept....My chapter here will end soon." I wondered what he meant. "Well, it's bound to come to a head..." He went into talk of "this church...and what people need in the Body of Christ."

August 17
(II Cor. 4:7–9) Lord, I have "this treasure" I know. Thank you. And I'm a clay jar, "hard pressed on every side..."

> I can feel so pressed down under the verbal assaults that come so often (including accusations that I'm not following you and he is), "but not crushed...struck down but not destroyed." O my Lord, the power is in me from you, keeping me *at it*, getting me up every morning, enabling me to take care of his needs, to take his verbal arrows...you, in me, live another day...

Wayne was totally confused in setting the table, bringing spoons when I said forks. He got ice but didn't know what to do with it, putting it in a towel. He put tartar sauce on an ear of corn and on the sweet potato. I asked if he wanted to put it on the salmon but he said, "No! This is how I want to do it."

August 18
> (Luke 18:38) "Jesus, have mercy on me." "What do you want me to do for you?" Lord, please spare Wayne a long, drawn-out ending stage; keep AD from putting him in bed for months (years); grant me life apart from AD to compile the thoughts and experiences of this journey and to make more booklets with paraphrases and devotionals... in your mercy... I give you glory (v. 43).

Today he was angry and accusatory about Vee coming. Just before she arrived, he was napping, so I awakened him by playing "In the Midst." When I told him he didn't have to be afraid, he scoffed, looking sad and forlorn. But when I returned, I saw that they'd had a good time. We made coffee, and he suggested a ride together. I suggested Kouw Park on the lake. It was awesome. We enjoyed each other like old times, he knowing me as wife. It was so, so good. But about 8:30 he asked where Chris was. Then he came with materials saying he was going to a meeting with people from the University of Wisconsin and headed for the door. I intercepted, finally getting him to stay in. He talked, and talked, pressing me, then telling me not to worry, saying, "You're doing fine." He's been talking of seeing, perhaps talking to his parents.

(Philippians 1:6) Lord, you began a good work in Wayne, in me, and we both know you will complete it. Please help us both be completers, finishers, I pray. I was told I'd have to "surrender and release him." I do, again. Help me know what that entails...

August 20
Father, we function all right, even though he sees me as helper, not as wife. The afternoon at Kouw Park was an isolated experience of recognition with joy in each other's company, rather than recognition with assault, accusation and verbal battering. It reminded me of *The Notebook* (Nicholas Sparks). Lord, is it all right to desire life for myself? Am I selfish by not wanting AD to take me along with him? And wanting to do things like compiling paraphrases and devotionals? I bring it again. I do ask for that ability... I'd like to be a person apart from AD. Please be merciful to me on this path, I pray, and help me with it, with taking care of everything, and with making decisions regarding that care. Father, thank you for welcoming me with this kind of processing. I don't know what I'd do without it.

Wayne was very lucid with George this afternoon and they discussed several things. But after supper I could not understand what he was saying. I gathered he wanted me to make coffee for people who were coming. I dithered, and he let it go. Then he asked me to put out dishes of ice cream. I turned, feeling pressed. Then he asked if I could help them sing. I lost it and hurried to a back room, crying out silently, "O Lord...!" The Lord settled me and I returned to help them sing three songs. Later, as I walked away from the piano, he got disturbed, saying something about needing me to lead singing. I said I had. He said it should have been five more songs! After a bit I offered him ice cream. That broke his pressing and he admitted to being so tired. We managed to do the bedtime routine.

After the group thing, he wanted to call his brother Ken. I helped him. We got a busy signal, but Ken called back. They talked, and then Ken wanted to talk with me; he asked if something was wrong. I just said Wayne had wanted to call. Later Wayne said he'd wanted to do it because of what he'd experienced – "They assaulted me." When I questioned what he meant, he told me two women assaulted him. I think he again meant me, Wife and Helper, and the assault was simply my dithering, my walking away from his pressing. He felt it as rejection, I guess, and was looking for a familiar connection for comfort.

At 2 am I awakened as he put the light on. He was wrapped in a towel, ready to shower. I was upset but managed to get him back into pjs. Still, he refused to get into bed. He said he was going to read in the chair. "I always read here...I always do it this way..." He was very belligerent. But then we both finally fell asleep about 3, he in the chair and I in the bed. About 4:15 he startled awake and stumbled into bed.

August 21
O Lord, you are still God, in all these circumstances also. You are still on the throne, ruling over all, still aware of us. You see these things and have a way for us. I think you'd say to me this morning, "This is just normal AD stuff." And so it is. Who am I to complain and think I should be done, or relieved? Countless people endure this. You knew it, you know it. You know what's ahead. And I plead again for you to lead my steps.

He so needs an audience. He talks and talks and talks, usually cornering me to make me listen. In the evening he said, "I'm so glad my mom doesn't see this. You're way too violent for her." "I'm too violent?" "Yes." He kept talking, which included, "There's definitely abuse going on." I asked if he feels abused, but he strongly denied that. I told him he'd said I was violent and that there's abuse. He pleaded with me to overlook word choices.

I cried going out to Ottawa Beach as Vee stayed with him (he had accepted her coming). I wasn't sure why – perhaps because of the way things are deteriorating for him, and because I was feeling so much loss...

August 25
Lord, you are teaching me to love; I was no good at it and still struggle to see another past my duty list. I pray you give me knowledge of when I'm doing that. He calls it "violence" and "abuse" when I speak a strong directive (it's strong, but not a yell or shout, which he also calls it). He's coming from how it makes him feel. But I'm wondering if it's also because he never experienced me doing that – it's a parental action, not that of a peer. And he's always balked if he suspected me being parental, so naturally he hates it. Please help me know...

We visited friends at Sandy Pines and enjoyed a boat ride. Wayne was exceedingly unsteady getting off the pontoon; he needed help with that and with getting back up to the cottage.

I thought washing the car would be a good activity to do together. He kept asking me where to wash; I'd tell him and then he'd ask again. I forgot that he'd immediately forget, and I got frustrated. Afterwards, I lost it when he refused to take off his wet shoes before walking into the house. He said, "IT'S MY HOUSE!!" When he said something about Chris, I said, "I'm Chris." "NO, YOU'RE NOT!!" He acted and spoke as though everyone knows I'm not and said it was really hurtful that I make that claim. I just got silent. He talked on and on, and then slowly let it subside. I suggested lunch. Later, he seemed to be apologizing, trying to explain that things happen to him. I said, "It's okay. We're okay. The Lord is carrying us."

I realized his siblings' visit had reawakened his recognition of me with the accompanying accusations and scoldings. Lately though when he talks about his wife he doesn't go further or get all agitated. Maybe we're back where we were before they visited.

* * *

Wayne didn't understand what I needed to do at the bank, so he got suspicious and accusatory, claiming things were being done deceitfully. "We need to find someone to go over things, to make sure." Then he said, "Who are you? No one has told me who you are." He also made spiritual accusation of me. I said I didn't want to tell who I am because he disbelieves me and suspects me. Who I am is too precious to experience that kind of treatment. He seemed to receive that and eventually said he'd follow along. I suggested Walmart. After going there, he was apologetic and attempted to explain. When he brought up spiritual things, I broke and got up to leave. That stopped him. Every day I wonder if he should go to Grand Brook. He also raises the question almost every day about being moved.

I was awakened at five by him turning on the closet light. He was looking for clothes. He'd already showered, he said, but there was no evidence of one. He started looking for his Bible, saying someone had taken it. Then he pleaded with me to take him home – "I miss my kids, my wife...I have twenty-two grandkids!" (There are twenty-two in our family including thirteen grandkids, with one married.) He spent a lot of time wandering around – searching, looking, looking...

I tried to shower, while he kept looking, looking. Finally, I accomplished it, and we sat down to talk. He spoke so softly, I kept asking him to repeat. He decided that meant I was opposing him, got angry and got up to leave. I strongly told him to listen to my explanation for wanting him to speak more loudly. But my strong statement was thrown back at me – "I've been spit in the face," and then he went into religious jargon, accusing me of being wrong before the Lord. We separated for a while. When we met in the hallway, he asked if his wife was around. I explained about being Helper and Wife. He said, "I know that's your god-line," mocking it, showing disgust for my claim. I walked away, and he went on with religious warnings. I pleaded, "Lord, have mercy on him. He doesn't know he's misusing you. And in your power, I choose mercy also..."

Later I went to him, which pleased him. He talked of doing what we can until a place can be found for him. He denied he was thinking about being moved because we can't handle things here. Sometime later he answered a question by saying strongly, "Because I'm moving!" He also spent time organizing his desk items for packing.

September 3
Lord – controlled, I feel controlled by him. He relentlessly demanded I take his scribblings and create something from them to send out to people (as a devotional). How do I get out from under? Pressing me to write for his audience, pressing me to sit and listen to his expounding, even as he indicates I'm just one of the listening group... Lord, I rebel within – why? Is it because it hinders my time, my schedule, my agenda? Is it because I don't trust it all, wondering if there's a spirit of religion in some things? Is it because I just don't have the energy or desire to work at responses to what he's saying (which is so confusing)? So, Lord, help me choose mercy again. Thank you for your mercy to me, new again.

I suggested a walk at DeWitt Nature Center which we enjoyed. Afterwards, as we were leaving, he insisted we'd left people there. I said I knew of no one being left there and drove home. At home, he started watching for them to come; he was very worried. Lor texted, so I told her about it. She said they'd pray. A few minutes later, Jeff came! Wayne's greeting was to tell him about the lost people. Jeff tried to divert, talking about soccer and Jonny's games, but Wayne kept returning to it. Finally, Jeff said he'd call them when he got in the car and look for them on the way home. That settled Wayne, but then he wondered about "going home" himself and "where he'd sleep." He accepted my saying that we'd stay here for the night, though also asking if my name was "Larry."

About 11:45 he needed help finding the bathroom. I realized he was going to shave and tried to talk him out of it, to no avail. He did finally return to bed, but he got up many times throughout the night. I realized I was ready for the day center to accept him.

Very early this morning, he was very restless, though he stayed in bed. At one point he said, "This is Wayne, Wayne Leys, L-e-y-s; who are you?" and then proceeded to describe how we should exit the room. He also looked around the place for the other people that were here. (Apparently, he keeps assuming he's already in, or close to being moved to a residential facility.)

Jeff took him for a hike and he wanted me to go also. "I don't like being separate." Twice today I tried to play a worship song, and each time he stopped me. Later, he was confused about his desk and his things there. He said, "something's going on, something's wrong. You need to get me out of here." It seemed he thought his confusion was caused by being in this house. Or maybe he thinks he is in some facility, and so there are changes?

I told him about my intention to go to our friend's daughter's wedding the next day. He lectured me in anger. I thought of yielding and calling it off, but as I sat with him, listening but saying nothing, I realized I had no fear of his accusations. I also realized he was addressing me as a sister in Christ, not as his wife, which bolstered my resolve. He was saying people in church together should not leave each other. I just listened, sitting with him. After a while the anger broke. Finally, after he'd talked long about "leaving being against the Lord," he asked if I wanted to say something. I countered that accusation, quietly and confidently saying church people are able to leave and return. So, it petered out.

The Lord showed me that I need to consider his feelings about confusing things, but I was not to be led by AD thinking.

September 7 (Labor Day) Maria's family came to stay with him for the afternoon, and I was picked up by friends. Before they came Wayne had gotten very upset about my leaving but had quashed it when they walked in. Just before lunch he wanted a hug, indicating he was okay with me. Jeff stayed with him in the evening till I returned about midnight. He did well with them and the next day we carried on as though it hadn't happened. He'd already forgotten it.

September 10
Lord, I realize you are helping me remain honoring, respectful of him, helping me to love. I know it is your provision, and I am humbled. I am *nothing* without you. There would be no fruit on the branches without your life flow. Even in the areas where I may have "eyes to see," it was you who enabled, empowered me...

Wayne so likes the song "My God and King" by Terry McAlmon. I always thought it sounded like a love song and now I realize it is. It's similar to that of Song of Solomon, and I remember that Wayne has always had that intimate kind of love for the Lord. He said this week after we sang it, "I don't know why, but that song affects me." It was good for me to remember who he is before the Lord.

As we drove into the Family Fare parking lot, he asked if I visit my father often. I wasn't sure of whom he was thinking, so just said I did visit but not as often as I should have. He was very confused at suppertime and knocked over his water glass. When I reacted too loudly, it upset him and he left. When he returned, he said he couldn't find his mom. I sympathized, realizing his search for his mom was a search for comfort. I urged him to finish his supper and he did. I then encouraged him to rest in the recliner, and I hugged him. He said, "I can't handle it when people are shouting at me." I apologized, realizing he'd *felt* that and knowing that correcting his memory of the actual event wouldn't make any difference.

September 11
Lord, again I pray for knowledge and discernment (Philippians 1:9) in finding a next step... I ask for opportunity to have him at Evergreen Commons Day Center, even as I admit I'd like to have that time for myself. Should I then cancel Comfort Keepers? Or keep it so Maria can have her time back? And now Jeff has more going on again – soccer games, then basketball, softball, more church meetings and work stuff. O Lord, please keep me from overloading them...

As I tried to nap while George was here, I was checking Facebook and saw an ad for an assisted living and memory care facility being built nearby! So, I sent the link to the kids. We all got excited about possibly having a facility so close.

On Sunday, after a night of many interruptions and little sleep, I decided we'd watch church online instead of driving there.

September 14
Thank you for the article that came yesterday, saying, "Hold on, for this is the place I've planted you. This is the position where I am developing you. I have appointed you to bear great fruit here. I am sending my angels to protect you!" Yes, Lord! I believe you have arranged this assignment. I believe you are working things in me through this, things that will become (are becoming?) "fruit." I believe you are surrounding me, protecting my health, my mind, my strength, my future, my usefulness to you (fruit). I receive this help anew this morning and ask you to make my love abound today with knowledge and discernment.

I realized again Wayne thinks in terms of having an audience. Everything must be presented to an audience. He often makes me *be* that audience. He so wants people to be given the great stuff he's thinking.

September 15 He had a meltdown. He was so sad and cried a lot, but I couldn't tell what it was about. He wanted Jeff, so he called him. Jeff came over and talked forthrightly about Wayne's desire that I be taken care of, that we are to make decisions regarding Wayne's care, and that the result may be moving him to a facility. Wayne nodded to it all. Later he said to me, "Maybe we should call my brothers and sister tonight. Chris can call her sister." I think he was assuming the move is right now. I could only cry out, "Father, it's so hard to know what to do in those moments. Please continue to supply, and I ask…that you keep him in peace through Vee's stay today."

Today I prayed at the construction site of the new memory care facility, but I just felt like crying. A Prayer Shield partner suggested I was feeling the sadness he was feeling. When I returned home (Vee had been here with him), he said he hadn't been told that I was leaving. I countered that, saying I had told him and so had Jeff but AD had caused him to forget. He remained quiet and sad and said he felt as though he was on the verge of something but also that he was stuck. I said the Lord was moving both of us forward toward the goal of being fully in his presence. He agreed. Later he got himself some ice cream, putting it on a paper towel.

Each morning he presses, presses me to send out a devotional for him, to find something in his scribblings that could be used.

September 16 I had an early morning dream. In the dream our whole family went to a fun house, it seemed. There were lots of people, and it was hard to get in. We each pushed in, falling into something soft. I saw Wayne fall in also but didn't see him again. I kept looking for him, realizing I needed money from him to buy tickets for each activity. I tried to go into some performance with two family members, but a man instantly put up barriers. I tried something else, but again barriers were put up. This is now the third dream since Thanksgiving of not finding him. I wonder if needing "tickets" has to do with my needing to get something yet from him or something to do while still having his income? What should I get at now that I wouldn't be able to do without him?

I looked back at the previous dreams of not finding him: the first occurred early morning after Thanksgiving. As the Christmas tree fell on me and he couldn't understand anything I was saying, I remembered the dream. Then a month later, on December 19 he really disappeared regarding mental ability. The second took place March 19, 2020, after which his recognition of me as wife was happening less and less. I realized the Lord was repeatedly showing me what's coming and was so thankful.

In the morning he asked, "Does this place have people come in who make the beds? Because then I'll leave it." It took me a few seconds to grasp what he was saying. Then I said, "Yes." He said "Okay."

When we sat down in church, he asked how I'd gotten there, as he recognized me then. He didn't get upset. That was new, and I felt relieved.

September 20 One of the Prayer Shield team sent the hymn, "O Jesus, I Have Promised to Serve Thee to the End." It made me ask, "So, Lord, my question is what is the 'end' of my AD service? Is it residential care, or death? If residential care, how will I know? O Jesus, I've said I'll do this 'to the end.' Please help me know."

It was a night of many interruptions. Twice I stopped him from shaving. At one point he cried out (while sleeping), "You forgot me!" Is there an unconscious fear of being forgotten, as he realizes he's forgetting?

I prayed again at the construction site. He accepted Vee being here pretty well, but then was quiet and sad for a long time. In the evening, there was a baseball game on TV as I read. He said, "This is boring." (He just sits.) So, I offered a game – Bananagram. He said, "Why? So, you can show that you can do it and I can't?" I showed sympathy, and he then backed away. I played the piano instead and he sang.

September 24
I got here, Lord! It feels as though miles have been traversed already: get him his toothbrush and paste, shower him, clothe him, feed him…walk with him…get to Family Fare…get him going in his journal…take my shower…think through the day's required actions… and so I'm here! Thank you that I can do all that; I know you give health and strength, and knowledge for it, and I am so very grateful.

He slept a lot today and was *on* in the evening. I played the piano to try to calm him. He wanted me to come sit in the office, which I did. He then asked if I was okay, saying he'd be glad to help, and if I wanted to talk about my needs, I'd be welcome to do so with him. I thanked him.

Once in bed, we read Psalm 69, prayed, and then he said, "You are not alone. You will receive blessing. If I'm not around, I'll come find you. I don't know what that means." We slept till he turned the light on at 2, saying, "Good morning!" I said it wasn't morning yet; he was surprised, for someone had said it was time to pack things up. I said I knew of no such order, so he came back to bed. But we both were awake for a long time. At times he whispered to people he saw there.

After our walk, I went to help him start his journal and discovered that all his things were gathered up on the desk, along with my Bible and journal (which he'd taken off the porch during the night). He again talked about moving. I said it wouldn't be today. He said, "Okay." He again said there was help available if I needed it.

September 25
He's certainly focused on ministry to people. Is he also, perhaps, at some level, concerned for me, realizing I'm carrying everything? Thank you for that, and for the times

> yesterday when I could *see* the real Wayne, though it wasn't obviously apparent. Please help me today and prepare me for the next level of disappearance, as the dream revealed.

September 27 Wayne was very belligerent towards me today.

> O Lord…once more I lift my rights to you: the right to sleep, the right to have my life without his dictating everything, the right to prevent him from going through my clothes, the right to have my quiet time stuff and household files private. These I bring anew and lay them at the cross. O Lord, please forgive self's rising, and its reacting to him. Why can he get away with everything? He can move important things, deny it, and get upset with me for reacting! With no fault! So, take me anew, I pray…renew my spirit, my strength for today… I give praise to you and am so grateful.

Driving home after church, he asked, "So, who was it that drove us to church?" "I did." There was no anger, thankfully. What a change. But he later said "this living arrangement" will probably change. When I asked if he meant this home, he said, "Yes." Maybe he's thinking I, his helper, will finish, and he and I, his wife, will go elsewhere?

At 5 am I found him standing in a puddle of pee in the bathroom.

He was angry when he realized Vee was coming but then did all right. She gave him time to himself on the porch and he slept. Meanwhile I arranged and paid for his funeral. I went in feeling *up*, thinking I was following the message of the dream, getting one of the "tickets" that were needed. I came out feeling very *down*, even yucky, thinking I was doing things behind his back. I visited with Jeff at his office. He told me more of his experience with Exodus 33, and we talked of a funeral. He told me Wayne asks about me when they walk: "Will Mom be there when we return? Was she there when we left?" I was touched but reminded again of his confusion regarding me.

I also prayed again at the new facility being built.

He told Jeff and Shelly, "I'm ready to go home." Jeff asked, "Where is home?" Wayne talked but without making sense, so we don't know what it was about. Might he even mean Home in the Lord's full presence?

* * *

October 1 He mentioned again there'd be a move, saying something about December 1.

> Is that the time frame? That's two months – so long, yet so short. Lord God above, you know, and you have made the way...You are leading, and I look to you, for strength for today, these weeks and months, for knowledge of if, when, where...for help with decisions, and Christmas??

Wayne keeps talking of moving or being moved; he doesn't forget this topic. I told him we know there will be a change sometime and are awaiting clarity from the Lord regarding it. So, we'll just carry on till we know. After I showered, he said, "Did you hear anything yet?"

I read that taking Communion is so good for Persons With Dementia, so I brought the idea of doing that with the whole family to Maria. She agreed and suggested we do it all together on Thanksgiving. Everyone readily supported it.

Wayne talked about baptism and then was evidently planning something. He called me into the office and had me sit in the recliner since "you're the mother." I sat down, and he began, pad in hand, to interview me. "How many children do you have?" I got flustered but tried not to show it and said, "Three, and they're all baptized." But it was too hard to "enter his reality;" I got up and left. He came a little later saying she had decided such and such, which I couldn't understand.

When we got to our church he recognized me, asking how I'd rested and how I'd gotten there. He talked and asked questions several times during the service. Then, during the ride home, he *hit* me, accusing me of causing marriage failure because I'd left. He mocked my explanations and rejected my saying AD was causing this. At home, we came to a truce, had coffee and rested. Then he needed to talk. He asked about being removed to a different living space "for Chris and him," and kept pressing. Finally, he said we need someone in charge to help us, to say who's right – he or I – and he pressed me to get hold of someone. I said Jeff was coming, and we would ask him. When I prepared supper for him, he stood up with it and offered it to everyone else in the room and finally ate a little. Jeff came and listened, then explained things; again Wayne received. But Jeff's car wasn't out of the driveway before Wayne started talking to me as helper, asking about our nighttime arrangements. Still, he submitted to me in getting ready for bed. And we slept! But I realized I can't do this unendingly; I was drained.

> **October 5**
> I remember the call to love – O Lord, forgive, I pray… I'm still trying to hang on to my wants and plans (I'd really wanted to watch the Chicago Bears), but I got less upset perhaps than I would have in the past? I know I'm *for* him (agape). I just don't always have the feelings, though they're there sometimes. So, Lord Jesus, please meet me, us, today. Help me care, care give, honor, and love, I pray…

Wayne asked, "Do you think I'll be out of here?" I said, "No, not now; there's been no indication of any change." He agreed. I asked if he thought these thoughts come to him from the Lord. At first, he said, "No," but then thought they were.

> **October 6**
> I'm at Ottawa Beach and am so thankful to be free for a bit from being *on*. But Lord, there are so many retired

people here, and they're all couples. They're doing what we used to do. But I had to leave my husband for a few hours in order to get quiet. Father, please help him in these hours and days as he too seems to think life feels like a waiting room. I await the facility opening up and being released from COVID restrictions. Wayne awaits a move that he senses is coming and asks about it each day. Dear Lord, please help us in waiting, in watching for your cloud to move. Meet him and give him peace, I pray. Meet me and give me ideas as to how to make the most of the time. (I got the idea from Maria's funeral message this morning to remember *now* who he was and not wait till a funeral to do so. So, help me in it, I pray – with the albums I put together? With Communion celebrating also with Community Life Church (CLC) friends this weekend? ...)

(Philippians 1:13) Paul writes that all know "my imprisonment is for Christ." I thought about Wayne being in a prison of sorts also, and thought that he's taken me into it too. All night, all the time I'm with him, I'm subject to its whims.

I've known this is your assignment – can it actually be *for* you? I can see the test for me, but for him? He's not responsible...and yet he does resubmit himself regularly to you. So, Lord, I do so again as well. I sense your call to me to "learn to love," and I know I still fail. I ask you to continue to meet me, to fill me, to empower me, to enable me to "lay me down" again. Please continue doing what you need to so that you shine through me "to those around me," family first... so that others "become confident in the Lord by my imprisonment...[and] are much more bold to speak the word without fear." (v. 14)

I prayed at the new construction again. Later, Wayne said he's wondering about loving me properly.
Our friend John took him to walk at Ottawa Beach. Wayne

fell there, and John couldn't get him up without a passer-by helping. Wayne was banged up quite a bit.

I goofed up, I guess. He piled everything from the shelf unit by his desk corner onto the desk. I reacted to it, saying I needed room to do office work. That bothered him. He suggested I use the little space between the computer and the window; I said that wouldn't work. We both got upset. We went to take our walk, and he really gave it to me. He said I'm a terrible member of this team. He was angry, accused me a lot and said I was sinning. I apologized for him experiencing such treatment. He suggested I do the office work on the bed. I said no, though I thanked him for the suggestion.

I showered and then he pressed me to write a devotional. I kept asking him "What on?" And he just gave "it's what we do" kind of talk. He still knows about sending out devotionals, but he has no idea what's involved.

I suggested we go to De Boer's Bakery and the lake; he loved that. On returning, I did some computer work while he methodically went through his stuff, stacking much of it on the bed.

I so often think, "I can't do this." He talks and talks and talks, and I have no idea what it's about. He's so restless, always looking, looking, looking; he can't settle. He moves things. It so seems to me to be evidence of more decline.

We had a night of many interruptions, and he couldn't always find the bathroom when he needed it. At 5 am, he needed help; I realized he'd put jeans on over his pjs. I started helping to remove them when he told me they were wet. I discovered the pjs were too.

He couldn't settle for breakfast. He kept looking, looking for something. I heard a loud noise in the office and ran to check; the recliner was on its side and he was on the floor, his head bleeding. We were both pretty shaken.

Late afternoon I tried to prepare crackers and cheese, which he likes, but I realized he'd put the cheese ball back in the fridge (I'd taken it out to soften). That was a "straw" for me as I *felt* all his times of moving and changing things, and I broke. He tried to comfort me. At supper he told me I could do what I wanted because he'd be gone. I asked if he was planning to leave? "Yes." "Why?" "Personal reasons." I asked his forgiveness and he gave it.

October 9
(John 3:16) "...God so loved that he gave..." That's it. Love results in giving. It's loving so much that one is willing to give what is most precious. Lord, I bring to you something *precious* to me (though of so much less significance, I know); it's my desire for order – in drawers, cupboards, closets – that he now rifles through. I react inwardly – "You can't do that! It belongs to me. It's my order. And I'll have to redo it when you're finished!" And so, I come, handing you my desire for order... and give it up in favor of loving him. Help me, Lord, I pray in your name and in your mercy.

The evening was long and hard. He said he wanted to go home and had a pile of stuff with him. I told him we were okay to stay here, so he sat down and dozed instead. After a while, I played and sang worship songs at the piano. He got up, stood in the darkened front hall, and listened. Then he worshiped, perhaps also blessing the group he seemed to think filled the room and trying to expound with his voice low (because there were other people around also). I asked him to talk louder, he got mad, accusing me – of what? I objected, so he prayed for me. I finally left the room, for his doing that makes me feel so pressed.

Last night at 11:30 I found him in the office wrapped in a towel. He said he couldn't sleep. He'd shaved and was now going to read. I talked him into returning to bed.

October 11 We had a terrific time with friends sharing food, worship and Communion. I'd typed out the Lord's

Supper introduction and asked Tom to help Wayne take us into participation. He held Wayne (who was very unsteady) as they walked around the circle serving the elements, and Wayne blessed each participant. It was an amazing time. Tom and Lor remained after the others left, and Wayne unloaded to them. He talked for forty-five minutes, showing anger, disgust (at Helper me for encouraging sexual connecting). We came to a truce after they left.

The next day the disgust talk resumed on our way to church. He asked if I was looking forward to worship. I said, "Yes!" And then he warned me about not doing it rightly. I asked if he thought there was reason why I had no right to worship, but he backed off. Inside the church he recognized me, and now attacked Wife me: "I don't know how you can stand among these people." That kind of lambasting of me continued all the way home. I said little except that AD was confusing his brain about me and that I was sorry for him in it. At home we both napped long. We were exhausted. Jeff and Shelly came with sundaes.

Wayne pleaded with me to get help for "these people." I asked what he meant. He said many feel defiled and talked on and on. I asked if he felt defiled. He said he didn't. He talked about people here being watched – "They're being watched; you're being watched; I'm being watched." I told him I received that as an alert and then said, "But the greater watcher is the Lord. He's watching over us for good." Wayne responded saying something about "her;" I said, "You mean Chris." "Yes. Speaking of Chris, I haven't seen her. She was here only one day last week…but I'm not angry."

October 12
So, my Lord and King, I bring all this to you, ask you to equip me for today and help me to bring assurance and love. Please visit him in his cell and give him peace. Please be preparing a place if he is to move somewhere…

Maria and I looked at the new facility – we were disappointed – and enrolled him in Evergreen Commons Day Center as they were finally receiving new clients.

October 14
Good morning, Father. It looks beautiful, but I feel worn out. I think it took a toll yesterday – getting disappointed with the nearby facility and then enrolling him in the day center – and I'm feeling drained. I'm also drained by his anger after Vee left, and I'm anticipating anger because of the day center. I admit, Father, I'm so tired of it, so, so tired from it, and the not knowing if the anger is toward me as helper or as wife, for it can be both in the same day and requires different responses.

He pressed hard in the evening. He started early saying he was disturbed about marriage. I asked, "Who's?" He said, "Mine; my wife is dead." And then he talked and talked and talked. I'd been a bit under the weather and was so tired; I couldn't take it. I begged him to let me go. He begged me to stay.

Maria told him about the day center. She said, "When I was last here you told me we should look at next steps." She laid out our decision and the action we'd taken. He was accepting, especially when hearing that our doctor thought it was good to do.

October 16
Father, it's so good to be renewed, somewhat at least! Thank you for your mercy that stopped the illness a bit. I sense it could escalate again and will take it easy today. I ask you to meet Wayne in the midst and enable him to be settled, so I can get rest…

October 17
Father, I'm tired again. I thought I had completely recovered, but here I am, tired. He was pressing right

away today – "What's the plan today? No one is planning, and nothing gets done. We have to figure out ways to help people and need to have people in to plan… you need to _____," – pressing, pressing, pressing… I told him it wasn't my job to run meetings or to find people for them for I'm his caregiver. He got ticked off, "O come on!!" The pressing, Lord, is what beats me down. I pray it be alleviated – let him find the people he seeks at the day center.

I again had the dream about not finding Wayne. This is now the fourth such dream in the last year.

Sundowning hit, with pressing, pressing, talking about getting hold of people for a group, pressing me to contact "her," or "him." I asked, "Who?" He said I should know and got disturbed with me for hesitating. Then he wanted his wife, pressing me to take him to her. Because I couldn't, he saw me as against him. I suggested calling Maria, but he wanted to call his wife. I told him it would be I who'd answer, and that is what happened. He didn't understand. Then he apparently called someone. He said later that Sarah had called, saying it was great to talk with her and congratulating himself on doing a great job with his daughters. I felt accusation of me in there. We came to a truce.

October 18
O Lord, when the pressing comes, I feel myself wilting with tightness in my chest… and his pressing me to get him to his wife – how long, Lord, how long? I feel as though I can't do this on and on and on. Will being at Evergreen help with his wanting to lead and help people in a group? Will it be even better to be in residential care? Should we actually do that? O Lord, I question myself even as I do this. How can it be? He lies here next to me, but since supper he's not been here, and he isn't who he was, even though now quiet… The dreams, yes, I understand…

The press to plan to get people together started right away this morning. He's ticked, for he wants to do this but knows he can't by himself. So, he presses me and gets disturbed by seeming inaction. It continued in the evening as well. He also talked a lot about people coming to move him. He's ready – over and over he gets ready. As I cleaned up supper dishes, he came with a jacket on saying he needed to go. "They" had said, "Come." I questioned and finally agreed to take him. We rode around Zeeland, but he didn't recognize any place that he thought he was being sent to, so we returned home. He came in looking for people. He wanted a key. I tried to divert him, afraid he meant car key, and suggested we sing. We sang two songs, but then he stopped it, though he said it was nice. He needed my attention and talked again about leaving. Somehow, I convinced him to get ready for bed.

He has had accidents in the bathroom the last two nights and used the bathmat to wipe it up.

October 19
Lord, thank you for this outlet. It may not always be prayer as I recount what has happened, but it is release, allowing me then to leave it with you and go on to the next care need. It is so good, and I thank you. Once again, I marvel at your provision: sleep, health, ability to do what's needed – it's so very good. Please continue to supply...

He told me the people who were with us last night really enjoyed singing with us!

He went to the day center willingly. Last night I explained what would happen, and he said it made sense. Three staff members came out to meet him, welcoming him as "Pastor Wayne!" But it felt pretty awful for me. I stood outside watching the two sets of sliding doors close, one at a time, and felt SEPARATION hit. It was another level in the process of separating. It reminded me of our years of working at a jail – entering the secure section required two sets of doors, and each banged shut behind you. The closing of the sliding doors felt like that banging, as though separation was hitting me more closely. I remembered the phrase "creeping separateness" from *A Severe Mercy* by Sheldon Van Auken, and ordered a copy of the book.

He came out saying he realized it could be good if one kept going, but he didn't want to. He'd prefer his family come to him at home. Still, he told me he knew the decision was mine and the kids' and he'd comply. Later he expressed disappointment. He'd thought it would be a church where he could do something. He said, "You find out they're in worse shape than you are, but I'm one of them." He added, "When I see you going past here, having a good time with others, I can't take it." I figured he was referring to my having had coffee with a friend the previous day, something I rarely did anymore.

October 22
Lord, I think I'm feeling the imprisonment today. I think yesterday, after he went in to the day center so well, I started assuming life could get a bit easier, for he'd be there (eventually) two mornings a week. I should have been more circumspect and not jumped so quickly. Lord Jesus, help me, fill me with strength today, I pray, to be honest and in the moment with him, not just looking ahead to what's easier. Help me be what he needs today, I pray. And Lord, I bring my discouragement to you, even as I sense the question, "Do you have a right... to be discouraged, to be close to anger?" The answer, of course, is NO. I have the right to be called a child of God and, therefore, to expect help. Thank you. Please be merciful to me today, to us, to him as well, I plead.

He fell twice. He misjudged where a dining room chair was and fell over with it. As I napped, Maria watched him try to get up from the recliner only to fall.

October 23
Lord God Above, thank you for a new day, for sleep, health, ability to function and to meet friends for breakfast. You are God, God over all, watching over, working for good, and I bow and turn to you for help for today and hope for tomorrow...

He asked about moving again this morning, stacking, and restacking his office things in preparation.

We made it to our church on Sunday where he recognized me but didn't say anything about it. As we drove away, however, he brought it up, saying he wouldn't say much except that the evil one is doing it and needs rebuking. I said it was AD, and that made him angry. At home I started helping him change. In anger he spoke of "the girl" that helped before, who even gets out socks, and apparently does it wrong. I knew he meant me and was bothered that he criticized my helping; I felt knocked down, as though my strength was hit hard. But I also realized he was revealing his sense of loss of autonomy – he even needs help with socks. That helped me back away from feeling wounded.

October 27 Again, I dreamed of being with him and then not being able to find him. This is the fifth time. I went to Ottawa Beach while Vee was with him. It was hard to leave because he was so sad; he'd given me a lingering hug, saying, "I love you so much."

> Lord, my love for him is now tearing me up. For a while I wondered if taking this kind of break is worth it because of his anger at and accusations of me. Now I feel horrible for him, sensing – feeling? – his sorrow, his fear about not having me there. Would it be better to just let him have my constant presence? But I'm not you! You are ever-present... Would that be asked of me if I am seeking to flesh out your love and care? Is that "laying down my life?" But I keep getting these dreams of him disappearing. That reveals separating, not being together, and he's always the one leaving, not I.

I prayed at the new facility construction, using Jeremiah 29:11: "Lord, you know your plans for Wayne and me, and they're plans to 'prosper' us, not harm, giving hope and a future. I agree and pray that you lead....'With my life laid down I surrender now. I give you everything...Your goodness is running after, running after me.' (The Goodness of God, Bethel Music)"

He usually asks what's on the schedule for the day. Today, as at other times, I told him he'd spend some time at that place downtown Holland that helps people with Alzheimer's. He accepted that and went into the day center really well. The article that came today said there's "strength and courage being poured out like rain right now..." I thanked the Lord for doing that here, realizing anew that he is so, so good.

I was thinking again of the change in my identity in our relationship. We'd always started sleeping with him having his arm around me, with me leaning against him and with him leaning on me. It was analogous for how we related. We leaned on each other for help for thinking through things we faced, examining together how we felt about things. That leaning bolstered my soul and his as well. But the leaning physically ended several years ago, for as he relaxed there'd be a jerkiness from him. I had to move in order to sleep. That too was analogous; as his thoughts and feelings were being jerked around by AD, it became harder and harder to lean on him mentally and emotionally. and a switch took place. I don't lean at all anymore; I am being leaned on. This morning he said he has days where he struggles and realizes he just needs to look to my lead, to entrust things to me. That was huge, but I know he won't remember it and will again struggle with my place.

He walked out of the day center saying he wasn't angry, but then angry feelings started coming out. He pleaded that he be able to stay home. It made us both feel very down; I wondered again about "laying my life down" to keep him with me at all times. I finally texted the kids about it. Jeff said the Day Center wasn't for him, it was for me. Then I realized I couldn't lay my life down if it was being lost in AD.

> **October 28**
> (Philippians 1:29) It has been *granted* to me that not only may I believe in you but also suffer for your sake. May it be *for* you, my Lord, my God, My Savior and deliverer, my strength, my supply, my waymaker...

He fell on our walk at Helder Park. He got going faster and faster with his head bent way down in front of him. Thankfully the fall was next to the car, so he could get back up by leaning on it.

October 29 He's been saying things like: "When do I next go to that place downtown?" "Will Chris come tonight?" "I'd like to go home." "This place doesn't look the same..." (that is, our living room).

> What does it mean, Lord? But I also realize the next disappearing (as shown in the dreams) has begun – there's more confusion and now also some incontinence. Is November a deciding month? It feels so with a family Communion celebration planned for Thanksgiving. Is that the culmination, the turning point? If so, please help me make the most of this time.... I bow in awe – that you know me...that you help me...that you have abundance for me...O Lord God above, I lift praise...

He had a bowel accident some time before I discovered his situation. He accepted my help in cleaning up, saying the underpants should be thrown away. I agreed and said I'd get him another one that could be thrown away. (I had purchased a package of Depends as I followed the "get ready" steps.) He accepted that and has been wearing it.

* * *

Jeff and Shelly took Wayne to church; I stayed home to keep my foot elevated above my head for a couple hours. It was good to get the rest and it helped with the foot's swelling. From reading *A Severe Mercy* I got the idea of revisiting who Wayne was and the "us" in each chapter of our life together, to celebrate it, and in time, grieve its passing.

After church he was in his own world. He was sure he'd lost people and he looked all over for them, even opening the car doors saying, "Come on out; we can go into the house." He pressed me a lot – why didn't I care about a missing child or someone needing Jesus. And there was again the plea for his wife. At one point he called, "Chris, I need your help!" I thought he'd fallen or something, but no, he wanted me to take his dictation and send out a devotional to his audience. He said, "I don't want to pressure you, but..."

> **November 1**
> Lord, am I losing my grip, my hold? I just don't know what to do under all that pressure and find I really don't want to do anything either. The night of little sleep affects me, so I don't handle things very well; in fact, today I was ticked. It can't be at him because AD is doing this, or is it in fact at him for these days are all about him? I bring it to you and give up anew my right to have what I want – to have good sleep and to not be pressed under his bidding. I bring it, Jesus, and once again "lay me down." I ask you to fill me by your Spirit, to strengthen me, to erase the need to have sleep loss made up, to reverse foot damage and keep the blood flowing. Thank you, Merciful Lord.

In the evening he wanted a discussion and called me into the office. He talked and talked and talked, so I broke in saying he could go on talking with his group – he'd indicated they were there – but I'd excuse myself. He came begging me to be part of it. "I ask you in the name of Jesus to be with us..." I reacted to such religiousness. I tried to divert him by showing him pictures of the toy giveaway at Community Life Church that we'd done for inmates of the jail. He didn't recognize any of it and didn't want me changing the subject. The group HAD to take place. Jeff came over, and Wayne talked and talked about the group. Jeff almost fell asleep.

John took him for a long walk at Helder Park. He said Wayne flagged down a worker driving a tractor. When the man stopped, Wayne hesitated and said something about being lost. John said Wayne had seemed interested because of the tractor. When he came home, he asked several times, "What's going on here?" He said we should call the police, but he hesitated because he wasn't sure what was going on. Much later I wondered if seeing the tractor took him back to his great-uncle's farm, thinking he was seeing Uncle John and excitedly tried flag him down. When he saw it wasn't Uncle John, he couldn't come up with "I'm mistaken," so said something about their being "lost."

He accepted Vee's coming and my return all right but was very quiet. A bit later he returned to the idea that we'll be removed from this home soon for lack of funds, also saying someone above me should review it all to see if my claims about our finances are correct. We had a nice evening though, listening to some worship music, and then I played some of John Elliott's first book on the piano.

November 3
I told the day center that I'd be bringing him also on Monday mornings starting on the 16th.

Lord, I have great peace about it. Is that right? It seems that if he were in his own world and it were pretty silent, it would be easier. But wow, that's scary. Still, he seems more and more unreachable, and perhaps he knows it's happening.... Lord, I wonder about a life review such as Van Auken engaged in after his wife died. Since Wayne seems increasingly less present, would that be a good exercise to start soon? Would that retrieve him for me, so I'm not always wanting relief from his pressing? Please lead, show me how to start, if at all...

I then got the idea to read the letters he'd sent me while we were dating. I had never reread them, but I knew exactly where I'd kept them for fifty-six years.

He came out of the day center saying, "There's people who go all over the floor, so I couldn't go there." I knew that was his reaction to them telling him *he* does that in the bathroom. We were barely out of the parking lot when he let loose and everything got wet.

Later he told Jeff that someone (on staff) at the day center had said, "Pastor Wayne, will you help lead this...?" It had made him feel good and needed.

I started reading his letters from our dating years. It was rather hard to do but also really good. I felt as though I was hearing him speak of his love for me. It so helped me see beyond AD to the person who had been filled with vim and vigor, with passion and love for the Lord and for life and ministry.

November 6
Lord, I can't get over the change in me regarding Wayne in his present condition since reading some of his letters. Thank you so for bringing it to mind. I then also ask you to help me in getting things compiled about this journey. How should I start? Thank you.

He often caresses me during the night but seems unsure who I am. This morning he said, "I would like to marry you; let's see if that would be possible." I said Okay.

November 9
Father, that Elijah feeling hit again – I can feel so alone, so by myself...in the AD care. I get breaks from it, but no one else is here during the night or cleaning things up all the time...O my Father, I'm so weak and so ready

to cry...and now we can't go to church again for there are more (COVID) cases. That makes Sundays so long. But next Monday we start another morning per week at the day center...

Tom and Lor came. They brought lunch and then took Wayne to the lake and to Dairy Queen while I napped. It was so good, especially to hear Wayne laugh so much.

November 10
Father God, I looked forward to this break, but it doesn't feel very good. In fact, I feel like crying. He looked so sad when Vee came and I left. O Lord, how long, how long will he suffer having some awareness of being left but without understanding? With no possibility of me giving explanation that would be received? How long? And do I keep doing it to him? I decided to suspend Comfort Keepers now and do two mornings per week at the day center. Will that help? Help him, that is? Or will it just keep telling him that that's all he's good for? Still, at home there's no stimulation anymore, so yes, this is better.

Courage – that's what you showed me two weeks ago – courage to leave for this time, to take him to the day center for activities. He doesn't accept activities I suggest except walking and singing, but no games, no looking at albums. So, it's better there. So, okay, I'll carry on.

I prayed at the new construction, admitting I still didn't have a good sense about the place, wondering if that was the Lord's leading.

He did really well at the day center and accepted my explanation of it being a group that helps Persons With Dementia bolster brain cells. He came out saying he'd had a couple of good conversations. He felt needed.

November 12
(John 10:11, 15, 17-18) "I lay down my life..." O Lord, thank you for doing so and for also taking it up again (17). Thank you for calling me to it and clarifying things along the way. Mostly, right now, I lay down the self-protection born of fear.... Thank you, Good Shepherd, who came not to steal life from me (10) but to give it to me, with abundance (10)! I praise you! I am yours. You know me. You have taught and are teaching me to know you and your voice (4).

I thanked the Lord that Wayne had been more peaceful for a couple of days, realizing I hadn't felt that pressing for a bit. Perhaps it also felt better because the Lord had helped me get out of another waiting room, where I was waiting for him to go to a facility. I asked for help then to see him *here*, to start organizing writings, to move furniture, to redo some rooms. So, I did those things, starting by moving furniture and having Wayne help me. It felt good. I knew I was no longer waiting.

He got his jeans wet three times today and his pjs during the night.

November 15
I asked on the 10th how long he'd have to suffer because of my leaving for a few hours. Then on the 12th I found myself telling the doctor I saw less fight in him. Now I see a correlation between that prayer and my seeing less anger in him. Thank you so for it. Perhaps AD is taking him out of awareness that he's now different and letting him just live in the present, in the AD-affected moment. Thank you for watching over him each step on this journey. (I'm realizing I should get overnight Depends.)

He came out of the day center happy to see me, joking with the staff. Later he wet himself twice. He tried to put clean jeans over his wet ones, doing the same with the underpants, as he refused my help. I got frustrated, exclaiming that I can't do this. Later he came, almost in tears, wanting reassurance probably, but instead he reached for me to tell me Jesus loves me. I resisted it being about me but finally settled down, and we got reconnected. Later I realized he had wanted to comfort me and that was the only way he could think to say it. In the moment, however, I just reacted. After a bit, he came wanting me to open up his phone – "There's a show about a murder." As he talked, it became evident he thought I was being accused of murder and maybe he should go to the police with me. So, I dropped what I was doing and sat with him, realizing he was *feeling* something destructive had happened and that I was the cause. He wanted to call Maria and did, telling her the same thing. Meanwhile, I texted her my explanation. She prayed with him and got hold of Jeff. Jeff came and told Wayne his one job was to do what Mom said to do. I felt punched in the gut by it all.

He went into the day center jovially, joking with staff, and came out well also. He later said it was a good time.

November 18
O Lord my God, you are so very good! Thank you for his entering the day center so well…it's so good to be at this point. And now the new threshold of fighting for dignity is with the clothes-wetting. Please continue to show me what to do. Yesterday's events had me thinking I can't do this, again wondering if a facility would be better… Please lead, Lord Jesus…

In the evening he fell asleep in the recliner, and I began to smell urine. When he awakened and realized it, he was willing to put on overnight Depends. The next day he accepted a daytime Depends and accepted me going into the bathroom with him each time. At supper he thanked the Lord that we didn't fight at all today. But later he started pressing me to get hold of his wife for him. I told him I was his wife, but he pressed more and more, getting increasingly disturbed about what I was doing to her. I had to walk away. When I returned, he was putting on his jacket. In response to my question, he said, "Yes I'm leaving; I have to find him." Who? "He was one of the best teachers..." He walked out, stopped at the end of our sidewalk, and waved his arms, apparently trying to get someone's attention. Our neighbor was working at her kitchen window. Did he think she could help him? (He was waving toward her.) When he then started walking down the street, I called Jeff, got my jacket on and followed Wayne. At the roundabout he turned and headed back. He saw me and walked back with me, acting as if I'd done something wrong. He headed to Unit #5 instead of our condo and was standing there as Jeff drove up.

Jeff heard the religious talk, the lecturing of me to take things to Jesus and be helped there. He stayed a while, doing some explaining, but also just trying to reassure Wayne. When Wayne went to the bathroom, Jeff said to me, "We'll do the Communion on Thanksgiving, and then we'll make some decisions." I cried. But I realized I'd also had that thought, admitting I can't do this alone and Jeff can't keep leaving his family this often.

November 20
O Lord, I've gone through such extreme feelings. For a while I seemed eager for him to go to a place. Then you mercifully turned my thoughts from me to him, took me out of the waiting room, sent love to him through me. You led me to be reminded how much he loved me from the very beginning (the letters) and that in my great insecurity I was a taker. You gave me desire for more time to deeply return that love. Thank you for such mercy. And now the kids say it's time, time to separate even more. I know I'm tired. The bathroom issues have now been added, and it happens several times each night. So please help me. Help me keep seeing him, honoring, loving him, and not filling my thoughts with how to move him, and what I'll then do. Please be

merciful, I pray, and protect me from health problems. I look to you, my Shepherd, to lead me also regarding the place – which one? six minutes away, or twenty-two minutes away?

November 21
Wayne said, "I know there's talk about what happens after this place." My heart went out to him, and I said, "Are you okay? I know it's scary. Are you afraid?" "NO," he said, "I'm not afraid." Yet we clung to each other. My heart turned to the Lord, "O Lord, you are so good in preparing him – thank you. And now that my heart will tear, it's time? Right? Best for him...again I ask you to go ahead and prepare the place..."

When we were getting ready for bed, he told me good night and turned to sleep somewhere else. I told him he slept right there, in the bedroom. He hugged me and cried a little. He said he didn't know if it was proper. I assured him it was. We were up at least six times during the night, and I struggled to get him changed each time. He couldn't understand my instructions, such as, "pick up this foot." My back is hurting from it all.

November 23
O Lord, I seem to be moving him quickly in my mind. Is that okay? Or am I deserting my post? Is it all right to use Grand Brook? It would be such a nice environment. Please be merciful and bless him these days, especially in the Communion celebration on Thanksgiving Day, and bless each of our family there also.

We got up only once last night!! But that one time was long and hard in the bathroom, as I struggled to get him cleaned up and changed.

(Thanksgiving Day) We were up just three times during the night and again it was very hard to get him changed and the bathroom cleaned up. The third time, I lost it and left. He came back to bed with the same clothes on, and we slept a while. When we got up, he stopped me from going into the bathroom, whispering, "Don't go out. I want to tell you it's raining." I realized he knew there was pee on the floor so I assured him I'd check.

It was also a morning facing the reality of the need for residential care. Though we'd had two good nights and days, I still knew the time had come, for I was really tired, and during last night's times in the bathroom he was very uncooperative, even belligerent.

November 26
Lord, you have given me ideas when I was up against new challenges, and you have shown me how to respond more and react less, but I messed up last night. And yes, I believe you have taught me to love, and I thank you, and I marvel. You laid out this last year, giving the dream repeatedly, preparing me, helping me "get ready," and I thank you. Now we have the opportunity to receive from you together, and I pray you touch each heart, open it to you, strengthen each to pick up a piece of the mantle today. (We had planned to celebrate Thanksgiving and Communion together, but Maria got a positive COVID test the day before, so we gathered in our own homes, celebrating Communion over Zoom. The Lord showed me that morning that it was an Elijah-Elisha moment (II Kings 2). We were in separate homes so that each of our kids could pick up the "mantle" from Wayne and serve his or her family. I shared that, and then we partook of the Lord's Table.) How I thank you! and again, stand in awe.

I asked the Lord to make the choice between the two facilities clear, knowing it was to be soon.

The evening brought much disturbance. Wayne wanted his wife, and wanted people to come and take him home; he was very strong about it all. Jeff had to come and assure him that he may stay here. Wayne admitted to him that he's scared.

Sarah had talked with both of the facilities we were considering. Her assessment was that one is for families, to be a family. The other is a corporation that has good protocol for care. I realized she put into words exactly what my sense was. I was relieved. It also came to me that if Wayne were making the decision, he would not put convenience (the closer place) over what we considered best for him. That also helped so much. I knew we would move toward Grand Brook Memory Care in Wyoming, MI.

He continued being belligerent and uncooperative regarding bathroom needs.

November 29
Lord, he admitted he's scared. I plead for him to sense your presence deep within and all around, to be filled with peace, even as you prepare him for change. I ask in your name...

November 30
Father, the day of beginning the preparation for moving him has come. I feel –what? Ready, yet not ready; thinking it's good, yet it's awful; thinking I'm ready to have less care and realizing I'll then be alone. Father, I believe you also would say it's *not good*. The good world you made is tarnished, and AD is one result. Separating what God has put together is another. Please meet me in this and forgive me if I'm giving up, abandoning him. Enable him to forgive me, to accept, to be filled by you with peace, grace, mercy... And now I pick up this load of making ready to move him. Please help me with it, I pray, and smooth the way through doctor's visits, Hospice, insurance, entry forms...

He came out of the day center happy but in one of their sweatpants. His jeans were still in the dryer. He told me of some things he did there with them, and then said, "I don't know why I'm working to keep myself alive." I thought, "O Lord, please encourage him today!"

* * *

The Lord showed me it's right to think of sending him to residential care, for my body was now reacting to all the physical strain of changing him, cleaning him up after accidents and to the lack of sleep.

> **December 2**
> (John 14:21) You will love the one who loves you and manifest yourself to him. Yes. Thank you. I plead for you to manifest yourself to Wayne, who loves you, as we navigate a transition and to me also in such change. Separation will be a ripping with no more touch, no hugs, sleeping alone... Separation began in the soul – no longer knowing me, nor connecting, nor being able to take everything (anything) to him – and now it moves to the physical.

Still, I wondered if I was being selfish, "throwing him away," though also realizing we weren't considering a traditional nursing home –it wasn't skilled nursing care. But then I recognized in myself a fear of what people might say – "she should have continued...," and things like that. I knew I'd done this judging myself of others and pleaded again for mercy.

Wayne had oral surgery and did very well with it. I later fell asleep and could sometimes hear him doing things, but I couldn't move, I was so tired. He had to change himself, completely. My being unable to help opened up an opportunity to talk about us both needing help, which would mean a different facility for him. He received that and even agreed, saying he was willing to check it out, and willing to do this. Jeff later reinforced the idea.

The executive director and nurse from Grand Brook Memory Care came to assess his compatibility and readiness for their program. It went really well. The nurse was a bit teary-eyed when Wayne said he'd conclude in prayer and then prayed for her children who were at home because of COVID. He was amazingly at peace about it all. They told us, and demonstrated, that their staff really loves serving and caring for Persons With Dementia and their families. I felt cared for and saw their respect for Wayne.

But then I seemed to freeze mentally. I couldn't rest when George came in the afternoon. At bedtime I understood and my unconscious feelings finally became clear – "This is yucky, this stinks, it's not your intention for your children, Lord." I remembered the same feeling when we started Comfort Keepers and again when starting the day center. Separation of two united before the Lord in marriage is not his intention. But the Lord reminded me that in each case it was the right thing to do, and we both adjusted. It just took <u>courage</u>. I was led to say to Wayne, "It's all right before the Lord to both seek help for this journey rather than just exist." We would both be doing more than existing if we took this step.

Sundowning occurred later. He talked and talked and then got ready to go to people he believed he could help, but they needed me also, he said. I hesitated, and said I was getting things ready for bedtime. Later he came saying, "I'm wrong – I got it mixed up," and apologized.

Sundowning occurred again the next night, as he pressed for a planning session to meet with people who need our ministry. After 8:30 he said he was going to them. I said it's almost time to get ready for bed. He pressed and got angry at me for disrespecting people who need us. When I walked away, he came, a bit sheepish, wanting to be right with me. I just said, "Let's brush our teeth." He agreed. Later he was apologetic – "I hurt you." I said he accuses me of things I'm not, and it's caused by the AD. He fell asleep but had a bowel problem in the middle of the night.

December 7
Lord God, thank you for the reminder from Psalm 121 – You are my (and his) keeper. You are keeping us close to you through this. Your keeping is helping: giving ideas in the moment, giving health every day, giving strength, giving leading for decisions. And Lord, how I praise you, Faithful One. Thank you. Please help now as a text from Grand Brook has brought it close again. It seemed to hit me in the chest. Yet at night I think, "how many more nights yet?"

Wayne was in his church realm all evening and then started getting ready for bed at 8:30, saying, "I'm tired." He wouldn't accept suggestions, got up about every hour all night, stayed up at 5:15, couldn't find the bathroom and peed in the bedroom, wouldn't accept my suggestion regarding showering, got dressed, did breakfast, then slept about hour in the living room – after spilling coffee and getting mad at me when I tried to take the cup. I could only say, "Thank you, Lord, for confirming the decision (regarding memory care); it now feels so right…"

It was another hard sundowning evening. Wayne kept talking of people needing his ministry, pleading with me to take him to them. At one point, he put on a jacket as though he intended to leave. He kept looking, looking, working at something. Finally, about 7:30 he asked to call his son, which he did. It sounded as if Jeff said he'd come after finishing his walk, so for over an hour Wayne looked for him, even going outside thinking he saw other people also. Finally, after 9 he sat down on the couch and fell asleep. At 9:30 I awakened him to go to bed. He didn't remember he'd been looking for Jeff.

He refused my help in the bathroom during the night, especially the first time, so I went back to bed. But when he was gone a long time, I went to check and found him leaning on the sink, the pj pants at his feet and pee on the floor in front of him. I said I'd get clean pjs, I did and then tried to help him put them on, but he refused changing the Depends. He was immovable, so I asked what he wanted to do. He reached over and closed the door in my face. I waited quite a while and then went back. He finally accepted clean pjs. He also accepted a shower in the morning, saying the Depends was re-usable. However, it was completely wet. He just didn't feel it.

December 10
Thank you for a nurse friend's agreement with the decision regarding residential care, and our doctor's also – how good that was. I'd been worried about what others would think. You forgave that, and now there are people actually agreeing. You are so, so good, and I lift praise...

The Prayer Shield also agreed with the decision, sending much love. But the further separation haunted me, even as I realized I continue to be "his sister in Christ," for whom he feels love and appreciation. Perhaps deep down he really does know me?

I was able to do the things needed to have him ready for residential care. It seemed he tried to express concern for me, asking how we make sure "you get from here to there?" I told him I'd be all right. Then he prayed.

December 12
Father, please meet me in my emotional core, help me *enter* everything, and not shirk it or stay out.... please continue to press in his spirit that we'll both be met by you, kept by you, carried by you. O Lord my God, how good your help has been and will be. But Lord, what all is coming? I'm focused on being able to sleep, to veg out...but there's a lot more to it, isn't there? I'll be alone for the first time in my life. Will I miss him, or feel sorry for myself? Please help me with focus yet on him, even as I get at things here. Thank you! I feel better. It's not just feeling; it's choice to *keep* him yet a big part of me. That really helps. How I thank you.

In the evening Wayne wanted us to take the car to seek the place where there was a group gathering – "we're late" – and expecting him to join them. He did much pleading, searching, talking, which I couldn't understand. We drove around, but he couldn't find the place and accepted being brought back here. Finally, it was bedtime. He fell asleep the minute his head hit the pillow and didn't even hear me read the Psalm and pray. He was cooperative during the night.

George's words to me came into clarity this morning. At the time I thought he was saying I was abandoning Wayne and that he hadn't abandoned his son like that. But now I realize that when he'd said to his son, "Our home isn't a medical or psych facility; you need one – which will it be?" he meant, "You'll have to leave in order to get help." So, he was not saying I would be abandoning Wayne!! That broke the power of accusation. I am not abandoning him or my assignment. Peace came at the end of the Advent week on peace.

Jeff's family came to sing carols; it was a fun and awesome time.

> **December 14**
> Thank you for the gift of peace in the midst of and about the circumstances. That's so, so good. This Advent week is about joy. Yes, when one experiences peace, joy is then felt. I am already questioning how it can be that I am not sorrowing more? Is it because I've sorrowed throughout the whole past year? Or because you've shown me our relationship will still exist though separated (such a helpful thought!) and that both of us will benefit? O Lord, please bring that peace to him and fill him with joy also.

It's his last time to the day center. While he was there, Jeff, Maria and I moved some furniture and things to Grand Brook. Maria and I stayed there to sign the contract and pay the down payment. I still felt peace.

Maria then went with me to pick him up from the day center. At home she talked with him about the coming move. He didn't get angry but he grieved, I think. He said this step came so fast and then objected, saying marriage means being together. I told him what the Lord gave me Sunday. Our relationship wasn't ending – we just both needed help. He accepted that. We cried, and we prayed. He said he'd do what we thought best. After a bit he said, "Well, let's get it done." Jeff and Shelly later reinforced it, again telling him, "This is what you told us to do. We're taking care of you, but also of Mom." Wayne again accepted and suggested we pray together, which we did.

In the evening, I found him disrobing in the old bathroom, so I went to get pjs. I tried to help, but he kept stumbling backwards. Within minutes he fell backwards into the deep therapy tub, knocking down the shower rod. Thankfully the stool was in the tub, breaking his fall. Otherwise, he would have gone all the way in, probably injuring his head.

December 17
O Lord God, I know it can take me so long to get here. There are bathrooms to clean up, duties to figure out, people to report to – all swirling till I have waded through it. Thank you for your patience, your mercifully receiving me "just as I am."

We went to Grand Brook to get COVID tests – they were negative. He liked the place, and enjoyed the family relations staff person. She welcomed him as Pastor Wayne, saying they could use his help with services, devotions and prayer at meals. He said he'd be glad to help wherever needed.

Driving home and later at coffee, he talked positively about it. Then suddenly he said, "The devil is a murderer and a robber." Later that day we learned a resident had tested positive for COVID. I thought, "Was that what it referred to, Lord? You worked so much good in us and for us these days, and your enemy is trying to steal it..." With the COVID case now there, all in-person visitation was stopped. That made me question our putting him in at this time. But then I thought that the environment would be building for him mentally. And I realized I was increasingly worried about safety here because of his falls.

Maria's family came with dinner and guitars. We sang worship songs, and it was so very good. Then Jeff and Shelly's whole family came in, so we repeated all those songs and added carols.

December 21 Maria, Jeff, Shelly and I talked with Wayne in our home, explaining it was the day to go, and then we prayed together. It was an awesome time. He said he thought this step was necessary, and he helped move things into the car, but he was very quiet the whole way there. When we got out of the car at Grand Brook, the extent of it hit him and he said, "This isn't right." I hugged him, told him I loved him, and all I could think to say was to ask him to forgive me. He pushed me away. After the staff met us in the side entrance, Maria asked him if we could give him a hug. Each of us did, but when I did, he resisted, saying, "Aren't you coming with me?" Then he was taken inside.

They later texted a picture, saying he was friendly when they got inside. The executive director texted that he was "like the glue that was missing," getting everyone talking and enjoying being together.

Jeff, Shelly, Maria and I ordered salads and stayed together for a while at my house. After they left, I couldn't settle, though I tried. So, I moved furniture in the office and then finally emailed our siblings and texted the Prayer Shield: "Well, we did it. It was beautiful, and it was awful. An amazingly good thing was that is felt like a finishing, not a quitting. I am so thankful."

Jeff and Shelly came over to watch a movie with me. Wayne's brothers wrote in agreement with the decision. I felt no accusation and was grateful.

But Father, what an awful thing – to be ripped apart and he not able to understand it. O Lord, please move him quickly into not being affected by it. Thank you so for the good time they reported he was having, and I plead for you to carry him through the night with no fear, getting help quickly to him if he gets up. I'm concerned most about that, yet so relieved I don't have to do it.

CHAPTER THREE

The Landing: Memory Care, Fatal Illness

I visited Wayne the next morning and then scheduled appointments for every day. He told me yesterday had been terrible, but he was all right. He kept wanting me to come in and asked why we couldn't be together at night. "Are you saying it's over?" But he didn't scold me.

December 22
Father, what a day it's been. I had been worried I wouldn't be able to enter this journey emotionally and had asked Lor to pray about that a couple of weeks ago. Boy, did I enter today! Sitting here this morning the breaking sun broke me. Then as I prayed with Wayne, he cried and said, "I love you so much," and I cried. In the car on the way home I returned L___'s call and cried with him. I cried when J___ called and wailing broke out periodically this afternoon and evening. Grand Brook posted a wonderful picture of Wayne saying, "We're so blessed to have Pastor Wayne as an addition to our GB family," and I cried out, "No! He's mine!" Later I was crying, "He's gone, he's gone." It was a deep, strong reaction, probably referring to the pre-AD Wayne and probably revealing a grief that has been in me for many years.

L____ told me, "I've found that peace and pain are bedfellows." So, so true. That peace has not left, or wavered at all, and I thank you, Prince of Peace. You came to reconcile, to make God's peace available to me...You came and you know this present pain too...

The next day they reported Wayne did great. He made a difference with others and prayed for meals. Wayne told me the people are wonderful. He didn't know me as wife.

December 24
Lord, it's Christmas Eve, but it seems just another day – that's okay, isn't it? You came and entered the ordinary, and life kept happening. I know you have been with me in my present *happening*, and my Father, I stand in awe. You are not far off, you are here; I am not alone, and Wayne is not alone. O Lord, I bow in praise of you, your faithfulness, your goodness, your mercy. That you hear... and respond...Lord, how can it be? I pray you help me today in connecting with Wayne and others, in resting – please free me to sleep – in doing what's required, but also in remembering your coming.

He was glad to see me and cried. But he said he knows he's to encourage people there in Jesus.

December 25 On Christmas day, after brunch, Jeff's whole family went with me to see Wayne. Because COVID had entered the building, we all gathered outside the window. He was brought to a deacon's bench there to visit with us, but another resident insisted on sitting with him. He was distracted by her, apparently thinking she needed him. He opened Shelly's gift, giving the card to the woman. Another woman was pushed by in a wheelchair, and Wayne immediately got up to take over the pushing. Finally caregivers took her and the woman on the bench away. He cried when he opened the picture of Door County I'd wrapped for him. When we sang "Silent Night," he closed his eyes and sang with us, saying, "Amen" when we finished.

> Ah Lord God, the visit was so sad, so strange, yet so encouraging. To see him so ready to help the needy women was, on the one hand, encouraging – it showed his taking up purpose in being there. On the other hand, it was reminiscent of all the times I've seen him think he should be the one to help a needy woman. Interesting, isn't it? And strange to watch his familiarity with that woman (which seemed to have come quickly). So, Lord, help me here too and protect him, fill him with peace...

I continued to visit him each day. Jeff came along one day and Maria, Ben, Judah and Asher another day.

December 29 When I got to Grand Brook, he looked better (he'd been showered), but he cried. The activities director came to the window with him and told me he'd sung for them the day before. She asked him to sing so she could record it. He started with "Onward Christian Soldiers" but forgot it after the first line. Then he closed his eyes and sang a spontaneous worship song, raising his arms in praise. It was awesome.

> **December 30**
> Omnipresent LORD God – you are present everywhere, fully, always. Again, how comforting to know you are with Wayne, fully, and at the same time with me, fully, and with each member of our family, fully. I lift praise, ever-present, very present Lord, Father, Helper. Thank you for such good sleep – nine hours! That's what I used to do and haven't done this whole year.... Thank you for protecting my health and strength...

I was able to ask how his nights are going. The caregiver said he "likes to wander and get naked." I reacted to that and asked her again. She repeated it, saying they find him trying to start the shower in a bathroom of an unused room, and then she left. Later I realized he wakes up, thinks it's time to shower and his default memory tells him to leave his bedroom to find the bathroom, something he's done for many years. I was pretty upset by the caregiver's description and her lack of understanding his thought process. But Wayne had smiled big at me while asking what my first name is.

December 31
(9 pm) I was alone all day except for some texts I received, and it felt lonely. I don't think I've ever spent a New Year's Eve like this. Still, I had a great visit with Wayne. Thank you for that. He was more with it, so to speak. He knew me as his wife and said so. He held the phone instead of forgetting to use it, and I could hear every word, though I didn't understand it. He cried periodically, not the heavy sorrow of other days but a reflecting, I think, on the loss of our full togetherness. He was even aware this time that I'd get cold out there. He said he knows he's to be there and spoke of his gratitude. O Lord, please meet him with peace deep in his soul and spirit. help him sleep, and rest...

2021

January 1 I went with Jeff, Shelly, Josh and Alyssa in the morning, seeing him through his room window. He cried when Josh and Alyssa said they loved him, and he enjoyed seeing the golf balls Josh had had made with the Leys Department Store logo on them. He smiled big, saying, "Isn't that a wonderful name?!" It was a good time.

I went back later with Ben, Maria, Judah and Asher. They all wore Packer gear, thinking it might spark a connection. But it made no impression on Wayne. Maria told him about preaching her candidacy sermon, but that didn't register either.

January 2
Lord, God, I lift praise to you – you are beyond comprehension... I yield to you my plans, desires, hopes, expectations for my life now, for being alone, for

2021 and beyond. I ask you to lead me, to protect, to guide choices and decisions... and I know again how greatly you did all this in 2020. I marvel anew – O Lord, my God, when I in awesome wonder consider...

I went to see Wayne with Jeff. He seemed down and cried a lot. He also spoke of wondering if he was being punished and then went on to other things. I came back to that question, countering it as a lie he was being given.

January 3 He seemed sad again and did not know me as wife. A staff member was with him, so I could ask why he wasn't wearing shoes or a belt. She said he'd backed away from having them put on him. It's still the getting-to-trust-them time, she explained. But she said he's comfortable there, more so than some others. And that was really good to hear.

January 4
Lord, thank you for helping me get started on compiling our AD story. I ask you to help me in this endeavor and to find ways to show him love. Please open up in-person visiting, I pray...

I talked with the nurse in the afternoon. She said he's doing really well, that he has joy. (I remembered asking the Lord to give him joy – "Thank you so, Lord God Above.") I also got things going for Palliative Care to come in and assess whether he's a candidate for their service.

January 5 He was really glad to see me again. He cried but then talked freely. We prayed, also putting on the armor of God, and then he launched into a spontaneous worship song. Again, it was awesome. He was so friendly, saying he'd been really down on the weekend but was feeling much better now. He knows the Lord is there and that he's meeting him, using him. He seemed bright-eyed, open. But again, he raised the question of whether he's done something wrong. I said that was accusation from Satan and quoted Romans 8:1. He cried, saying, "Thank you!!!"

The nurse told me that as he prayed for breakfast, he broke out in song and then cried. She asked him if they were sad tears. "No, this is just great! Everyone is together!"

January 6 The executive director called me early to tell me Wayne had fallen, hitting his head. She said he needs stitches and had called for EMS to come for him. She followed them to Metro Hospital where a CAT scan was done to rule out concussion. I turned to the Lord, "O Lord, please meet him, and me. Please pour your peace into him, over him. Enable him to rest in you now and to find rest when returning to Grand Brook. Lord, I am so thankful others are helping him…"

The nurse said Wayne was really wobbly today, tired from the trauma. They gave him a couple stints in a wheelchair just to start getting him familiar with being in one. He liked the fact that he could propel it with his feet.

When Jeff and I saw him about noon, we brought slices of Meisfeld summer sausage, some Gibbsville cheese and three more books. A staff member sent a picture of him eating the Sheboygan treats, saying he loved it.

January 7
O Lord, what a day; how injured he looked, and the bruise on his head will most likely get more black and blue. But you had led us to put him in Grand Brook and they took care of it, and are continuing to take care of him, very well. Thank you so for having us make that step, for providing so much for his care, for freeing him to feel so comfortable, and for giving me so much sleep last night (nine hours!).

Tom and Lor visited him with me. When he saw them, he knew them! And then immediately he let frustration surface and maybe some anger, as he talked and threw down the papers he was holding, saying, because of _____ (non-understandable) he needed to talk with Tom. It was hard to see, but we knew he felt safe with them, and therefore could unburden. They loved the place and the staff that they saw.

> **January 9**
> (Deuteronomy 32:4) You are The Rock, and what you do is perfect, just, faithful, upright. This you were in Moses' estimation, and this I know you to be. My Lord and my God, I bow...You have been so faithful to your promises regarding your children. I have experienced you staying with me, helping, guiding, comforting, supplying...and I bow in the awe of gratitude. I worship you...

He was so happy to see me but prayed for me as "my sister here." A physical therapist met me there so I could sign consent forms. Then she began working with him. She'll come three times a week.

January 10 He cried just about every time he looked at me today. I think I was Helper me in his thinking. He asked me to give him three names of people to pray for and then he talked a lot. I suggested one of our grandkids and then asked if he would pray for her with me right then. We did. He asked also how we are going "to make it." I said, "Only with Jesus. He has your hand. He has my hand. He is our way, He is your way, my way, the way." I quoted some scriptures. He was very loving.

> Thank you, Lord. I realize I need to concentrate on his spirit. I'll bring a scripture verse, maybe a song, and we'll pray for people, especially grandkids, together. Thank you for that, and I pray you lead me each day.

> **January 11**
> (Psalm 103:10) You do not deal with me, your child, according to my sins, nor repay me according to my iniquities. O Lord, whatever would we do, could we do, without your mercy and the newness of it every day....

> So, Merciful Lord, please cover me now, go with me, help me in blessing him...

He was very glad to see me. He cried only one time, briefly. He talked quite a bit about someone -— I wondered if it was the physical therapist? I sang "All the Way My Savior Leads Me" (Fanny Jane Crosby), and we prayed together for another of the grandkids, getting into other things as well. After a few more minutes he said he thought he had some ministry to do and needed to go.

> **January 12 (Wayne's birthday)**
> O Lord, thank you so for Wayne, for how he loved me and enabled me to find freedom, for how he loves you and yields to what you have for him, for how he served you and your church and still serves you by serving others. Lord, please bless him today, help him know he's loved, I pray. Meet him with your love, your presence, and fill him with peace, with joy.

He cried when he saw Jeff and was happy to see Shelly. He talked quite a bit, moving it into prayer. He told the Lord that Chris hasn't come for a long time. Jeff interrupted to tell him Mom is here. He then looked up and recognized me, bringing joy to us both. He asked why we weren't coming in (he hasn't asked that since the day after he moved there). After a while he told us he had to go...

I brought a cake which they had after lunch. A staff member emailed that he was all smiles as they sang to him this morning, sending a picture of him in front of the cake and gifts.

> Lord, help...grief hit as I greeted Jeff and Shelly this morning...and just now as I saw the pictures of his party – it hurts. Life isn't supposed to have this kind of thing, but AD came with the Fall, I guess. Death will separate us, but this...?

January 13
Father, I realize this morning why seeing the pictures of the birthday party hit me. Maria had said he looked as if he thought the experience was silly, and that's probably how he felt (he always did regarding such things). Yesterday when a friend asked how she could specifically pray for me, I said, "That I may show him dignity." At the time, I wasn't sure why I said that, but now I realize it came from what I saw in the picture. Naturally, there'd be indignities in memory care. So, I do pray you help me lift him and reinstate a sense of dignity. That's also why, I see now, I said to Jeff that I pray you take him out of it all, mercifully...O Lord, please meet him, lift him by your Spirit conveying to his spirit he is valued to you, to us...

I had a really good time at Grand Brook with Maria and Marissa. On the phone this morning I told Wayne Marissa was coming and he said to tell her he couldn't wait. And it was good. She'd brought a frame with three pictures of him and her together, and Maria brought sugar cookies she'd made from his mom's recipe. He smiled and laughed with them. He looked better, was dressed better. He was brought to the window in the new wheelchair, but when he was finished with us, he got up and walked away. He played with my blown kiss again.

January 14 He cried a lot and talked a lot, moving it into prayer. His wound is healing well. He was in the wheelchair. When I suggested singing, he agreed and we sang "When Peace Like a River." I suggested praying for another grandchild, which we did. His talking included, "I don't want to die yet..." and something to the effect of, "what are we going to be doing?" I talked about this place doing things that help AD. He agreed.

January 15 We talked a bit. He said they're having a Christmas celebration tomorrow and something about working on a tree. I read two of his birthday cards to him and he seemed to like that. He talked and moved into praying, so I did also. The caregiver tried to get him to look at me for kiss-blowing, but when he looked my way, he didn't seem to see me or notice my blown kiss.

January 16 I went to see Wayne with Jeff, Shelly, Josh and Michaela. Wayne seemed very pleased they were there, especially the kids. He talked a lot. Jeff mentioned Elijah running in fear from Jezebel and the still small voice of the Lord meeting him. He started us singing "Be Still and Know."

January 17 On this Sunday I prayed, "O Lord, please meet Wayne and powerfully fill him today. Help him know your presence, your love for him, your peace deep within..."

Jeff, Izzy and I went this afternoon. Wayne came walking to the window but seemed unable to go in a straight line. He leaned heavily on the caregiver. He saw us but it didn't seem that he knew us; he looked blank for a couple of minutes. He started talking, but then I told him to look up and see that Izzy was there. He did, and smiled big, "When did you get here?" When we sang "How Great Thou Art," he hummed the tenor. Jeff prayed. Wayne then ended the visit and got up to leave, but his legs gave out as he tried to walk away. He just went down, hitting his head on a door frame. We made multiple attempts to get someone's attention, and finally he was helped. That was really hard to watch from outside a window.

January 18
Lord, please settle over Wayne with your peace more and more. Help him accept the wheelchair, I pray. And Lord, as this quick deterioration unfolds before us, please shorten the days, I ask in your mercy, the days of misery. Carry him, please, and me...

He fell again today, his "legs just giving out under him," they said. They put him in the wheelchair I'd ordered for him. However, he fell again in the afternoon, though he didn't get hurt. His blood pressure apparently dropped, and he wouldn't eat. When Maria, Judah, Asher and I visited in the afternoon, he seemed unaware for most of the time. He perked up a bit seeing Asher and Judah, but he didn't talk much or pray.

The physical therapist told me this morning that as she works with him, he can get very distracted by any voice he hears. He wants to turn to help, but that can cause losing his balance. She said he prays all the time.

(5:30) The nurse called. She thinks Wayne may have a Urinary Tract Infection. There's increased confusion, his blood pressure is dropping, and he could be dehydrated. She was checking that.

(6:30) She called again saying he needs fluids, so she'd called the EMS. The ED went with him to the hospital. There they did an X-ray, gave him an EKG, a CT scan, and fluids. They also checked blood counts. There was indication of internal bleeding, so they gave him a blood transfusion.

The doctor called late in the evening to say the bleeding could be coming from the GI tract and that his falling may have been caused by that. She said they'll check blood counts regularly and check the GI tract tomorrow.

January 19 Jeff took me to Metro Hospital but was not allowed to go in with me because of COVID restrictions. Wayne was very confused, very fidgety, and often tried to take off cords. At times he seemed to know I was there, but he hardly opened his eyes all day. At noon, he was taken down for an endoscope, but twice he had massive bleeding before they could take him for the test. Changing and cleaning took a while. Hemoglobin was checked also, more blood was ordered, and a transfusion started. Then his blood pressure tanked too low to sedate him for the procedure. The anesthesiologist said they'd have to send him to ICU to be resuscitated so the procedure could be done. I was startled, saying we had a DNR (Do Not Resuscitate) order in his file. He said they'd talk with me about that in ICU.

Very soon they took him to ICU, where they hurriedly

got him ready to have the endoscope. A doctor told me he had looked at our forms and I think he told me those forms wouldn't stop what they intended to do. I seemed to be walking, listening, functioning in a fog. I cried and told him I wished our kids could have been with me.

Their actions got the blood pressure up enough to sedate him so they could perform the procedure there. Very soon the endoscopy team came with their machines.

> (3:30 pm, in the ICU waiting room during the procedure) O Lord, that was an awful sight – that black, black stool and then the black liquid… and the blood pressure 'way down… (I later learned it had gone down to 57/38.) I admit I wondered if you were answering our prayer about not prolonging his misery by already beginning to take him home. Lord, was it all right to have that thought, and all right to have thanks about it? These days have not been nice for him – he's had so much confusion about what's happening to him and so much discomfort from the wires and plugs. And the previous two days were not good either at Grand Brook. So, I pray your good carry him, and lead us. Lead me. Lord. If I have to make a decision, please let the kids be in on it somehow… (The Lord answered that prayer very soon.)

They found a large bleeding ulcer in the stomach and were able to cauterize the vessel, removing also some blood. But because there was so much blood present, they were not able to take a biopsy. I was told there's no guarantee it won't happen again.

Sarah, Maria and Ben had gone to my house that afternoon, and they, Jeff, Shelly and I had supper together there. We then discussed the things they had looked into that afternoon. We had all been surprised by the use of the word "resuscitate," and we now knew we had to get more specific in what we'd agree to do, or not to do for Wayne. We all agreed we had no desire to put him through anything more and needed to outline our future choices. It was so very good to have them all with me, especially since no one could accompany me to the hospital.

January 20-22 He stayed at Metro Hospital these days. He fought everything they tried to do, including attempts to get blood pressure readings and take blood (they checked hemoglobin levels every six hours). He wouldn't eat and fought a physical therapist's attempt to get him up. It was all so frightening for him. He didn't understand.

He kept his eyes closed most of the time, sometimes dozing, but usually he was talking to Jesus. At one point, he said the first part of the Lord's Prayer but couldn't remember the rest. He sang the first part of the Doxology but again stopped, not remembering how to finish. So, then he'd sing a worship song that he made up in that moment. Turning to Jesus in these ways seemed to be his way of dealing with the frightening situation. His long-term memory of that practice in his life was still intact.

> **January 20**
> Lord, I feel the weight of yesterday finally. The ICU doctor said they'd have to go in and cauterize the bleeding or "he'd bleed out." He would have died! But I stopped it by agreeing to blood transfusions and the cauterizing. I didn't know that that was also considered resuscitating. So did you in fact offer him (and us) a release, and I said "No?" O Lord, I didn't know, I didn't know... and you know that. So, now what? Tonight, the kids and I will talk again. Please lead and prepare us all. I know you're responding in mercy, and I thank you. Do we let it go if it occurs again? But maybe it won't? O Lord, did I pray that his misery not be prolonged and then reject your answer? Did I take control away from you? But I didn't know... Again, I plead for your mercy to give him a path home again, if that's what this episode was about, and to forgive my refusal of your offer, if that's what I did.

Please reach for him again since you've now given us a clearer understanding.

January 21
Lord my God, I'm so weak – I didn't sleep nearly enough. You are God, you are over all, you decided the number of our days even before one occurred. And I know you receive me anew with new mercies… Thank you so for our kids. They've rallied around me, around us, and are intent on loving their dad to the finish. Were you finished on Tuesday? I know think not, for these measures are also in your hand, and you knew our DNR wasn't complete. Thank you so for showing me that. You are so merciful to me, so loving in your leading. I admit also that I had a fearful thought that since we missed a good way, so to speak, to die, he'll now have to have the hard way, the slow and prolonged AD way. But Lord, you aren't human. You don't operate that way. So, I reject that in the name of Jesus. Lord, please help me today with the conversations with a doctor so I don't miss anything. Fill me to be blessing to Wayne, to bring all our love to him…

We learned from the doctor that they did the procedure because that was considered "diagnostic;" it was not a heroic life-saving measure. That helped me, greatly. I conveyed to him that our kids and I had decided we didn't want to put Wayne through anything more and, therefore, wanted to take no more proactive measures. He totally agreed and stopped everything at that point.

January 22
Lord God, thank you for carrying me. I was so tired, and maybe still am. He'll get moved today. I pray that you make it smooth and easy for him. Please come in peace, and fill us with your strength for the move and for his adjusting back. Please help him feel that he has returned home and enable him to place trust in those who care for him. Lord, it seems this has been conquered, unless

it's cancer. I wonder about his quality of life now – will it actually be better, without the effects of the ulcer? Will it then be prolonged... Again, Lord, I'm sorry for him that we weren't prepared for his release from life Tuesday, and again I pray that you in your mercy carry him till your day of finishing, that you keep him from the horrors of that last stage AD, and that you give him quick passage. Bless him with dignity and honor till then.... So, my Lord, thank you for time, time with him, time to get ready with more specific directives, time for grandkids to see him. Bless him. Thank you and for your great mercy to me, your covering of mistakes I made in this, and your giving me new possibilities. O Lord, please help me hear you, to know the way you're wanting me to go.

Late afternoon, Wayne and I arrived back at Grand Brook after Jeff and Sarah had greeted him coming out of Metro Hospital. At Grand Brook, Ben, Maria, Judah, Asher, Shelly, Josh, Alyssa, Michaela and Izzy greeted him and hugged him as he was taken in.

We all came to my home to have pizza. The executive director called about seven saying Wayne was "very uncomfortable, out of control," and they couldn't have him there like that. She worried he'd push the wheelchair over and said either he'd have to be sent back to the hospital to be sedated or go on Hospice. She'd already talked with the nurse, who said to call Hospice, but I didn't know that at the time. She asked for Jeff to come to help control and settle him, for we women (Sarah, Maria and I) wouldn't be able to – he was too strong. She'd give Jeff a COVID test and told me Hospice of MI would be calling me.

Jeff was able to help settle him in the hospital bed the nurse had already ordered for him. He prayed and read scripture. Wayne fell asleep.

Hospice, meanwhile, called me, asking for Wayne's history. She said the after-hours clinical team would review the hospital records to see if he was Hospice-appropriate. If so, they would send someone. If not, he might have to return to the hospital to be sedated. Since the hospital had told me he was fine to return to normal life, I thought Hospice would decline serving him.

Jeff called about 9:20, saying Hospice had been there, determined he had two to seven days to live, and we all needed to come right away for it could even be tonight. Sarah and I scrambled to get things together and left. We both seemed to move as if in a trance, especially since the hospital had indicated Wayne was ready to resume normal life. Sarah drove but kept my hand in hers the whole way there. Maria and Ben, who had only been home an hour or so, drove back. Grand Brook put four mattresses on the floor in an empty companion suite where they'd put Wayne's hospital bed. We didn't sleep a whole lot; Ben left about 2 am, not wanting Asher and Judah to wake up with both parents gone.

January 23 Grand Brook welcomed in our grandkids (only one wasn't able to make the trip), giving each a COVID test. They could come by twos with their parent and me. Wayne had some times of recognition. Sometimes he harmonized as we sang. His eyes couldn't focus enough to see Jonny and Izzy, so Jeff stood between them. Wayne then said, "Oh, there's Jeff," and his eyes brightened. Different groups sang and Wayne hummed the tenor part. There was a lot of crying. After it finished mid-afternoon, Ben took me home to get some more things while Maria stayed; Jeff went home to celebrate Topher's birthday with his family; Sarah went home to Illinois with her family. Wayne was very agitated for several hours, but when Jeff and I returned about 6:45, he had just settled. He never really was awake again after that.

January 24
The kids and adults all cried, but it was also an awesome time. O Lord, how merciful you are to me, to him. You heard my cry for this very mercy (Psalm 31:22), and you mercifully met me in the questions of Tuesday night and Wednesday. Lord, truly you are good to your children,

truly you have good, truly you act in love, you are for me and your own. You did not turn on me if indeed I was slow to understand what was happening on Tuesday. But you are now doing what we'd asked. You will carry Wayne through this door. He will not be alone and neither will I. And I ask you to open a way for us to have an honoring funeral in the midst of COVID. Meet us all through this day with strength, protection of health, unity among us, agreement about arrangements. To you be the glory, honor and praise.

January 25 Sleep apnea occurred quite a bit last night, so Jeff returned to spend the night. But Wayne rallied. Jeff left in the morning and Maria went to get Biggby coffee so I could have some alone time with him. I read the letters I'd written to him and cried my love. I told him I'd be all right, and he could let go. Midmorning, apnea returned with long periods of no breathing. We thought he was going. We sang, spoke to him, thanked him… and went to the back room to give him some privacy. But then he started breathing better again.

Tom and Lor drove up, just wanting to be in the area and to pray. They texted Maria about it and she got the idea of bringing them to the window. Wayne turned his head towards the window when he heard their voices. Later, the activities director brought some of the residents in to see him, pray with him, for they were showing concern.

January 26 George came to window visit also, which also blessed Wayne, I believe. I'd had to reschedule an appointment last week and now needed to do so again. Last week I'd said my husband was in the hospital. Now I said, "My husband is dying." Afterwards, I said to Maria, "There. I said it." Since the hospital had cleared him, I realized I'd been doubting that, even denying it? Now, saying it made it real.

We invited his siblings to do a Zoom visit, and they did. There were shared memories and many tears.

In the evening, we were singing, praying and reading

scripture when it came to me, we were in spiritual battle. It continued for quite a while. Finally, it was over.

The next day, January 27, we realized Wayne was no longer fighting, and I had the sense that I was *finished,* that is, I didn't need to look for more to say or do for him, I was at rest. Jeff decided to go home, thinking he'd stay there overnight. The Hospice nurse came after lunch and also noticed he was no longer fighting. She said he had "minutes to hours" left. It seemed Wayne was also at rest. Maria told Jeff and he returned. But again, Wayne rallied. (Having been a singer and a jogger, his heart and lungs were strong.)

January 28 Jeff and I each went home midafternoon and decided to stay home overnight. We both felt okay doing that. Maria had some powerful times during the night with him, especially using II Kings 2.

January 29
Father, you have sustained me, kept me in health throughout these eleven days of watching, waiting, wondering…I can't do any more here…

Maria got the idea to anoint Wayne with oil, so she texted for me to bring a bottle. We did that when we got there. We prayed, sang, and Maria read QA 32 of the Heidelberg Catechism: "Why are you called Christian?" That too was a powerful time.

The Hospice nurse saw some struggle in his breathing and increased the morphine dosage.

I realized this morning that I hadn't thought of him as someone with AD all week. I hadn't had to interpret his communication and behaviors. I could just give him love, gratitude, and bring the Lord's love through ministering to his spirit and soul. I was overwhelmed with the discovery.

January 30 Maria and I slept quite well there (Jeff had gone home), sensing we didn't have to keep alert anymore.

The Hospice nurse this morning said she believed he

would leave some time in the next twenty-four hours. Maria went home, feeling released to go to her family. Jeff and Shelly returned, staying there with me. After supper, as we were all close to him, Jeff reminded him of their telling each other they had no regrets in their relationship. This had been done at the Promise Keepers' Convention at Soldier's Field in Chicago. Now Jeff said, "Still true, Dad. No regrets." A tear escaped Wayne's eye. I then said some things and Shelly whispered, telling him it was okay to go. The very shallow breaths became spaced out more and more. I saw a grimace, and he opened an eye a bit. Jeff sensed connection. Then it all stopped. We watched and watched and watched. Nothing. Jeff went to look for a staff member. She came in, examined him, and nodded at me. I burst into tears. She hugged me and then Jeff did. It was 6:45 pm.

We called family. I texted the Prayer Shield, saying, "It is finished. He is free. It was so peaceful, without struggle." We packed our bags.

The Hospice nurse came and declared him gone at 8:12 pm.

The funeral director came. Jeff helped place his body on the gurney for the drive to the funeral home. We followed it out, watched it go into the car, and saw the car drive off. We headed home. As did Wayne.

January 31
O Lord, you have been good...you heard my cry, my plea to spare him the last horrors of AD. You did it. You answered and gave that to him, to us, to our family. That you would listen to me, O Lord, how can it be? And Lord, I'm still so fragmented in my thinking, I can't settle my mind. Thank you for meeting me anyway, for providing the strength for these last two weeks, and the four weeks prior to that and the year before that, and keeping me in health throughout. So, I plead for your continued supply through these coming days...and as I go on...

AFTERWORD
Subsequent Remembrances

I thoroughly appreciated all who came, all who reached out to me and to our family when Wayne died. For some time afterwards, I found myself rereading cards and notes, relistening to messages, reliving the reminders of what Wayne had meant to each person. It was so good to thus recover him, so to speak, to know again the Person With*out* Dementia. I found myself wanting to remain in this remembering, even while feeling pressed to compile this our AD story. I also wanted the reader to know who Wayne Leys was before AD – the person, the pastor, the friend loved by many. So, I've included here some of the comments received (used by permission or taken from the public record and given in no particular order):

Mike Hendriksen, Downers Grove, IL – Because of the impact that his wisdom and teachings had on people, you didn't need to be with Wayne to have Wayne with you.

Hal Hildebrand, Colorado Springs, CO – Wayne was the man who led my wife and me to the Lord. He taught me how to study the word of God and practice what I learned. I am deeply grateful for his influence on our lives.

John Rozeboom, Grand Rapids, MI – Wayne was a friend and colleague in all the years I was with Christian Reformed Church (CRC) Home Missions, whose love, help (especially when he was on the CRC Big Board), and his bias for having a good time made everything better.

Bill Lenters, Chicago, IL – [We're] not exactly classmates, but close enough. Wayne was always a step ahead of most of us in terms of sanctification. It wasn't a competition but his walk matched his talk. A rare find. Not an ounce of sanctimonious pride in him.

Allen Likkel, Lynden, WA – I will be forever thankful to God for placing Wayne in my orientation group at Calvin College as we began our pilgrimage of study and life together at that point. It was the gift of a lifelong friendship. Wayne was a primary influence in my surrender to God's call to me to become a missionary-pastor. I figured that if a fun-loving character like Wayne could be a pastor, then maybe there was room for me as well.... While living in distant places from one another throughout our ministry journeys, whatever the time lapse, a renewed conversation and time together was a full and immediate experience of a very special friendship.

Kathy Roosma, St. John, IN – Rev. Leys was my pastor in the early 80's when my husband, John Boss, and I attended Elmhurst Church. Both of you were very instrumental in our walk with the Lord and helped us to grow stronger in our faith because of your leadership. Rev. Leys was always willing to listen and offer gentle, godly advice. Our paths have not crossed in years, and yet, Rev. Leys and you have left a mark in my life and heart.

Sister Vivian Whitehead, Joliet, IL – I just heard that Wayne has gone to meet his God!... It has been my joy and inspiration to have shared life and ministry with him (and you).

Beth Nyhoff, Denver, CO – Ken and I were sharing with one another the profound influence Wayne had on our lives... He reached into our hearts in a way that pointed us to Jesus and his word, filling a longing that we didn't fully even realize we had. Wayne mentored Ken by making every council meeting a teaching time. He helped us both understand the immeasurable depths of scripture, always more to learn. Wayne inspired a hunger for God's word.

Beth Fink, Milford, MI – What a godly man [he] was! I am grateful for the spiritual care and concern he showed us during our high school years with an early morning Bible study. He shared his love of scripture and his desire for all of us to read and treasure it.

Jody Bolkema, Sioux Fall, SD – I remember all the Greenfields getting together at Aunt Chris and Uncle Wayne's house...All the families were spread out in the parsonage and the church. In the morning Uncle Wayne went through the house and church blowing into a French horn. He sounded like a sick elephant while waking up the clan.... Uncle Wayne's faith was evident and so was his fun. He taught me you can have fun being a Christian. I'm thankful for his life, service and love for God.

Dianne Butler, Atlanta, GA – Maybe Wayne's own words best capture a sense of the trusted advisor and treasured friend he was. Two things were always present: an unwavering focus on the Lord's priorities and his own sense of humor. Both were invaluable to his counsel. I sought his guidance as an insecure, young mom and he delivered uncompromising clarity and thoughtfulness. Like the time he answered my questions with, "The Lord needs faithful daughters. Unfaithful daughters are a dime a dozen." Zero judgment, and the choice was mine. Or after sharing a message of Jesus' warnings about "wolves in sheep's clothing," he paused and made the most unforgettable statement, one that was so uniquely "Wayne:" "We need to be aware of the wolves, but I don't worry about them. God will take care of them. I'm concerned about the sheep who THINK they're wolves. They're living like wolves, because that's all they know." That was a life-changing perspective for me.

Bruce Ryskamp, Grand Rapids, MI – In my life I've only known a few people whom I can call my "truth tellers." I could always trust these people to give me the "unvarnished" truth whether it be spiritual, personal, or business. Wayne was one of those exceptional people. His willingness to always tell me what he thought, regardless of how I might react or how it might impact our relationship changed my whole career path. I had just turned down a job offer from Zondervan but had no peace about it, so I asked Wayne to have breakfast with me. I told him I did not want to leave my job, my church, my community, my friends...sharing solid reasons for my decision. But, I asked, why don't I have peace? His answer cut right through my heart; he said, "Maybe God has not given you peace because he wants you to accept that job." Thirty-two hours later I called Zondervan and accepted. Looking back now thirty-eight years, it is so obvious that God used Wayne to guide me in making one of the best decisions in my life. Wayne was not only a loyal friend but a mentor, spiritual teacher and counselor to me and I will forever be grateful for knowing this servant of God.

Gregg DeMey, Elmhurst, IL – Our staff talked about Wayne's legacy...and recognized the deep debt of gratitude that we each owe for the spiritual leadership and change that he brought to Elmhurst CRC. Watching Wayne's online funeral service confirmed some of the great gifts and qualities that I sensed in spending time with him on a handful of occasions... qualities he also imparted to the life of the church:

> That a sense of spirituality and playfulness should go hand in hand
> That God's word is our go-to source in life
> That serving the vulnerable is a privilege and joy
> That facing outward is the best posture for Jesus' Church
> That Christians can be creative and even a little mischievous
> That the Holy Spirit's fire can animate our daily lives
> That the Holy Spirit's wisdom will get us through the toughest times.

* * *

Some months along in this remembering, after I'd finished writing our AD story, I found a letter in our files from Wayne to me, a letter he'd written on our 22nd wedding anniversary, over thirty-two years before he died. It was an amazing find for me, a gift from the Lord, for it showed me again his answer to my questions about demonstrating my love for him, questions reflected in the preceding story.

"Dear Christine,

This day is most important to me! For me it is a celebration of gratitude to God for the greatest gift I have ever received from him, the gift of your love, the gift of you.... One of the ways in which we reflect the very attribute of God is in a love that is "there." God is reflected in our love together, [and] in your love for me that is a love that is 'there' [See Ezekiel 48:35] .... After twenty-two years together, I know of no one with whom I want to be more than you. When others years ago spoke of the need to get away from their wives for a while, I found that to be strange. Today when I hear that, I hurt for them. Surely, we have discovered that the word was right when it compares our relationship of love to that of Christ and his church. Only, my task is much easier than that of the Lord Jesus! To desire to lay down my life for you is hardly a difficult task. I love you in this way. But I believe that kind of love has only been made possible because you have loved me. What I'm saying, my bride, is that you have liberated me to love. The process is going on, but it would not without you.... So, my love, congratulations! You made it through another year with this bungling Sheboyganite! We don't have a savings account but at least we are still having fun. I loved you so much on that day, that I just had to get you away to Traverse City quickly. I'd do it the same way if it was to be done today. Most of all we need the truth of the Lord Jesus. But after that, all I <u>need</u> is you.

I love you, Christine Leys! I always will, and I am excited about the 23rd year. We adventure together and the adventure is never dull.

Wayne"

ACKNOWLEDGEMENTS

We're told children are gifts from God. Wayne and I were blessed with three wonderful gifts: Jeff, Sarah and Maria. We could not have made it without them in the last year of walking this path called Alzheimer's. They gave themselves to coming regularly, to investigating help for us, to helping settle Wayne, to relieving me. They supplied food, encouragement, and fun in the midst of our COVID-shutdown-affected last year of AD. What a gift each was to Wayne and to me through what was sometimes a miry slough. Thank you, Jeff, thank you, Sarah, thank you, Maria. And thank you for the love, support and help from their spouses: Shelly, John, Ben and for the love and enjoyment of life from our grandkids: Josh and Alyssa, Michaela, Topher, Benjamin, Annika, Marissa, Emma, Jonny, Aiden, Izzy, Colin, Judah, and Asher.

A heart-felt thank you goes to my friend Deanne Bolt for being the first to read this chronicling of our AD story and for encouraging me to go further with it. And an enormous thank you goes to Linda Kolk who cleaned it up.

I am also deeply grateful for all who prayed for us throughout this journey (and the previous ones). They are too numerous to mention. By singling out a few, I do not mean to minimize the tremendous help to us from all the others, for we were both aware of being carried by those prayers through our AD journey. However, I must mention the small group the Lord appointed for me, the team I came to call my Prayer Shield. I sensed this appointment from him in April of 2020 and knew immediately who was being given the assignment. I have described this in the preceding pages. So, a deep and awe-filled thank you to Cindy Hendriksen, Connie Negen, Dianne Butler, Kaye Scott and Lor Visser.

We were tremendously grateful for those who gave themselves regularly to us in order to bless us both by spending time with Wayne, giving value to his personhood and helping him remember who he was throughout AD's robbing. We had many breakfasts and lunches with friends who continued to love him and I am still grateful. There were also four who gave me regular times to get a break, to take a nap, to be spiritually renewed. Thank you, John Hutt, George VanderWoude, Tom and Lor Visser.

I cannot imagine what my life would have been like had I not been given Wayne as my life partner. He was gifted by the Lord to see things in people that the Lord saw, things of which the person herself was yet unaware. He saw the actual me and helped me become the things he saw. In pastoring he did the same for many others. I know many are deeply grateful to him for that. But most of all, I am. One of the letters I read to him in Hospice illustrates that gratitude:

1-4-21

"Dear Wayne,

I was reminded recently of what a shy person I was when we met; so shy, even fearful, no, very fearful! So fearful I didn't dare have people notice me – what would they think or say? Would they laugh? That frightened me the most. Then you noticed me, and you smiled, a warm, welcoming smile, a smile that said, "You're worth getting to know." I was so grateful to be received. You showed me how to laugh and have fun as you showed me I could trust you.

Some time later, however, you worried about me still being so reticent with people. But you made a decision to stay by my side for you said you saw other qualities, good and admirable qualities. So, you stayed and continued to build my trust. More and more I could let go of those fears though it took a while. You believed in me, you entrusted yourself to me, you loved and accepted me so that I could, little by little, entrust myself to others but first, to you.

The Lord used you to teach me about love, to learn to receive love, to accept it unconditionally, and finally to receive the truth that my fear was fear of man, the opposite of the fear of the Lord. Because of your intention to love me, I could find freedom – freedom to love and enjoy the Lord, my husband, my family, my ministry.

And I will always be grateful... I love you, Chris"

My deepest gratitude is for my Lord, my very present help. How can it be – that he knows me, that he sees me, that he supplies me, that his mercy to me is new every morning, that his love and grace flow freely, daily? As so many others have learned, I know that my story is actually the story of him. He is the one who is good, who has good, who meets me, his child, in the midst:

> In the midst of uncertainty – Grant me hope.
> In the midst of questioning – Grant me light.
> In the midst of loneliness – Grant me strength.
> In the midst of o'erwhelming flood – Grant me Life.
>   You are my Hope, O Lord;
>   You are my Light, O Lord;
>   You are my Strength, O Lord,
>   You are my Life.

READING LIST

I am grateful also for the books I found helpful along the way:

Stop Alzheimer's Now, Bruce Fife, N.D. (which Jeff and Shelly brought over right after the diagnosis; it's about diet, and helped identify brain-boosting foods)

Dementia, Living in the Memories of God, John Swinton (I was greatly helped by this book, including by his call to see the Person With Dementia as a person yet and not as one who has "lost his mind, or himself.")

Second Forgetting, Remembering the Power of the Gospel During Alzheimer's Disease, Dr. Benjamin Mast

The Story of My Father, A Memoir, Sue Miller

The Notebook, a novel by Nicholas Sparks

Still Alice, a novel by Lisa Genova

A Memoir of Parting, Carol J. Rottman

My Journey into Alzheimer's Disease, A True Story by Robert Davis

The Soul of Care, Arthur Kleinman

Keeping Love Alive as the Memories Fade, The 5 Love Languages and the Alzheimer's Journey, Deborah Barr, Edward Shaw, Gary Chapman

Being Mortal, Atul Gawande (Thank you, Bill Stroo, for bringing this to our attention, and stopping over to help us talk about some of it.)

The 36-Hour Day, Nancy L. Mace and Peter V. Rabins (This gave very practical help; I read it twice, and referred to it repeatedly.)

Creating Moments of Joy, Jolene Brackey

Article:
"Alzheimer's: The Elusive Mind Stealer," National Center of Continuing Eduction, INC

CPSIA information can be obtained
at www.ICGtesting.com
Printed in the USA
JSHW040106180522
26047JS00001B/18